The Concept of Modernism

The Concept
of Modernism

Astradur Eysteinsson

Cornell University Press

Ithaca and London

Copyright © 1990 by Cornell University

First published 1990 by Cornell University Press.

International Standard Book Number 0-8014-2371-6
Library of Congress Catalog Card Number 89-46170
Printed in the United States of America
*Librarians: Library of Congress cataloging information appears on the last page
of the book.*

To my grandparents,
Ástráður and Sigríður Proppé

Contents

Acknowledgments

THIS BOOK is a product of a decade of thinking through modernist issues and writing on modernist literature. My involvement in modernist studies over this period has taken several forms: writing a dissertation and several papers and translating modernist works as well as teaching modernist literature and discussing its implications with students and colleagues.

My work has been supported by grants from the Icelandic Science Fund and the research funds of the universities of Iowa and Iceland.

I thank my friends and colleagues Rudolf E. Kuenzli (University of Iowa) and Martin Regal (University of Iceland) for their careful reading of my manuscript and their many helpful comments. I am also indebted to my father, Eysteinn Þorvaldsson, especially for going with me through the trial of translating Kafka into Icelandic, an effort that opened fascinating vistas on modernism at a decisive moment for me. Among the many people with whom I have had fruitful discussions I am especially grateful to Thomas E. Lewis, Geoffrey Waite, Brooks Landon, Gerald L. Bruns, Cheryl Herr, and Jeffrey Gardiner. I also acknowledge my debt to Susan Bassnett, under whose guidance I started thinking seriously about these matters eleven years ago at the University of Warwick, England. And most of all, I owe a great deal to my wife, Birna Kristjánsdóttir, for generously allowing me to interrupt her own work several times, and to my son, Andri, for interrupting mine.

ASTRADUR EYSTEINSSON

Reykjavik, Iceland

The Concept of Modernism

Introduction

ALTHOUGH THE CONCEPT "modernism" may seem intolerably vague, it has come to serve a crucial function in criticism and literary history, as well as in theoretical debates about literature. There is little doubt that of all the concepts used in discussing and mapping twentieth-century Western literature, "modernism" has become the most important, either as used by itself or as a part of the kindred concept "postmodernism."

One must of course be aware that until quite recently "modernism" was not a widespread concept, especially not outside the spheres of Anglo-American and Scandinavian criticism, and even today one may not encounter it frequently in the works of, say, German and French critics and scholars.[1] It may actually be the pressure exerted by critical and theoretical discussion in the United States that has recently made Continental-European critics more conscious of the concepts of "modernism" and "postmodernism." At the same time, we know that when for instance German scholars use the words "mod-

---

1. This book does not concern itself with the "modernismo" of South American and Spanish literature. Despite some parallels, the differences between the two concepts are too many to warrant their critical coalescence. Moreover, the use of the concept in Hispanic criticism, while it was established early in the century, has had virtually no influence on the formation of the critical paradigms of modernism that I discuss. For a survey of the Hispanic concept, see Ned J. Davison, *The Concept of Modernism in Hispanic Criticism* (Boulder, Colo.: Pruett Press, 1966).

ern" or "die Moderne" in the specific context of nontraditional twentieth-century literature, they are employing it in a way that parallels the use of "modernism" in English. The same goes for some other terms. It now seems obvious, for instance, that when Georg Lukács wrote about "Avantgardeismus" he was in fact dealing with "modernism" but resorted to the concept of the "avant-garde" for lack of a better term at that moment in critical history (that is, in the mid-fifties).[2]

The same lack of terminological consensus can be observed in pre-1960s Anglo-American criticism. Edmund Wilson's *Axel's Castle* (1931) is generally considered one of the first significant critical works to outline and define a modern(ist) paradigmatic shift in literature, but the term Wilson uses for this new literature is not "modernism" but "symbolism." Similarly, Joseph Frank's seminal essay "Spatial Form in Modern Literature," first published in 1945, never uses the concept "modernism" but seems to rely on the term "modern literature" as a frame of reference for the historical and aesthetic shift that Frank sees in the use of "spatial form."

As a concept, however, "modernism" has rapidly been gaining ground, and certain critical works that never even employ the term, such as those of Wilson and Frank, are now generally held to be landmark studies in literary modernism. There is a rapidly spreading agreement that "modernism" is a legitimate concept broadly signifying a paradigmatic shift, a major revolt, beginning in the mid- and late nineteenth century, against the prevalent literary and aesthetic traditions of the Western world. But this is as far as we can assume a critical and theoretical consensus to go. Beyond this point we face strikingly variable and often seemingly irreconcilable theories concerning the nature of the revolt. Hence it is not enough to admit that "vague terms still signify," to quote Michael Levenson's opening words in *A Genealogy of Modernism*.[3] Vague but widely used terms

---

2. This is indeed reflected in the English translation of Georg Lukács, *Wider den mißverstandenen Realismus* (1958): *The Meaning of Contemporary Realism*, trans. John and Necke Mander (London: Merlin Press, 1963), where "Avantgardeismus" is translated as "modernism."

3. Michael Levenson, *A Genealogy of Modernism: A Study of English Literary Doctrine, 1908–1922* (New York: Cambridge University Press, 1984), p. vii.

not only still signify, they are compelled to signify in highly relevant ways.

In the opening chapter, therefore, I ask what modernism has been made to signify, and how. Examining several different theories of modernism, we shall observe how they relate to one another and how they contribute to the making of various, often mutually conflicting, modernist paradigms.

Chapter 2 proceeds to observe the various modernist paradigms as interpretations (and fabrications) of *literary history*. As a concept used for literature, "modernism" signals a historical change on the literary scene. Even when the concept is used with no reference whatsoever to literary history, its respective placement and function within a literary-historical context are always indicated or assumed. It is primarily through this context, laden with issues of tradition, modernity, and canonization, that the concept of modernism acquires its full significance: that of highlighting and "naming" the complex relation between nontraditional or postrealist literature and history in the broader sense. This literary-historical context is certainly not always obvious or readily accessible, but we may attempt to point it out or "reconstruct" it as the locus of theoretical conflict over the concept of modernism.

Controversy over the concept and its role in literary history is frequently reflected in current debates about postmodernism, as is demonstrated in detail in chapter 3. Several proponents of postmodernism use that concept to signify the rejection or the end of the modernist era. For example, in "The Literature of Replenishment," John Barth states that any discussion of postmodernism must "either presume that modernism in its turn, at this hour of the world, needs no definition (surely everybody knows what modernism is!) or else must attempt after all to define or redefine that predominant aesthetic of Western literature . . . in the first half of this century."[4] Barth does not seem to be aware that the very claim that modernism was the "predominant aesthetic" of the first half of the

4. John Barth, "The Literature of Replenishment: Postmodernist Fiction," *Atlantic Monthly* (January 1980): 67.

century is a redefinition, one that silently dismisses the not uncommon view of modernism as an *oppositional* aesthetic.

However, what may appear as forced signification on Barth's behalf actually springs from the widespread critical assumption that modernism has now solidified into a stable category. In 1974 Maurice Beebe declared: "We can take some comfort in the realization that we can now define Modernism with confidence that we shall not have to keep adjusting our definition in order to accommodate new visions and values."[5] In light of the controversy over modernism during the past decade or so, such complacency, which is also reflected in Beebe's conservative definition of modernism, has come to seem totally ungrounded. From another perspective, as we shall see, Beebe's understanding of modernism as a settled category stems quite logically from certain powerful critical attempts at fixing modernism into an unquestionable, and unquestioning, aesthetic practice.

The comments of Barth and Beebe call attention to the important dialectical relationships between modernism and the critical apparatus brought to bear on the concept and, on the other hand, between modernism and other key concepts used to designate and map literary-historical currents of our century. Beside the term "postmodernism," these are primarily the concepts of the avant-garde and of realism.

The much-debated relation of the avant-garde with modernism constitutes the arena of my critical inquiry in chapter 4. Most relevant discussions of avant-garde practices prove to generate equally relevant perspectives on the concept of modernism, and the various estimations of the avant-garde tend to weigh heavily in critical appraisals of modernism. The two concepts obviously have a strongly reciprocal relationship which calls for a scrutiny. I find it necessary to resist tendencies to conflate the two terms or to see the avant-garde as a subcategory of modernism. It is equally important, however, to come to terms with approaches that seek to drive a critical wedge between modernism and the avant-garde. Surveying and refuting such approaches, I shall attempt to uphold a dynamic reciprocity between the two concepts.

5. Maurice Beebe, "What Modernism Was," *Journal of Modern Literature* 3 (July 1974): 1065.

The discussion of the multifaceted concept of realism, in the final chapter, should help us realize why any deliberation of modernism as a literary or aesthetic concept belongs within a broader cultural framework in which modernism is to be seen as a semiotic and historical project. Expounding and employing the concept of realism is, broadly speaking, a way of understanding and naming the connection between the mimetic powers of literature and the prevalent social contracts of signification and communication. Realism is therefore a key term that in various ways highlights the social background against which modernism receives its significance as a "negative" practice, or as a poetics of the nonorganic text. Toward the end of my book these prominent aspects of modernist aesthetics will be brought to bear, in a dialectical manner, on a brief but broad inquiry into modern cultural configurations.

While this book inevitably has to enter the domain of classificatory criticism, my primary aim is not to settle questions concerning the placement of individual works and writers. To be sure, the basis and background of this work involve my awareness of modernism in history and my inevitably implied reading and understanding of modernist works. But this is neither a history of modernism nor an interpretation of a selection of modernist works. My main focus is on the formation of a salient concept, with a view to the critical and theoretical forces at work in engendering the respective paradigm. Moreover, as an observer of such concept formation, I make no claim of excluding myself from the discourse/debate at hand. On the contrary, as a participant in the controversy over the concept of modernism, I cannot dissociate myself from the wider sociohistorical implications of that controversy.

For we are not just involved in questions of an isolated concept and its role in literary classification. What is at stake in the controversy over the concept of modernism is nothing less than the attempt to embrace conceptually—and thereby in a sense gain control over—those cultural and aesthetic agitations and changes which are seen to put a distinctively "modern" mark on literature and art, or even on Western culture in general. I say "gain control over" because I do see the debate about modernism as a *struggle* over the *meaning* of significant changes that most critics recognize, starting in the latter half of the nineteenth century, but reaching an explosive stage in the first three decades of the twentieth. Modernism, in other words, is the "name" given to these changes, but as a significant name it has proven to be a highly troublesome signifier.

The changes "named" by the concept took place in a tumultuous era: an era of Western imperialism, enormous advances in science and technology, world war, communist revolutions, crisis in the capitalist economy, the rise of fascism. The turmoil of this era signals in several ways the "creation" of the contemporary world, and no reading of our world can overlook the way it emerged from these historical disruptions. The sweeping breadth of the concept of modernism seems to indicate that changes of enormous proportions are also seen to have occurred in literature and art. If this is so, and I tend to agree that it is, then any appraisal of these changes is going to be crucial for our understanding of the present literary and cultural situation.

Positioning modernism parallel to the tumultuous aspects of modernity, however, can lead to an unproductive view of its semiotic practices. The changes that can be observed in modernist aesthetics, the disruptions and breaks with tradition that it seems to call for, do not directly *reflect* social modernity or lend us an immediate access to its distinctive qualities. Most of us do not experience modernity as a mode of disruption, however many disruptive historical events we may be aware of. I find it more to the point to see modernism as an attempt to *interrupt* the modernity that we live and understand as a social, if not "normal," way of life.[6] Such norms are not least buttressed by the various channels and media of communication, and this is where the interruptive practices of modernism ap-

---

6. The notions of a common subject ("we") and a collectively shared ("normal") way of life, even when limited to Western bourgeois reality, are bound to seem spurious in an age that many of "us" think of in terms of pluralism and endless "differences." It would be even more idealistic, however, to assume that the age of such notions has passed. Suffice it to say, at this stage, that the signs for "norms," while they remain functional, are always "under erasure." For a useful discussion of signs under erasure, see Gayatri Spivak's "Translator's Preface" to Jacques Derrida's *Of Grammatology* (Baltimore: Johns Hopkins University Press, 1976).

pear in their most significant and characteristic forms. In refusing to communicate according to established socio-semiotic contracts, they seem to imply that there are other modes of communication to be looked for, or even some other modernity to be created.

The Making of
Modernist Paradigms

THIS CHAPTER does not offer a comprehensive survey of the uses of our concept, but rather a critical inquiry into dominant, paradigmatic conceptions of what constitutes modernism. I shall examine how modernism has been understood and what the concept has been made to signify, or, to put it differently, how we collaborate with historical reality (including texts designated "modernist") in constructing the paradigm called "modernism."

The term itself appears to provide us with a semantic base on which to ground such an endeavor. "Modernism" signals a dialectical opposition to what is not functionally "modern," namely "tradition." But this pivotal characteristic seems to be progressively less prevalent in recent critical discourse, in part because we now often perceive modernist literature itself as a "tradition." Actually, the antitraditional aspects of modernism and their implications were played down at an early stage by writers and critics seeking an aesthetic order in which to ground a modern poetics. Thus, while the rage against prevalent traditions is perhaps the principal characteristic of modernism, and one that has provided it with a name, this feature has always been counteracted by a desire to forestall the anarchistic implications of such a stance. I am not thinking primarily of the attempts of Eliot, Pound, and others to create alternative, often highly personal and idiosyncratic, "traditions." This in itself can be seen as just another way of undermining the authority of tradition and unveiling the arbitrariness of the traditions that the modernists felt they were up against. I have in mind, rather, the more strictly formal-aesthetic politics of critics and commentators on modernism (some of whom were also practicing modernists). In their various guises, these approaches constitute a broad and powerful critical paradigm.

The Rage for Order

In his famous essay "Ulysses, Order, and Myth," which appeared in 1923, T. S. Eliot lays the groundwork for a great deal of subsequent criticism and appraisal of modernism. He contends that Joyce's use of Homer's *Odyssey* has the importance of "a scientific discovery," making *Ulysses* not a novel, because "the novel is a form which will no longer serve; it is because the novel, instead of being a form, was simply the expression of an age which had not sufficiently lost all form to feel the need of something stricter." This "something stricter" is the use of myth as "a way of controlling, of ordering, of giving a shape and a significance to the immense panorama of futility and anarchy which is contemporary history."[1]

Here Eliot strikes a chord that has been sounded in innumerable theories of modernism to this day. Modernism is viewed as a kind of aesthetic heroism, which in the face of the chaos of the modern world (very much a "fallen" world) sees art as the only dependable reality and as an ordering principle of a quasi-religious kind. The unity of art is supposedly a salvation from the shattered order of modern reality. The aesthetics of modernism have been made to look like a solution to Stephen Dedalus's problem in *Ulysses*, when he complains that history is a nightmare from which he is trying to awake. Eliot's aesthetics in fact strongly resembles Stephen's, presented in an ironic manner by Joyce in *A Portrait of the Artist as a Young Man*: "The esthetic image is first luminously apprehended as

1. Frank Kermode, ed., *Selected Prose of T. S. Eliot* (New York: Harcourt Brace Jovanovich/Farrar, Straus and Giroux, 1975), p. 177.

selfbounded and selfcontained upon the immeasurable background of space and time which it is not. You apprehend it as *one* thing. You see it as one whole. You apprehend its wholeness. That is *integritas.*"[2] This organic theory of art, derived partly from classical, partly from romanticist aesthetics, is echoed in different ways in a great number of works on modernism—very often through a reference to Eliot's essay or Joyce's novel—and is frequently taken to constitute the center of the revolutionary *formal* awareness and emphasis that most critics detect in modernist works.

In "Spatial Form in Modern Literature," Joseph Frank says that for T. S. Eliot "the distinctive quality of a poetic sensibility is its capacity to form new wholes, to fuse seemingly disparate experiences into an organic unity."[3] Frank finds that a spatial form of this kind is indeed the distinctive mark of "modern" literature, undermining the "inherent consecutiveness of language" (10) and suspending "the process of individual reference temporarily until the entire pattern of internal references can be apprehended as a unity" (13). In so doing modern literature locks past and present "in a timeless unity" and achieves a "transformation of the historical imagination into myth—an imagination for which time does not exist" (60).

Maurice Beebe relies partly on Frank in defining modernism, which he sees as being distinguished by four features: formalism and aesthetic autonomy; detachment and noncommitment or " 'irony' in the sense of that term as used by the New Critics"; use of myth as a structuring device; and a development from Impressionism to reflexivism, centering its attention upon "its own creation and composition."[4] There is no mention at all of the historical or social relevance of modernist

2. James Joyce, *A Portrait of the Artist as a Young Man* (New York: Penguin Books, 1976), p. 212. As an implied author Joyce is of course not uniformly ironic throughout the novel, but he wields the narrative voice in such a way that there is a fluid play of identification with and distance from the young aesthete. In view of their mode of presentation, it is surprising how literally Stephen's aesthetic theories have been read by critics as the author's forthright statements, if not his manifesto.

3. Joseph Frank, "Spatial Form in Modern Literature," *The Widening Gyre: Crisis and Mastery in Modern Literature* (New Brunswick, N.J.: Rutgers University Press, 1963), p. 10.

4. Beebe, "What Modernism Was," p. 1073.

works, to which Beebe actually refers to as "the closed worlds of Modernist art" (1077).

Such a portrayal of modernism, especially in the Anglo-American context, is clearly influenced by New Criticism, which Beebe does not fail to invoke. Eliot's position of authority, both as poet and critic, is also instrumental in this particular New Critical construction of the modernist paradigm. It is crucial not so much because of Eliot's view of the use of myth as a structuring device[5]—the New Critics were not all that interested in mythology—as because of his persistent emphasis on form as an autonomous vehicle of aesthetic significance. From a certain perspective, modernism, in its rejection of traditional social representation and in its heightening of formal awareness, would seem the ideal example of New Critical tenets and of the New Critical view of the poem as an isolated whole, whose unity is based on internal tensions that perhaps remain unresolved but nonetheless do not disturb the autonomy of the work. Indeed, when critics use the term "modernist criticism" they often seem to be referring to New Criticism, and they appear unaware that there need be no "natural" connection between modernist works and this particular critical or analytical paradigm.

To this day, however, critics persist in reading modernism through the spectacles of New Criticism. Recently this tendency has been apparent in the discussion surrounding postmodernism (see chapter 3), which is frequently seen as rejecting *this particular kind* of "modernism," together with the aesthetics of the organic, unified, autonomous and "pure" work of art. Of course, one might point out another, similar connection between modernist literature and modern criticism and theory, namely that between modernism and Russian formalism, whose emphasis on the autonomy of the literary work—based on an opposition between "poetic" and "ordinary" or "communicative" language—prefigures that of New Criticism

5. As I shall discuss later, Eliot, in his essay on the mythic order of Joyce's *Ulysses*, is actually not at all interested in the interpretive implications of mythological parallels or allusions. He is mainly concerned with securing a structural grid on which to latch the work that can find no such coherent structural means in the chaos of modern history. Hence, myth comes to serve as an aesthetic substitute for the "lost" whole of historical reality.

as well as that of a great deal of structuralist work. But as we shall see, the implications of Russian formalist poetics are more intricate and productive with respect to modernism than are those of New Criticism.

Outside History

Many modernists have to a great extent shared the "purist" views of formalists and New Critics, and have even forcefully uttered ahistorical notions of poetic autonomy in their essays and other commentaries. But nothing obliges us to take such views as adequately representative of their own work or of modernism in general. Too seldom have literary scholars demonstrated a skeptical view of such auto-commentary, as Mary Louise Pratt does in her criticism of the "poetic language" fallacy. Having shown how formalist/structuralist theories are echoed in the critical writings of modernists like Rilke, Valéry, and Mallarmé, she concludes:

> It is one thing for the poet, or even the poet-critic, to claim that his art exists in a universe of its own and bears no relation to the society in which he and his readers live. It is quite another for the literary analyst to unquestioningly accept such a view as the basis for a theory of literature. The poet's declaration that he no longer wishes his work to be associated with "society" or "reality" or "commerce" or "the masses" is hardly grounds for the critic to decide that the associations have in fact ceased to exist or ceased to pertain to the critical enterprise.[6]

That modernist literature has severed ties with society, reality, or history has indeed been a basic assumption behind a great deal of criticism of modernism—not only criticism that could be labeled formalist or New Critical, but, significantly, also historically minded criticism, in particular a certain brand of Marxist criticism. According to Robert Onopa, for instance, one of the premises of modernism, partly inherited from ro-

6. Mary Louise Pratt, *Toward a Speech Act Theory of Literary Discourse* (Bloomington: Indiana University Press, 1977), p. xviii.

manticism, "is the notion that the *uses* of art are very much like the uses of religion."[7] The use-structure of religion—consisting in salvation from and transcendence of reality, the fallen world—provides modernism with "an escape from history" (364). Onopa does not fail to relate this religious aesthetics to New Criticism:

> Organic theory, Richards' dissociation of poetic use from poetic content, and Eliot's notion of impersonal poetry all were elaborated by New Criticism, perhaps the most complete view that the work of art exists outside of, and should be treated outside of, history, since art is self-contained and generates its own laws. Once outside of history, the work is available as a paradigm of paradise, the antithesis of the fallen world, and, as a product of man, a means for him to transcend the fallen, time-bound world. (372)

Daniel Fuchs states: "The modernist aesthetic invented the New Criticism, in which judgments of form preceded judgments of meaning,"[8] and Robert Weimann goes so far as to label "modernist" the various kinds of formalist criticism that he feels have been dominant in the twentieth century, such as New Criticism and the critical works of T. S. Eliot. "Modernism," in Weimann's vocabulary, seems to stand for a rejection of any objective continuity of literary history in favor of a spatial aesthetic, be it within the literary work itself or on the level of present appreciation of the literature of the past.[9] Modernism, it would seem, like Stephen Dedalus, is striving to escape from the nightmare of history, trying to rule out the dimension of time. Lillian Robinson and Lise Vogel approach this issue from a slightly different angle but reach a parallel conclusion: "Modernism . . . seeks to intensify isolation. It forces the work of art, the artist, the critic, and the audience outside of history. Modernism denies us the possibility of understanding ourselves as

7. Robert Onopa, "The End of Art as a Spiritual Project," *TriQuarterly*, no. 26 (Winter 1973): 363.

8. Daniel Fuchs, "Saul Bellow and the Modern Tradition," *Contemporary Literature* 15 (Winter 1974): 69.

9. Robert Weimann, *Structure and Society in Literary History: Studies in the History and Theory of Historical Criticism* (Baltimore: Johns Hopkins University Press, 1984), esp. pp. 71–78, 201–10.

agents in the material world, for all has been removed to an abstract world of ideas, where interactions can be minimized or emptied of meaning and real consequences. Less than ever are we able to interpret the world—much less change it."[10]

Ironically, it was on precisely such grounds that Ortega y Gasset valorized the "dehumanization of art," the almost complete dissociation of "human sensibility" from "artistic sensibility" that he saw modern art having achieved.[11] Thus, it sometimes appears that the most radically historical and the most radically formalist critics fundamentally agree on the basic characteristic of modern(ist) art and literature, one group condemning what the other celebrates. But while Ortega is, or at least pretends to be, modestly (and aristocratically!) resigned to the subsequent status of art as "a thing of no consequence" (49), critics such as Robinson and Vogel often seem to find this state of affairs immensely threatening: it is as if by being displaced "out of history" we are lifted from a state of security and comfort and put in a bewildering place that defies interpretation, much like Kafka's heroes. It is noteworthy that some critics might want to see this as a thoroughly "historical" experience and argue that such a displacement is a moment of being shocked "into history." The latter notion is one we shall come back to, especially in discussing the theories of Theodor W. Adorno.

History with a Vengeance versus "Pure" Aesthetics

Critics who vehemently attack modernism for being ahistorical, on grounds of its preoccupation with formal order, often open the floodgates of history through their very characterization of modernism. In an essay on expressionism written in 1934, Georg Lukács attacked its abstract, ahistorical, irrational, and mythical forms, claiming that the new fascist powers should find in it a suitable aesthetic to draw on in forming a

---

10. Lillian Robinson and Lise Vogel, "Modernism and History," *New Literary History* 3 (Autumn 1971): 198.

11. José Ortega y Gasset, *The Dehumanization of Art and Other Essays on Art, Culture, and Literature* (Princeton, N.J.: Princeton University Press, 1968), p. 11.

new culture.[12] Although three years later the Nazis denounced expressionism as "decadent art," this analogy between modernism and fascism has persistently been drawn, partly because several modernists have actually tended toward, or even openly supported, fascism. In one of the two essays that started the expressionist controversy in the German expatriate magazine *Das Wort* in the late 1930s, Klaus Mann attacked the famous poet Gottfried Benn, arguing that his overemphasis on form reflected the authoritarian order and discipline of the fascist state.[13] It later became a commonplace to elaborate on this formal-ideological connection in generalizing about modernism, well-known examples being Fredric Jameson's *Fables of Aggression: Wyndham Lewis, the Modernist as Fascist*, and Frank Kermode's discussion of modernism in *The Sense of an Ending*. Kermode argues that modernists find in myth and in the "formal elegance of fascism" a means to create closed, immobile aesthetic hierarchies; such form expresses "order as the modernist artist understands it: rigid, out of flux, the spatial order of the modern critic or the closed authoritarian society."[14]

But in light of the eagerness displayed in critically establishing a connection between modernism and fascism, it is baffling how rarely its further historical and formal implications are probed. First, where does this formal-ideological nexus place modernism with regard to the prevalent capitalist-bourgeois culture of the twentieth century? Second, how, and under what conditions, can aesthetically elaborated form (*as form*) become the vehicle of a specific ideology? And third, do readers of modernist works actually or predominantly experience the strict formal elegance that proponents as well as adversaries of modernism so often concentrate on? It is highly significant that while modernism is often accused of being a *cult of form*, it is also (not infrequently by the same critics, such as Lukács)

12. Georg Lukács, "Größe und Verfall des Expressionismus," *Essays über Realismus* (Neuwied and Berlin: Luchterhand, 1971), pp. 109–49.

13. Klaus Mann, "Gottfried Benn. Die Geschichte einer Verirrung," in Hans-Jürgen Schmitt, ed., *Die Expressionismusdebatte: Materialien zu einer marxistischen Realismuskonzeption* (Frankfurt: Suhrkamp, 1973), pp. 39–49.

14. Frank Kermode, *The Sense of an Ending: Studies in the Theory of Fiction* (New York: Oxford University Press, 1966), pp. 114, 111.

attacked for *formlessness* and for distorted and anarchic representation of society, disintegration of outer reality, and disorderly manipulation of language. It is at this point that the whole notion of modernism moving the communicative act of reading "outside of history" shows itself to be a contradiction in terms, for the very detection of either exaggerated formal maneuvers or distorted representations of reality assumes some kind of "norm," a symbolic and semiotic order that underlies our every act of social communication.

It is not surprising, therefore, that in writings on modernism the theory of aesthetic autonomy frequently appears to coexist with that of cultural subversion, or a questioning of the very foundations of the reigning social order. This, it seems to me, is a central paradox of modernist studies. In an essay in the widely read symposium *Modernism 1890–1930*, Malcolm Bradbury and John Fletcher remark how modernists strive for "that making of pattern and wholeness which makes art into an order standing outside and beyond the human muddle, a transcendent object, a luminous whole."[15] In another essay in the same anthology, written by Bradbury and James McFarlane, modernism is seen to signal "overwhelming dislocations," one of "those cataclysmic upheavals of culture" that "question an entire civilization or culture."[16] This underscores, I believe, the most important task facing modernist studies: we need to ask ourselves how the concept of autonomy, so crucial to many theories of modernism, can possibly coexist with the equally prominent view of modernism as a historically explosive paradigm. This dichotomy, hardly recognized by most critics, is characteristic for the divergent approaches to modernism as, on the one hand, a *cultural force*, and on the other as an *aesthetic project*. But if we refuse, as I think we must, to acknowledge any strict boundaries between the two, then the Dedalian view of the work of art as a "transcendent object" and an isolated aesthetic whole is invalidated as a critical basis for modernist studies; it is an abstract notion that is bound to be unsettled or

15. Malcolm Bradbury and John Fletcher, "The Introverted Novel," in Malcolm Bradbury and James McFarlane, ed., *Modernism, 1890–1930* (Harmondsworth, Eng.: Penguin Books, 1976), p. 407.

16. Malcolm Bradbury and James McFarlane, "The Name and Nature of Modernism," in Bradbury and McFarlane, ed., *Modernism, 1890–1930*, p. 19.

deconstructed when the work is received and disseminated, when it enters the "human muddle."

Clement Greenberg, in his well-known essay "Modernist Painting," provides us with a good example of how critics often seek to skirt the problem of cultural dislodgment: "The essence of Modernism lies, as I see it, in the use of the characteristic methods of a discipline to criticize the discipline itself—not in order to subvert it, but to entrench it more firmly in its area of competence."[17] Hence, "each art had to determine, through the operations peculiar to itself, the effects peculiar and exclusive to itself" whereby "each art would be rendered 'pure,' and in its 'purity' find the guarantee of its standards of quality as well as of its independence" (102). The effects peculiar to painting lie in its flatness or two-dimensionality, but those of literature would analogously rest in the "materiality" of language or of "the word," as opposed to its communicative function; very much, of course, the argument of the Russian formalists. But Greenberg is caught in a kind of intentional fallacy: he asserts that the modernist self-criticism of each artistic discipline does *not* take place "in order to subvert it," but he fails to provide any arguments or evidence concerning this nonintention, or, more important, concerning its nonsubversive *effect*. Ironically, he would hardly bring up the issue of subversion if he did not consider it a potential result of this self-critical function of modernism.

Despite the obvious weaknesses in his argument, Greenberg's theory has become a standard approach to modernism, thus buttressing an immensely powerful critical paradigm in modernist studies, a paradigm moreover that is now accepted by various less formalistically oriented critics. In fact, this paradigmatic construction is often simply accepted as an objective observation. Thus, Hal Foster, arguing for a "postmodernism of resistance," has no qualms about talking about the modernist striving for "the purity of each art," a purity clearly analogous to and arising from the sanctity of individual modernist works, which he describes as "unique, symbolic, visionary" and as "closed systems."[18] Moreover, this ahistorical pro-

17. Clement Greenberg, "Modernist Painting," in Gregory Battock, ed., *The New Art: A Critical Anthology* (New York: E. P. Dutton, 1966), p. 101.

18. Hal Foster, "Postmodernism: A Preface," in Hal Foster, ed., *The Anti-*

jection seems to have found its way into theories ostensibly approaching modernism from a very different angle. Alan Wilde, in his self-declared phenomenological approach, establishes for the "absolute irony" of modernist works a concept of the "anironic," which is based on a moment of fusion and harmony, a "formal symmetry," a self-contained aesthetic whole that balances out the modernist perception of fragmentation: "Unable to make sense of the world but unwilling to forgo the ideal model of orderliness, the absolute ironist folds back on himself in the sanctuary of his art."[19] This reading of the modernist paradigm is only a thinly disguised reworking of the New Critical approach, according to which the modernist work manages to garner for itself a total aesthetic autonomy in its unresolved ironic tensions, its "equal poise of opposites" (35).

We should now be ready to turn to critics who are less likely to be hampered by aestheticist, formalist, or New Critical theories and who do not turn so blind an eye to the historical significance of modernist aesthetic practices.

Complementing History

R. A. Scott-James notes that "there are characteristics of modern life in general which can only be summed up, as Mr. Thomas Hardy and others have summed them up, by the word *modernism*."[20] Scott-James has in mind a highly self-conscious, bleak mode of sociocultural expression that he sees as being on a threatening rise in the domain of literature. His book, published in 1908, was of course written before the wave of the more radical formal experiments in modernist literature and art, but it significantly prefigures a good deal of critical response to modernism as a historical and cultural force, in contrast to the various aesthetic appraisals that largely limit

---

Aesthetic: Essays on Postmodern Culture (Port Townsend, Wash.: Bay Press, 1983), pp. x–xi.

19. Alan Wilde, *Horizons of Assent: Modernism, Postmodernism, and the Ironic Imagination* (Baltimore: Johns Hopkins University Press, 1981), pp. 33–34.

20. R. A. Scott-James, *Modernism and Romance* (New York and London: John Lane, 1908), p. ix.

themselves to the formal characteristics and achievements of modernist writing. The former, instead of viewing modernist aesthetics as more or less divorced from history, seeks to inquire into the various ways in which modernism either parallels, interacts with, or reacts to social modernity. Such studies set up modernist paradigms that appear radically different from the formalist ones, although the latter have arguably had the upper hand on the post–World War II critical scene, at least within the Anglo-American sphere.

Naturally, such cultural inquiries do not constitute a uniform approach to modernism. There is, however, widespread agreement as to the constituents of modernity to which modernism is felt to be responding. I have already alluded to some decisive moments in the general historical framework of the so-called modern experience. Its more detailed "physical" signs and symptoms have often enough been enumerated and packed into summaries; I have selected the following pregnant specimen, taken from one of the most spirited books on the issue of modernism, Marshall Berman's *All That Is Solid Melts into Air*:

The maelstrom of modern life has been fed from many sources: great discoveries in the physical sciences, changing our images of the universe and our place in it; the industrialization of production, which transforms scientific knowledge into technology, creates new human environments and destroys old ones, speeds up the whole tempo of life, generates new forms of corporate power and class struggle; immense demographic upheavals, severing millions of people from their ancestral habitats, hurtling them halfway across the world into new lives; rapid and often cataclysmic urban growth; systems of mass communication, dynamic in their development, enveloping and binding together the most diverse people and societies; increasingly powerful national states, bureaucratically structured and operated, constantly striving to expand their powers; mass social movements of people, and peoples, challenging their political and economic rulers, striving to gain some control over their lives; finally, bearing and driving all these people and institutions along, an ever-expanding, drastically fluctuating capitalist world market. In the twentieth century, the social processes that bring this maelstrom into being, and keep it in a state of perpetual becoming, have come to be called "modernization."[21]

The visions and ideals nourished by these "world-historical processes," Berman goes on, have "come to be loosely grouped together under the name of 'modernism.' This book is a study in the dialectics of modernization and modernism." One might feel that "modernism" is in fact used all too "loosely" here, but Berman's study typifies one approach to modernism, namely, a general view of it as a dialectical counterpart of social modernity, partaking of both the fascination and the destruction that characterize modernization. And although Berman's work could not be said to represent an aesthetic "reflection theory," modernism (being a broad and seemingly dominant cultural trend) is for him a kind of mirror image of social modernization.

Several other scholars have elaborated on the dialectics of modernization and modernism. Hugh Kenner points out how modern science has changed the world outlook in art as well as its formal characteristics. He argues that modernist poetry, like modern science, draws on "patterned energies"[22] as well as on qualities of space discovered in the twentieth century. Elsewhere he points out that the radically altered "quality of city life" obligated a "change in artistic means."[23] He mentions the "Machine," the "Crowd," electricity, telephone, new means of transportation, and other aspects of modern technology, and goes on to discuss how these elements influenced the structure of James Joyce's work (and not just his subject matter). "The deep connections between modernism and modern urban rhythms" are nowhere more evident than in *Ulysses*," Kenner concludes (28). Such rhythms and sounds are also prominent in other major modernist novels, some of which followed in the wake of *Ulysses*; one thinks for instance of Döblin's *Berlin Alexanderplatz* and Dos Passos's *Manhattan Transfer*. But the

21. Marshall Berman, *All That Is Solid Melts into Air: The Experience of Modernity* (New York: Simon and Schuster, 1982), p. 16.

22. Hugh Kenner, *The Pound Era* (Berkeley and Los Angeles: University of California Press, 1971), p. 153.

23. Hugh Kenner, "Notes toward an Anatomy of 'Modernism,'" in E. L. Epstein, ed., *A Starchamber Quiry: A James Joyce Centennial Volume, 1882-1982* (London: Methuen, 1982), pp. 4–5.

structural connections between modernism and modern city life also reach back in time beyond *Ulysses*, and are often traced to Baudelaire's poetry.

Thus, critics have frequently elaborated on the *parallels* between urban life, modern science, and technological progress on the one hand and modernist art and literature on the other. James Mellard notes that when "the new science exploded the world, it exploded with it the novel as well."[24] The problem with modernist paradigms invoked by drawing such direct analogies between modernism and modernity (scientific or more broadly social) is that modernism, and the social experience it utters, assumes the role of a reverberation and even reflection of social modernization. Such an analogy can easily miss the sociocultural and ideological positioning of modernism with regard to social modernity, or can reduce it to a unilaterally reproductive or symbolic act. The latter tendency, in fact, is clearly exemplified by critics who see in the formal fervor of modernism a reflection of fascist discipline or totalitarian ideologies.

One can of course point to several parallels between modernization in social life and in art. It is well known, for instance, that certain modernist groups, in particular the Italian futurists, reveled in the technological aspects of modernity and celebrated in their work modern machinery, the increased tempo of urban life, in some cases even modern warfare. But we must not let such cases obscure the undeniably troubled relationship that generally exists between modernism and modernization. In "What Was Modernism?" Harry Levin asks in conclusion, playing on Stephen Dedalus's famous pledge in *A Portrait of the Artist as a Young Man*, whether it has not been the endeavor of the modernist generation "to have created a conscience for a scientific age?"[25] "For" may be a misleading preposition here, should it suggest that this conscience is uniformly activated *by* the "scientific age" or by modernization in general. Is this highly disturbed conscience not a critical reaction to modern-

---

24. James M. Mellard, *The Exploded Form: The Modernist Novel in America* (Urbana: University of Illinois Press, 1980), p. 30.

25. Harry Levin, "What Was Modernism?" *Refractions: Essays in Comparative Literature* (New York: Oxford University Press, 1966), p. 295.

ization, presenting its otherness, its negativity, that which is negated by the prominent modes of cultural production?

Answering this question involves, of course, determining the semantic and significatory status of "modernization," of sociocultural modernity. In the introductory essay to *Modernism 1890–1930*, Bradbury and McFarlane assert: "Modernism is our art; it is the one art that responds to the scenario of our chaos."[26] It is noteworthy that their criterion seems to be that our age indeed constitutes a "chaos." This is arguably a modernist criterion, but risks restricting modernism to a mirroring relationship with this "scenario of our chaos." In fact the authors do go on to draw the kind of analogy discussed above: "It is the art consequent on Heisenberg's 'Uncertainty Principle', of the destruction of civilization and reason in the First World War . . . of existential exposure to meaninglessness or absurdity," to quote but a few items from their list. Later on, however, they seem to eschew this reductive analogy, when they argue that modernism is to some extent centered in "a notion of a relationship of crisis between art and history" (29). Such a relationship of crisis would explain why modernist art can *not* simply be the reflecting counterpart of history, or of social modernization. This relationship, and hence the conscience that modernism may have created for (or against) our scientific age, is clearly too troubled and distorted to be possibly mapped on to classical and mimetic models of the relationship between art and reality.

Mimetic notions, however, have sometimes been used as an apology for modernism. In his seminal anthology of 1919, *Menschheitsdämmerung*, Kurt Pinthus asks about modern poetry: "Must it not be chaotic, like the age out of whose torn and bloody soil it grew?"[27] Later Georg Lukács was to *attack* modernism on mimetic grounds. In his contribution to the expressionist controversy in *Das Wort*, he claimed that expressionism had drastically failed to reflect adequately the "objective totality of reality,"[28] and that like other modern movements of the

26. Bradbury and McFarlane, "The Name and Nature of Modernism," in Bradbury and McFarlane, ed., *Modernism, 1890–1930*, p. 27.

27. Kurt Pinthus, *Menschheitsdämmerung: Ein Dokument des Expressionismus* (Hamburg: Rowohlt Taschenbuch, 1959), p. 25 (my translation).

28. Georg Lukács, "Es geht um den Realismus," in Schmitt, ed., *Die Expressionismusdebatte*, p. 198. I find Lukács's formulation important: "Das Problem der

imperialist era it reflected only the "tattered surface" of capitalist society in an "unmediated" manner (201–202). Thus, expressionism "disavows every relation to reality" and declares a subjective war on all its contents (207). The paradox here is that expressionism supposedly disavows its ties to reality while also reflecting, in its unprocessed rawness, the "tattered surface" of that reality, that is, capitalist society.

The problem lies in Lukács's reflection theory, which appears to assume that "reality" can actually be rendered ("mirrored") without being mediated. But in his early works Lukács had already argued that the reality that people may perceive as being unmediated will generally not appear to have a "tattered surface" (it is no coincidence that in the essay at hand he denounces both his *Theory of the Novel* and *History and Class Consciousness* as youthful, "idealistic" and "reactionary" works [218–219]). In order to survive and reproduce itself, capitalist ideology requires a smooth surface, one which, in the process of its mediation, takes on the guise of a *normal* human condition.[29] In *Wider den mißverstandenen Realismus* Lukács states that in modernist writing everyday life under capitalism, the bourgeois norm, is, to a large extent justifiably, presented as a "distortion" (in terms of petrification as well as fragmentation) of the human character. But, says Lukács, literature must have a clear social-human "concept of the normal if it is to 'place' distortion correctly," see it in its correct context, "that is to say, to see it as *as* distortion."[30]

The concept of the "normal" is central here: it is inconceivable that capitalist reality could be continually "lived" as a distortion, for then the distortion would have no background of normalcy against which it would be recognizable. If, however, the reality of the bourgeois-capitalist era is lived as a more or

---

objektiven Totalität der Wirklichkeit." It has been trimmed down to "question of totality" in the English translation: "Realism in the Balance," trans. Rodney Livingston, in Ernst Bloch et al., *Aesthetics and Politics* (London: New Left Books, 1977), p. 33. Subsequent page references are to the German version.

29. Such normalcy, however, is radically ruptured in the case of extended "physical" crisis, especially that of war, which is of course the historical background for Kurt Pinthus's remark quoted above.

30. Lukács, *The Meaning of Contemporary Realism*, p. 33. Cf. the German original, *Wider den mißverstandenen Realismus* (Hamburg: Claassen, 1958), pp. 32–33.

less accepted *order*, as "the normal," then Lukács's view of the modernist distortion of life calls forth implications radically different from those he seeks to establish, since modernism can only present society as a place of distortion by working against a dominant concept of the normal. This is a dialectics that Lukács will not acknowledge, since his concept of "the normal" is of a specific ideological order and not the one operative in bourgeois society (although his career can be partly seen as trying to reconcile the two). Lukács is thus in agreement with a host of other critics in taking modernism to task for distorting reality, for failing to adhere to normal conditions of human life, for creating a sense of chaos in its depiction of the world, and for causing a perceptual crisis in the receiver.

Aesthetics of Subversion

Lukács's approach to the issue of modernism is contradictory, but his contradictions are illuminating. They illustrate how the historical conception of a modernist paradigm can (and has tended to) vacillate between mimetic notions of a modern "chaos" reflected in one way or another by modernist works and an understanding of modernism as a chaotic subversion of the communicative and semiotic norms of society.

Not all those who judge modernism critically from the vantage point of social norms are as hostile as Lukács, and some are among the most perceptive commentators on modernism. In what remains one of the most interesting and insightful essays on modernism, "The Brown Stocking" (the final chapter of *Mimesis*), Erich Auerbach brilliantly analyzes Virginia Woolf's novel *To the Lighthouse* as a representative literary approach to, and "realist" reworking of, modern reality. *To the Lighthouse* might seem to be an ideal example of the "aesthetic whole" in modernist art, ending as it does with the boat reaching the lighthouse and with Lily Briscoe's line being drawn in the center of her painting: "With a sudden intensity, as if she saw it clear for a second, she drew a line there, in the centre. It was done; it was finished. Yes, she thought . . . I have had my vision."[31] Auerbach, however, not limiting his interests to

31. Virginia Woolf, *To the Lighthouse* (London: Panther Books, 1977), p. 192. *To the Lighthouse* has actually been used as an example of a "close alliance" between

strictly formal matters, finds that the novel tends toward chaos, toward the breaking down of cultural unity or "whole." In this as well as in other works that break with traditional methods of representation, he sees signs of "confusion" and "a certain atmosphere of universal doom" and "something hostile to the reality which they represent."[32]

Another liberal humanist, Lionel Trilling, approaches modernism in a not dissimilar fashion. "On the Modern Element in Modern Literature" describes how wary he was when first offering a course on modern literature to his students, since it seemed to him that its "modern element" entailed quite ominous portrayals of human irrationality and cultural subversion that were obviously hostile to the dominant views of social order of which he and his students were a part.[33] The conservative culture critic Daniel Bell, making the issue more explicitly ideological, claims that for over a century modernism has persisted in "providing renewed and sustained attacks on the bourgeois social structure."[34]

In this respect Lukács, the Marxist, is basically in agreement with Bell. Using Kafka as an archetypal example, Lukács claims that modernists reduce social reality to nightmare and portray it as an angst-ridden, absurd world, thus depriving us of any sense of perspective. We have already seen how Lukács, who constantly argued that Marxist ideology had to build on and critically utilize the bourgeois heritage, claims that literature must have a clear social-human concept of the "normal," and that this is precisely what modernism denounces. Lukács shares with Auerbach and Trilling the notion that as a cultural force modernism leads to the inevitable subversion of traditional humanism (a topic we shall take up again later in this chapter). But what we see in this variety of responses to modernism is significantly the very reverse of Eliot's view of the

---

modernism and New Criticism; see Joanne V. Creighton, "The Reader and Modern and Post-Modern Fiction," *College Literature* 9 (1982): 216–18.

32. Erich Auerbach, *Mimesis: The Representation of Reality in Western Literature*, trans. Willard R. Trask (Princeton, N.J.: Princeton University Press, 1953), p. 551.

33. Lionel Trilling, "On the Modern Element in Modern Literature," in Stanley Burnshaw, ed., *Varieties of Literary Experience* (New York: New York University Press, 1962), pp. 407–33.

34. Daniel Bell, "Beyond Modernism, Beyond Self," *The Winding Passage: Essays and Sociological Journeys, 1960–1980* (New York: Basic, 1980), pp. 275–76.

paradigmatic breakthrough achieved by Joyce in *Ulysses*. Whereas Eliot saw Joyce imposing a strict aesthetic order upon the futility and anarchy of contemporary history, these critics judge modernism as an anarchic force attacking and even severely undermining our social order and our habitual way of perceiving and communicating reality.

Crisis of the Subject

Approached from such angles of social norms, modernism is judged not as an aesthetic complement of social modernity, but rather as a vehicle of crisis within the "progress" of modernization. The signs of this crisis are generally felt to reside in a modernist preoccupation with human consciousness (as opposed to a mimetic concern with the human environment and social conditions), and they are perhaps most pronounced in the use of the "stream of consciousness" technique in modernist fiction. Thus, in view of previous literary history, modernism is felt to signal a radical "inward turn" in literature, and often a more thorough exploration of the human psyche than is deemed to have been probable or even possible in pre-Freudian times. But this inward turn is also widely held to have ruptured the conventional ties between the individual and society.

According to Lukács, modernism, aided by contemporary theories of existential philosophy, presents the individual as being eternally and by nature solitary, extricated from all human, and in particular from all social, relations, existing ontologically independent of them.[35] Consequently, by showing the individual as being "thrown into existence," modernism basically negates outward reality, and equates man's inwardness with an abstract subjectivity. This "reading" of the modernist presentation of human individuality consolidated early on into a prominent paradigm. In the words Ortega y Gasset used for the will-to-style of modern art, it is often characterized as the "dehumanization of art." But the dismantling of conventional presentation of individuality has led to a certain dichot-

35. Lukács, *Wider den mißverstandenen Realismus*, p. 16; *The Meaning of Contemporary Realism*, p. 20.

omy in modernist aesthetics as well as in theories of modernism. On the one hand, it seems that modernism is built on highly subjectivist premises: by directing its attention so predominantly toward individual or subjective experience, it elevates the ego in proportion to a diminishing awareness of objective or coherent outside reality. It is customary to point to the preeminence of such subjectivist poetics in expressionist and surrealist literature, and more specifically in certain techniques, such as manipulation of "centers of consciousness" or the use of "stream of consciousness" in modern fiction.

On the other hand, modernism is often held to draw its legitimacy primarily from writing based on highly antisubjectivist or impersonal poetics. T. S. Eliot was one of the most adamant spokesmen of a neoclassical reaction against romantic-personal poetry: "Poetry is not a turning loose of emotion, but an escape from emotion; it is not the expression of personality, but an escape from personality." Hence, "the progress of an artist is a continual self-sacrifice, a continual extinction of personality," and "it is in this depersonalization that art may be said to approach the condition of science."[36]

In his study of the "genealogy" of English modernism, Michael Levenson has shown how "modernism was individualist before it was anti-individualist, anti-traditional before it was traditional, inclined to anarchism before it was inclined to authoritarianism."[37] But such differences and developments can easily be overemphasized and are sometimes based on misleading notions of the author's "presence in" or "absence from" the work as it is received. In *Ulysses*, for example, it is near impossible to detect a narrator or narrative perspectives that can decidedly be said to represent the author. In that limited sense, the text might be called antisubjective or impersonal (and Joyce was indeed a spokesman of a "poetics of impersonality"), but at the same time we experience in the work radical modes of subjective representation of reality, to the extent that outside reality comes to lose its habitual, mimetic reliability. But so does the "reality" of individual experiences mediated

36. T. S. Eliot, "Tradition and the Individual Talent," *Selected Essays, 1917–1932* (New York: Harcourt, Brace, 1932), pp. 10, 7.
37. Levenson, *A Genealogy of Modernism*, p. 79.

through the text, and in this respect the effect of such "subjective" methods is clearly related to that of the "loss of self" or the "erasure of personality" that exhausts many characters in modern fiction, such as Ulrich in Musil's *Mann ohne Eigenschaften*.[38] This foregrounds a decisive point: what the modernist poetics of impersonality and that of extreme subjectivity have in common (and this outweighs whatever may separate them) is a revolt against the traditional relation of the subject to the outside world.

In one sense, therefore, Lukács is not far off the mark in stating that the ontological degradation of the objective reality of man's outside world (Außenwelt des Menschen) and the corresponding exaltation of his subjectivity necessarily result in a distorted structure of the subject.[39] The problem is that Lukács takes this subject to be an already given, natural entity, whereby he forfeits a critical distance that might elucidate modernist treatments of subjectivity. Gabriel Josipovici, for instance, claims that modernism brings about a deep questioning of the bourgeois self that "was in fact a *construction*. It was built up by impulses within us in order to protect us from chaos and destruction."[40] And this has of course been a basic view of a great deal of recent criticism and theory, much of which has in fact vehemently reinforced modernist deconstruction of bourgeois identity.

It is a widespread notion that chaos and destruction are the only alternatives that modernism has held up for individuality and the traditional bourgeois self. Again, we can look to Lukács for a critical (and highly polemic) "construction" of a modernist paradigm. His views are representative not only because his approach to modernism has assumed a central place in much sociological and Marxist criticism, but also because of his strong ties with traditional bourgeois humanism, the critical branch of which has often reacted with great reserve, if not

38. See Wylie Sypher, *Loss of the Self in Modern Literature and Art* (New York: Vintage Books, 1962), p. 74.

39. Lukács, *Wider den mißverstandenen Realismus*, p. 22; *The Meaning of Contemporary Realism*, p. 24. Lukács talks about a "Verzerrung" in the "dynamischen Struktur des Subjekts."

40. Gabriel Josipovici, *The Lessons of Modernism and Other Essays* (Totowa, N.J.: Rowman and Littlefield, 1977), p. x.

hostility, to modernism. In dealing with expressionism in the thirties, Lukács was mainly responding to the "formalism" of its poetry, but when he comes to write *Wider den mißverstand-enen Realismus* his emphasis is on fiction, and his views are largely shaped and sharpened by his reaction to modernist modes of characterization. He attacks modernism for not creating believable and lasting "types," but instead effecting a fading of characters into shadows or congealment in ghostly irrationality. By reducing reality to a nightmare, possibly in the nebulous consciousness of an idiot, and through its obsession with the morbid and the pathological, modernism partakes in "a glorification of the abnormal," in "anti-humanism."[41]

Again Lukács involves us in an insightful paradox. While he finds modernism to have severed the essential ties between subjective experience and objective reality, he still sees in its portrayal of the human character an *aggressive* social (that is *anti*social) attitude, which he and several other critics have judged to betoken a crisis of humanism. One is reminded again of the words of Robinson and Vogel on how the modernist intensification of isolation undermines our interpretive facilities. Humanist critics are often of the same opinion. Eugene Goodheart finds that the "lesson of modernism" lies in providing "an exacerbated sense of insecurity about the world . . . and if one institutionalizes this lesson in the university, one is getting not moral guidance, but subversion."[42] Like some other critics, Goodheart finds an early sign of this tendency in Dostoevsky's *Notes from Underground*: "Dostoevsky's underground man violates every rule of moral and intellectual decorum in order to achieve a sense of individual vitality. . . . He regards the moral sense as a disease from which he is trying to purge himself" (10). The nameless (anti)hero of Dostoevsky's work, who begins by stating that he is sick and who seeks to distance himself from all "normal" behavior, is often seen as the prototype of the modernist "hero," in whom heightened

41. Lukács, *Wider den mißverstandenen Realismus*, pp. 63, 31, 29, 32; *The Meaning of Contemporary Realism*, pp. 58, 31, 30, 32. The English translation is at times inaccurate, and sometimes condenses the text to the point of leaving out relevant things.

42. Eugene Goodheart, "Modernism and the Critical Spirit," *The Failure of Criticism* (Cambridge, Mass.: Harvard University Press, 1978), p. 10.

consciousness and social isolation and paralysis go hand in hand, as do the exaltation of individuality and its erasure.

Modernism and Its Discontents

Notes from Underground is among the books Lionel Trilling finds characteristic for the "modern element" that he sees as socially subversive, hostile to the positivism and the "common sense" of our bourgeois era. Trilling comes to the conclusion that characteristically *modern* literature, and the "freedom" it seeks, are incompatible with our society.[43] Several humanist critics have highlighted the discontent of modernism at the hands of social order, the extraordinarily bleak view of modern culture and society they find embodied in modernism. According to Richard Poirier, "modernism is associated with being unhappy."[44] Part of the fame of Eliot's *Waste Land* springs undoubtedly from the fact that its title is felt to be typically evocative of the pessimistic view of modern culture often associated with modernism (which its adversaries sometimes call "wastelandism"). Modernist writing—and here it is often felt to be greatly influenced by Nietzsche—in its preoccupation with "alienation, fragmentation, break with tradition, isolation and magnification of subjectivity, threat of the void, weight of vast numbers and monolithic impersonal institutions, hatred of civilization itself" (these are, according to Daniel Fuchs, the "general characteristics of modernism"[45]), would seem to be the music played to the imminent decline of Western culture.

Other critics, elaborating on the dark vision that modernism is felt to usher in, lay more stress on how it opens the gates to the forces of the irrational, and some lament the concomitant destruction of reason. The modernist interest in human consciousness was not least directed at the recently "discovered" subconscious layers of the life of the mind. It is noteworthy that

43. Trilling, "On the Modern Element in Modern Literature," p. 433.
44. Richard Poirier, "The Difficulties of Modernism and the Modernism of Difficulty," in Arthur Edelstein, ed., *Images and Ideas in American Culture: The Functions of Criticism* (Hanover, N.H.: Brandeis University Press, 1979), p. 125.
45. Fuchs, "Saul Bellow and the Modern Tradition," p. 75.

Lukács, in discussing the modernist obsession with the pathological, sees in it a tendency conspicuously analogous to Freud's psychological theories.[46] Several modernists were of course influenced by Freud, and we can no doubt extract from modernist studies various significant aspects of a "Freudian" theory of modernism. But modernist explorations of the darker regions of the mind frequently go hand in hand with the kind of cultural and historical revolt often associated with Nietzsche. This approach to modernism is perhaps most forcefully presented not in a piece of academic criticism, but by Thomas Mann in *Doktor Faustus*, which is indeed a book about music composed for an era of decline and destruction.

Doktor Faustus although a novel, is one of the most important books *about* modernism, written by an author who was continually contemplating the cultural implications of modernism in art and literature (whether Mann was himself a "practicing" modernist is by no means as obvious as some critics seem to think; his whole relationship with aesthetic modernity is extremely complex). In *Doktor Faustus* he amalgamates his views of modernism into a novel whose "hero" is both a modernist artist and a kind of reincarnation of Nietzsche, whom Mann considered the preeminent cultural precursor of modernism. I believe we can find in this novel a rich melting pot of paradigmatic notions about modernism.[47]

In the composer Adrian Leverkühn we find, first of all, a familiar *biographical* image of the modernist artist. Leverkühn typifies the isolation of the artist from modern society. He suffers from "Weltscheu," as he calls it; in a way he symbolizes the separation, so often associated with modernism, of the world of art from the "real" or "outside" world. Not only does he ignore a public audience, "because he altogether declined to imagine a contemporary public for his exclusive, eccentric, fantastic dreams,"[48] but he seems to have only scorn for the

46. Lukács, *Wider den mißverstandenen Realismus*, p. 29; *The Meaning of Contemporary Realism*, p. 30.

47. I am not the first critic to note the relevance of Mann's novel for the whole debate around modernism. Gabriel Josipovici states in the preface to *The Lessons of Modernism* that his book is "the result of a long struggle to come to terms with . . . Thomas Mann's Dr. Faustus" (p. ix).

48. Thomas Mann, *Doctor Faustus: The Life of the German Composer Adrian Leverkühn as Told by a Friend*, trans. H. T. Lowe-Porter (New York: Vintage Books, 1971), p. 165.

outside world: "He wanted to know nothing, see nothing, actually experience nothing, at least not in any obvious, exterior sense of the word" (176). His aesthetic views are characterized by the subjective-impersonal nexus mentioned above. He refuses to discuss his music as a personal expression, yet his art is said to arise from "his exclusive, eccentric, fantastic dreams" (165). His biographer, Serenus Zeitblom, finds a perfect expression of this paradox in Leverkühn's last work: "The creator of *'Fausti Wehe-klage'* can, in the previously organized material, unhampered, untroubled by the already given structure, yield himself to subjectivity; and so this, his technically most rigid work, a work of extreme calculation, is at the same time purely expressive" (488). Zeitblom experiences a kind of solution of the paradox we have already mentioned: how modernist works often seem to involve an interplay of spontaneous reactions of subjective faculties and a "distancing" effect caused by elaborate formal mediation. This becomes a central issue for the dichotomy of order and chaos that runs through the novel.

Already at the beginning of his career Leverkühn finds Western culture a wasteland. He wonders whether epochs that really experienced *culture* could have known the concept itself. For unconscious presence, "naiveté," may be a prerequisite of culture.

> What we are losing is just this naïveté, and this lack, if one may so speak of it, protects us from many a colourful barbarism which altogether perfectly agreed with culture, even with very high culture. I mean: our state is that of civilization—a very praiseworthy state no doubt, but also neither was there any doubt that we should have to become very much more barbaric to be capable of culture again. Technique and comfort—in that state one talks about culture but one has not got it. (59–60)

Leverkühn's music can be seen as a search for this barbarism that would bring back "Kultur" into a decadent modernity. It is significant that Zeitblom's biographical task, as he sees it, is very much like that of many students of modernism, that is, he is seeking to reestablish the "lost" connections between the world of art (in this case the art of Leverkühn) and the world of history: "The subject of the narrative is the same: 'the outer world,' and the history of my departed friend's connection or lack of connection with it" (397). But Zeitblom's own sense of history and the world around him is inextricably tied up with a strong tradition from which he is unable to distance himself. Leverkühn might actually be alluding in part to Zeitblom when he says that "the nineteenth century must have been an uncommonly pleasant epoch, since it had never been harder for humanity to tear itself away from the opinions and habits of the previous period than it was for the generation now living" (25).

Leverkühn, however, being almost painfully self-conscious of the habitualized modes of existence (and this awareness is in itself often considered a major characteristic of modernism), revolts against the aesthetic traditions of the nineteenth century. While still a student he asks why "almost all, no, all the methods and conventions of art today *are good for parody only?*" (134). In reporting on one of Leverkühn's works, Zeitblom notes: "There are altogether no thematic connections, developments, variations. . . . Of traditional forms not a trace" (456). But what troubles Zeitblom more than Leverkühn's formal innovations is the fact that they carry with them, in his major works, a deep questioning of prevalent notions of human existence, indeed, a radical decentering of man. Leverkühn wants his music to depict a universe in which modern man is peripheral, while the elemental and the primal dominate; he describes for Zeitblom his fascination with outer space and the depths of the ocean with its monstrous creatures, which he would like to bring to the surface (269–70). The psychological implications are unmistakable, and Zeitblom, in his "allegiance to the sphere of the human and articulate" (269), is frightened by the kind of intellect he finds in Leverkühn, which "stands in the most immediate relation of all to the animal, to naked instinct" (147). Thus, Leverkühn's sophisticated and self-conscious aesthetics is not to be severed from the totemic and the cultic or the most primitive levels of human consciousness, and Zeitblom must acknowledge that aestheticism and barbarism are intimately related (373). But as the two coalesce, Zeitblom realizes that they also negate traditional aesthetics and the humanism that has formed its bedrock and that is the foundation of his own view of life. To Zeitblom, who describes himself as "by nature wholly moderate, of a temper, I may say, both healthy and humane, addressed to reason and harmony" (3)—indeed an archetype of "the normal" as promoted by Lukács—Leverkühn's aesthetics and art is the threatening "other," the demonic (a key word in the novel), a Faustian expression of forbidden desires that lead Leverkühn into a pact with the devil. (We seem indeed to have traveled to the "other" side of the notion of modernist art as religious sanctuary!)

In seeking the connections between Leverkühn's music and the turbulent age, Zeitblom is acutely aware of his friend's perception of historical ruptures, aware that World War I signaled for him "the opening of a new period of history, crowded with tumult and disruptions, agonies and wild vicissitudes," and that "on the horizon of his creative life ... there was already rising the 'Apocalypsis cum figuris'" (315), an apt name for his magnum opus.

From his own perspective (which incidentally closely resembles that of Stefan Zweig in *Die Welt von Gestern*), Zeitblom also sees the world undergoing an apocalypse; the world of yesterday, a world that had seemed to point toward unequivocal progress in every sphere of life, is disintegrating:

> I felt that an epoch was ending, which had not only included the nineteenth century, but gone far back to the end of the Middle Ages, to the loosening of scholastic ties, the emancipation of the individual, the birth of freedom. This was the epoch which I had in very truth regarded as that of my more extended spiritual home, in short the epoch of bourgeois humanism. And I felt as I say that its hour had come; that a mutation of life would be consummated; the world would enter into a new, still nameless constellation. (352)

Zeitblom is unwillingly but inexorably pulled toward drawing an analogy between the worldly powers, principally fascism, that are shattering the bourgeois-humanist world and the art of the friend he holds in such high reverence; an art that so obviously is also hostile to the products of that succumbing world. Mann has placed the question of the ideological role of modernism in a blatant, although ambivalent, historical context. Zeitblom appears to commit one version of the reflection fallacy discussed earlier, but he does so in a way that reverses the alleged modernist reflection of the "closed," rigidly hierarchized order of the fascist state. For Zeitblom, Leverkühn's modernism is the musical accompaniment to the brutal, chaotic, barbaric attacks launched on bourgeois humanist order in the "practical" sphere of life.

What prevents Zeitblom from seeing beyond this mirror relationship is not least his inability to view critically the ideological implications of those powers of reason which he associates with humanism. He sees no continuity, only schism between Western capitalist society and the emerging forces of fascism, and he is also unable to fathom the resilience and survival of Western capitalism and of the bourgeois humanist subject that is so ineluctably tied up with that social form. All he sees is its imminent destruction and the total lack of any viable alternatives. Mann's own perspective is of course to be dissociated from that of his biographer-narrator, Mann's very example of the surviving bourgeois subject, indeed of "the normal," and it is only against the background of Zeitblom that we can appreciate the "abnormality" or subversion of Leverkühn's art and life. Mann's dialectics is strikingly incorporated into the structure of the novel: he has a traditional humanist-realist narrator filter and mediate the norm-breaking art and aesthetics of a radical modernist. Thus, Mann places himself at a distance from Leverkühn, while to a certain extent he also treats Zeitblom with Leverkühn's methods of irony and parody, showing, for instance, that Zeitblom's relation to history is no more "innocent" than that of Leverkühn. Despite all his humanist values, Zeitblom is prone to the kind of nationalist fervor and desire for social order from which Nazism tapped so much energy.

Discontent as Negation

I do not want to try to determine what Mann's total depiction of modernism in *Doktor Faustus* amounts to, rich and ambivalent as it is. But from the way he plays his two "heroes" against one another, Mann appears to concur with the observation, which modernists are often felt to play out in their works, that humanism has entered an era of deep crisis; that in a capitalist world of increasing economic conflict, social strife, and war, the heritage of bourgeois humanism and all the values it was taken to ensure are evidently at sea. While modernists have repeatedly been attacked for antihumanism in their portrayal of a fragmented subject in an estranged or morbid universe, they have often seen their aversion from traditional humanism as necessitated by a historical development that called this subject and its values into question. Hermann Broch called the final chapter of *Die Schlafwandler* "The Breakdown of Values" (Zerfall der Werte), and in a commentary on the novel he describes this topic in the following terms:

> At the center of this final volume is the "breakdown of values," the historical and epistemological portrayal of the four-century-long process which under the guidance of rationality dissolved the Christian-platonic cosmology of medieval Europe, an overwhelming and terrifying process, ending in total fragmentation of values, the unleashing of reason together with the eruption of irrationality in every sense, the self-laceration of the world in blood and suffering.[49]

Broch significantly points out the double-edged relation of modernism to the whole program of the Enlightenment. Modernism is arguably both an heir to the project of the Enlightenment and a revolt against its historical process. This ambivalence is variously manifest in the presentation of the modern "subject." Modernism cannot really make the "loss" of the bounded bourgeois subject and the breakdown of its values a part of its discourse without in the first place invoking the validity, however tentative, of that subject and those values. To quote Terry Eagleton:

> The contradiction of modernism in this respect is that in order valuably to deconstruct the unified subject of bourgeois humanism, it draws upon key negative aspects of the actual experience of such subjects in late bourgeois society, which often enough

49. Hermann Broch, "Der Wertzerfall und die Schlafwandler," pub. in an appendix to Paul Michael Lützeler, ed., *Die Schlafwandler: Eine Romantrilogie* (Frankfurt: Suhrkamp, 1978), p. 734 (my translation).

does not at all correspond to the official ideological version. It thus pits what is increasingly felt to be the phenomenological reality of capitalism against its formal ideologies, and in doing so finds that it can fully embrace neither. The phenomenological reality of the subject throws formal humanist ideology into question, while the persistence of that ideology is precisely what enables the phenomenological reality to be characterized as negative.[50]

Modernism thus invokes the bourgeois subject, but it does so more through negation than affirmation. Hence—and this sums up the various aspects of the crisis of the subject discussed above—modernism can be seen as the negative other of capitalist-bourgeois ideology and of the ideological space of social harmony demarcated for the bourgeois subject. This appears to cohere with the historical theory of what Matei Calinescu has termed "the two modernities," according to which modernism is judged in the light of its opposition to the "progress" of social modernity. We have already seen how such a dualism characterizes some critical approaches to modernism whereby modernism is seen as subverting and negating the cultural and ethical heritage of traditional bourgeois society. According to Calinescu:

> At some point during the first half of the nineteenth century an irreversible split occurred between modernity as a stage in the history of Western civilization—a product of scientific and technological progress, of the industrial revolution, of the sweeping economic and social changes brought about by capitalism—and modernity as an aesthetic concept. Since then, the relations between the two modernities have been irreducibly hostile, but not without allowing and even stimulating a variety of mutual influences in their rage for each other's destruction.[51]

Critics who emphasize how modernism negates the cultural "contents" of bourgeois society as well as the status of its

50. Terry Eagleton, "Capitalism, Modernism and Postmodernism," *Against the Grain: Essays 1975–1985* (London: Verso, 1986), p. 144.
51. Matei Calinescu, *Faces of Modernity: Avant-Garde, Decadence, Kitsch* (Bloomington: Indiana University Press, 1977), p. 41.

subject—Trilling will serve as an example—often do so in terms of thematic, ethical, sociological, psychological, philosophical, and ideological issues. The question remains whether this is an appropriate basis on which to ground such a negation and hence a modernist paradigm. Surely we can imagine a traditional realist text that fulfills the thematic requirements of such a negation. It seems, therefore, that in order for us to begin finding the edges of modernism, we have to relate the above issues to modes of presentation, to language and formal mediation, winding our way back to the question of "modernist form."

In the above-quoted article, Hermann Broch goes on to say of his *Schlafwandler* trilogy: "While 'Pasenow' still holds on to the style of the old family novel (although forged into a thoroughly modern one), 'Esch' already shows signs—in strict parallel to the historical process of disintegration in the forms of life—of the disintegration and blowing-up of narrative art which reaches an extraordinary breakthrough in 'Huguenau'" (734–35). Broch thus draws a "strict parallel" between his narrative and the historical process of the disintegration of life. This constitutes one more variant of the reflection theory: in the "explosion" of narrative forms we are to see reflected the dissolution of bourgeois forms of life. What is involved here, however, is not a reflection of the prevalent perceptions of the "progress" of social modernity, but rather a "reproduction" of its negative or its "other"; that is, of social experience that contradicts the "official" ideology of coherence and progress that is interwoven with technological and capitalist-economic development. This cultural negation, moreover, is manifested in the revolt against traditional narrative modes. Hence, while in cultural terms modernism can be seen as constituting the "other modernity," this cultural function, by necessity as it were, entails a negation of prevalent literary and aesthetic traditions.

A powerful instance of such a negation occurs toward the end of *Doktor Faustus*. Zeitblom notes of Leverkühn's last work, *Fausti Weheklag*: "He wrote it, no doubt, with his eye on Beethoven's Ninth, as its counterpart in a most melancholy sense of the word. But it is not only that it more than once formally negates the symphony, reverses it into the negative" (490), for Zeitblom also finds a reversal of the "Watch with me" of Gethsemane; Faustus does not want anyone to stay awake with him or tempt him to be saved, not because it is too late, "but because with his whole soul he despises the positivism of the world for which one would save him, the lie of its godliness" (490). Leverkühn's work is a negation not only of Beethoven's paradigmatic symphony but of society's general "positivity," which is annulled by its negative reversal. Once one knows that Theodor W. Adorno was Mann's musical advisor in writing *Doktor Faustus*, it is hard not to think that he had a hand in Mann's formulation of negativity. Indeed, this seems to be confirmed in "Zu einem Porträt Thomas Manns," in which Adorno describes how he "rebelled" against Mann's original description of *Fausti Weheklag*: "Not only in view of the over-all situation of Doctor Faustus's lamentation, but with regard to the novel as a whole, I found the heavily loaded pages too positive, too uninterruptedly theological. They seemed to lack what was called for in the decisive passage, the force of a determinate negation as the only permitted sign of the other."[52] He then relates how Mann changed the text to the liking of his advisor.

Adorno's Aesthetics of Negativity

So far we have traced several modernist paradigms as they have been constructed by critics and scholars in the context of twentieth-century literature—first those that, in a mode strongly related to New Criticism, judge modernism on the basis of strictly formal aesthetics, according to which modern-ist works are characterized by a largely nonreferential dis-course and an ahistorical formal autonomy. Touching on cer-tain Marxist readings of such an "escape" from history, we then moved through approaches to modernism as a historical coun-terpart of social modernity on to various readings of it as a culturally subversive enterprise that revolts against dominant notions of the bourgeois subject or of bourgeois-capitalist his-torical development.

Jochen Schulte-Sasse claims that "the two most prevalent

---

52. Theodor W. Adorno, *Zur Dialektik des Engagements: Aufsätze zur Literatur des 20. Jahrhunderts II* (Frankfurt: Suhrkamp, 1973), p. 144 (my translation).

(and also most interesting) theories of modernism [are] those proceeding from Adorno and from French poststructuralism."[53] This is a rather surprising statement. Rightly or wrongly, although in many cases it can and should be approached as a theory of modernism, poststructuralism (especially in the Anglo-American sphere) has been discussed mostly in light of theories of postmodernism, with which it is more or less contemporary. Adorno's work, especially outside German-speaking countries, has hardly been at the forefront of the discussion surrounding modernism. His theories certainly deserve to be placed at the center of that debate, however, not least since they focus acutely, within a coherent aesthetic framework, on important ideas and problems that are often more loosely expressed by others.

Adorno's theories of art, in particular his *Ästhetische Theorie* (1970), are shaped by—are indeed almost concomitant with—his approach to modernism. I have chosen to ignore in this context how this undermines the generality of his aesthetic theory, for instance with regard to premodernist art. The most fruitful way to look at *Ästhetische Theorie*, this most significant, although unfinished, work of Adorno's ripe years is to read it as a theory of modernism. Also, before proceeding, I would like to note that Adorno's term "die Moderne," is clearly equivalent to our use of "modernism,"[54] its first signs being visible at around the mid-nineteenth century, especially in Baudelaire's work, although it reaches its heights only in the twentieth century and is still fully in the foreground in Beckett, who is one of Adorno's chief examples of "die Moderne."

In his opening chapter Adorno states that the communication of works of art with the outside world, from which they

53. Jochen Schulte-Sasse, "Foreword: Theory of Modernism versus Theory of the Avant-Garde," in Peter Bürger, *Theory of the Avant-Garde*, trans. Michael Shaw (Minneapolis: University of Minnesota Press, 1984), p. xv.

54. On at least two occasions, Adorno actually uses the concept "Modernismus" for a kind of epigonal, imitative modernism; he clearly assumes it to be a rather pejorative term. See *Ästhetische Theorie*, ed. Gretel Adorno and Rolf Tiedemann (Frankfurt: Suhrkamp, 1970), p. 45; *Versuch, das Endspiel zu verstehen: Aufsätze zur Literatur des 20. Jahrhunderts I* (Frankfurt: Suhrkamp Taschenbuch, 1973), p. 167. The same use of the term can be found in Renato Poggioli, *The Theory of the Avant-Garde*, trans. Gerald Fitzgerald (Cambridge, Mass.: Harvard University Press, 1968), pp. 216–18.

"blissfully or unhappily" seclude themselves, takes place through noncommunication, and this is how they manifest their fragmentation.[55] This view of artworks as fractured and communicating through noncommunication obviously points to features of modernist art, a view that is substantiated when Adorno seeks to pinpoint the social nature of art. He sees art as being social neither solely through its mode and state of production nor through the social derivation of its material content. "Rather, it is social primarily because it stands opposed to society." This function is facilitated through the autonomy of art, for by crystallizing its autonomous qualities "rather than obeying existing social norms and thus proving itself to be 'socially useful'—art criticizes society just by being there. Pure and immanently elaborated art is a tacit critique of the debasement of man by a condition that is moving toward a total-exchange society where everything is a for-other." The asocial aspect (das Asoziale) of art "is the determinate negation of a determinate society."[56]

We see here pivotal elements of Adorno's view of the sociocultural function of art. Its social context is that of an ever-expanding, monolithic capitalist society, moving toward a system of total exchange as well as total rationality, which is equivalent to absolute reification in matters of social interaction. It is a system in which the very notion of meaning has become wholly contaminated with the capitalist ideology of total exchange. In the face of this human debasement, art's basic mode of resistance is in a sense that of opting out of the system's communicative network in order to attack it head on from the "outside." In one of his essays Adorno even goes so far as to say that "the topical work of art gets a better grip of society the less it deals with society."[57]

Adorno's complex dialectics, however, by no means rests on a one-sided purism, for the qualities of art that promote its "autonomy" also arrange themselves in such a way that they *reflect* social conditions. This happens through a process of nega-

55. Theodor W. Adorno, *Aesthetic Theory*, trans. C. Lenhardt (London: Routledge and Kegan Paul, 1984), p. 7; cf. *Ästhetische Theorie*, p. 15.

56. Adorno, *Aesthetic Theory*, p. 321; cf. *Ästhetische Theorie*, p. 335.

57. Adorno, "Voraussetzungen," *Versuch, das Endspiel zu verstehen*, p. 115 (my translation).

tive mimesis, not unlike that discussed in the context of Broch and Mann. Adorno states in *Ästhetische Theorie* that modern art has no interest in a direct reflection of the social surface; it does not "want to duplicate the façade of reality," but "makes an uncompromising reprint of reality while at the same time avoiding being contaminated by it." Kafka's power as a writer, he adds, is precisely that of this "negative sense of reality."[58] In a separate essay, Adorno rejects any attempt to see in Kafka's work the physical reflection of a modern bureaucratic society. Rather, the shabbiness depicted in Kafka "is the cryptogram of capitalism's highly polished, glittering late phase, which he excludes in order to define it all the more precisely in its negative. Kafka scrutinizes the smudges left behind in the deluxe edition of the book of life by the fingers of power. No world could be more homogeneous than the stifling one which he compresses to a totality by means of petty-bourgeois dread; it is logically air-tight and empty of meaning like every system."[59]

Here we can observe another dialectical twist in Adorno's theory: by arguing that modernists like Kafka present the "negative" of society (presenting what Adorno in fact sometimes calls "the negative of negativity"), he hands meaninglessness over to the "logically closed" capitalist system. In this society, logic and rationality have turned into their opposites. In *Ästhetische Theorie* Adorno notes that the fact that mimesis is practicable in the midst of rationality, employing its means, manifests a response to the base irrationality of the rational world and its means of control. For the purpose of rationality, of the quintessential means of regulating nature, "would have to be something other than a means, hence a non-rational quality. Capitalist society hides and disavows precisely this irrationality, whereas art does not." Art holds forth the image, rejected by rationality, of its purpose and exposes its other, its irrationality.[60]

While we may not agree with Adorno's pessimistic view of the inevitably destructive social process of human rationality, which he saw as being typically represented by the Enlighten-

58. Adorno, *Aesthetic Theory*, p. 28; *Ästhetische Theorie*, p. 36.

59. Theodor W. Adorno, "Notes on Kafka," *Prisms*, trans. Samuel and Shierry Weber (Cambridge, Mass.: MIT Press, 1981), p. 256.

60. Adorno, *Aesthetic Theory*, p. 79; *Ästhetische Theorie*, p. 86.

ment, his is a compelling explanation of the "irrational" element in modernism, an element that some critics can only blindly reject. (On the other hand, one might also note that his pessimism—appearing more radically in *Dialectic of Enlightenment*, which he coauthored with Horkheimer—runs parallel with the bleak view of the modern human situation that critics, particularly traditionally humanist critics, see as prominent in modernist literature).

The modernist reversal of society's rational negativity, according to Adorno, finds an authentic expression in the objectification of a subjective experience of society. This experience, as Eagleton puts it in the above quote, does "not at all correspond to the official ideological version" of bourgeois society, but is in fact its negative "reflection." Such objectification, therefore, must not take on the shape of the ostensibly objective portrayals of subjective experience in realist representation, for, as Adorno notes in discussing Beckett, the negativity of the subject as a true objective gestalt can only manifest itself in a radically subjective configuration (Gestaltung). It cannot emerge in an "allegedly higher objectivity."[61] If I understand Adorno's typically dense formulation correctly, it provides us with the most elaborate illustration yet of the subject-object nexus in modernist representation. While subjective experience is to be mediated through objectification, that is, as an objective gestalt (and it is at this level that Adorno discards the relevance of the author's personality), this objectification, in order to express the negativity of the experience, must be constructed in a radically "subjective" manner—it must not take on the shape of "rationalized" objective representation to which as social beings we are accustomed. Thus, on one level of representation, for instance in Kafka's work, the outside world is forcefully objectified through all the surface elements familiar to us, but on another level this objectification does not concur with our habitualized perception of the "objective" world, and hence takes on the shape of a radically subjective construct. This subjective "Gestaltung" effects the erasure or

61. "Die Negativität des Subjekts als wahre Gestalt von Objektivität kann nur in radikal subjektiver Gestaltung, nicht in der Supposition vermeintlich höherer Objektivität sich darstellen." Adorno, *Ästhetische Theorie*, p. 370; cf. *Aesthetic Theory*, p. 354.

explosion, discussed above, of the bourgeois subject, while at the same time reflecting, in a "negative" manner, its social enchainment.

It follows that Adorno is perhaps the most prominent representative of the view that modernism, in Fredric Jameson's words, is not so much "a way of avoiding social content . . . as rather of managing and containing it, secluding it out of sight in the very form itself."[62]

The Function of Form

Adorno has sought a solution to a paradox mentioned earlier in this chapter; he has gone far toward reconciling the oppositional conceptions of modernism as, on the one hand, an autonomous aesthetic practice and, on the other, a historical-cultural force. But on at least one level, it seems to me, this solution may have been bought at too high a price. While Adorno's outright rejection of intentionality and the validity of authorial-subjective expression may be justified, he goes too far in erasing the notion of any kind of *social consciousness* behind the creation of the work. Artists and writers, according to Adorno, should not think of themselves as critical agents, they should concentrate on formal matters, for what is socially determinant in works of art "is content that articulates itself in formal structures."[63] Through the socially unconscious wielding of form, history would find its way into works of art, since it is an inherent part of them, whereby the works constitute themselves as an unconscious historiography of their age.[64] There is a sense in which this certainly holds true, but as a general rule it borders on an essentialist reflection theory, and even though we may agree that form, in one way or another, is

62. Fredric Jameson, "Reflections in Conclusion," in Ernst Bloch et al., *Aesthetics and Politics* (London: New Left Books, 1977), p. 202.
63. Adorno, *Aesthetic Theory*, p. 327; *Ästhetische Theorie*, p. 342: "Gesellschaftlich entscheidet an den Kunstwerken, was an Inhalt aus ihren Formstrukturen spricht."
64. Adorno, *Ästhetische Theorie*, p. 272: "Sie sind ihrer selbst unbewußte Geschichtschreibung ihrer Epoche; das nicht zuletzt vermittelt sie zur Erkenntnis." Cf. *Aesthetic Theory*, p. 261.

always historical, we do not have to share Adorno's rejection of artists and writers, such as Brecht, who self-consciously use their formal constructions as vehicles of more "obtrusively" foregrounded social issues.

Adorno's theory of form, aside from the function of form as a vehicle of the negative historiography of the age, shares a good deal with that of the Russian formalists, even though they have more obviously contributed to the construction of other modernist paradigms. Like the formalists, Adorno distinguishes between aesthetic or "poetic" language and the language of everyday communication. Adorno says of aesthetic language that its purposefulness, divested of practical purpose, lies in its language-semblance, in its purposeless conceptual lack, its difference from significatory language.[65] Antisignificatory language is of course part and parcel of Adorno's very concept of form, which designates a pronounced confrontation of art and empirical life.[66]

The antithesis in Adorno's writings between aesthetic and significatory language need not, however, stem from the formalists, for in his aesthetics this antagonism is a fundamental element of social negativity. But as such it does play the role of a kind of "defamiliarization," to use a formalist concept that has been prominent in the theoretical discourse surrounding modernism. Modernist writing, through its autonomous formal constructions, places us at a "distance" from society, making it strange, whereby we come to see its reverse, but true, mirror image, its negativity.

Hence, Adorno's aesthetics of negativity, by linking artistic autonomy to a dialectical social mimesis, seeks to reconcile the two major functional implications of the formalist theory of defamiliarization. Victor Shklovsky, in his seminal essay "Art as Technique," notes that "habitualization devours works, clothes, furniture, one's wife, and the fear of war," and states that art, through its defamiliarizing practices, "exists that one may recover the sensation of life."[67] This formulation would

65. Adorno, *Ästhetische Theorie*, p. 211; *Aesthetic Theory*, pp. 202–3.

66. Adorno, *Ästhetische Theorie*, p. 213; *Aesthetic Theory*, p. 205.

67. Victor Shklovsky, "Art as Technique," in Lee T. Lemon and Marion J. Reis, ed., *Russian Formalist Criticism: Four Essays* (Lincoln: University of Nebraska Press, 1965), p. 12.

appear to have significant social bearings; indeed, defamiliarization could be seen as a major arsenal of devices to be directed
against reified ideologies. It is precisely this aspect of the defamiliarization theory, as Peter Bürger points out in discussing
its inherent duality, that Brecht developed further in his "Ver-
fremdungstechnik."[68] But Shklovsky immediately adds: "The
technique of art is to make objects 'unfamiliar,' to make forms
difficult, to increase the difficulty and length of perception
because the process of perception is an aesthetic end in itself
and must be prolonged" (12). Shklovsky is here under the sway
of the general formalist tenets of aesthetic autonomy and the
separation of poetic from "ordinary" language. It is of course
this "purist" side of defamiliarization, according to which
"making it strange" only means ensuring the total separation
of the work from social affairs, that one can then trace throughout the methodologies of twentieth-century literary criticism,
and nowhere as clearly as in Anglo-American New Criticism.
We have already discussed how such aesthetics of sanctity and
wholeness have been projected onto the emergence of the modernist paradigm.

But the Russian formalists' broad significance for critical
approaches to modernism is by no means limited to issues of
defamiliarization. They were among the first literary scholars
to realize the significance of Saussure's dissociation of "natural" links, within the sign, between the signifier and the signified. Thus, they helped initiate a period of semiotic inquiry
into the relationship between the levels of reference and meaning, an inquiry that has also been carried out, in a different way,
by modernism in art and literature. But despite the fact that the
formalists had intimate ties with the literary experiments of
contemporary Russian futurism, we must be cautious in drawing self-explanatory parallels between modernist literature and
modern literary theories or critical methodologies. The Russian formalists can certainly be judged as instigators of a semiotic revolution, but what they inquired into at a theoretical
(analytical and metalinguistic) level regarding production and

68. Peter Bürger, *Vermittlung—Rezeption—Funktion: Ästhetische Theorie und Methodologie der Literaturwissenschaft* (Frankfurt: Suhrkamp Taschenbuch, 1979), p. 98.

function of meaning in literary language is more immediately acted out as a *crisis* of meaning in the realm of modernist literature, as is apparent when its site of troubled signification is observed in the context of social norms of language use.

From this perspective one could argue that it is only with the emergence of poststructuralist activities that theory "catches up with" the literary practices of modernism in this performative sense. Modernism could certainly be seen as the aesthetic embodiment of the "crisis of representation" that structuralists, and particularly poststructuralists, have greatly elaborated on recently and to some extent "performed" themselves. While Anglo-American advocates of poststructuralism have frequently taken it to be a part of a postmodernist revolt against the burden of a modernist tradition, some of them have acknowledged the often blatantly modernist tendencies in the methods and language-play of poststructuralist critics. Gregory Ulmer, for instance, states that "the break with 'mimesis,' with the values and assumptions of 'realism,' which revolutionized the modernist arts, is now underway (belatedly) in criticism, the chief consequence of which, of course, is a change in the relation of the critical text to its object—literature."[69] And a consequence of that change is our difficulty in determining to what extent poststructuralist practices present us with a theory of modernism, or a construction of a modernist paradigm— for to some extent the borders between theory and practice have been erased.

At the risk of oversimplification, however, we can extract from the variety of poststructuralist work two major concerns that relate to the issues we have been discussing in terms of modernism: the crisis of language and representation and the crisis of the subject. The source of these two manifestations of crisis, which poststructuralists generally see as being intimately related, is frequently sought through modernist texts. Julia Kristeva, for instance, using early modernist texts as her examples, demonstrates how an archaic, instinctual, incestuous, maternal process of "signifiance" in norm-breaking liter-

---

69. Gregory Ulmer, "The Object of Post-Criticism," in Foster, ed., *The Anti-Aesthetic*, p. 83. See also Ronald Schleifer, "The Poison of Ink: Modernism and Post-War Literary Criticism," *New Orleans Review* 8 (Fall 1981): 241–49.

ary works violates the authorized codes and the symbolic function of social signification, allowing the subject to slip out from under "the constraints of a civilization dominated by transcendental rationality."[70] Kristeva also notes that this process is dangerous for the subject and must be "linked to analytical interpretation" (145), but other poststructuralists—perhaps none more than Deleuze and Guattari in *Anti-Oedipus*—valorize a total release of the subject from repressive rationality.

Similarly, it would be possible to approach Jacques Derrida as a theorist as well as a practitioner of modernism, and to see modernism in its totality as a deconstructive practice in the Derridian sense. Thus, we could read texts such as *Ulysses* (not to mention *Finnegans Wake*), *The Waves*, *The Sound and the Fury*, and *Das Schloß* with an emphasis on how they undermine the human desire for stable centers of representation by constantly displacing signifiers, frustrating immediate "presence" of meaning, decentering the subject or whatever constitutes a production of convention-bound reference, and dispersing it in the linguistic field. Modernist texts present elaborate witness to the notion, so basic to Derrida's endeavors, that "the verbal text is constituted by concealment as much as revelation."[71] (This notion, differently formulated, constitutes the foundation of Adorno's theory.)

Here one might object that a possible result of this approach—and here we are touching on *one* of the reasons for Derrida's large following in the United States—would be determining the central thrust of modernism to be an incessant language game, playing one skittish signifier against another. This makes modernist studies risk reverting to the New Critical idea of the work as a self-bounded whole, vibrating with unresolved internal tensions. Another problem is that according to a radical deconstructive philosophy of language, not only modernist works are characterized by the various implications of "différance," but indeed every verbal text. This might seem

70. Julia Kristeva, "From One Identity to an Other," *Desire in Language: A Semiotic Approach to Literature and Art*, ed. Leon S. Roudiez, trans. T. Gora, A. Jardine, and L. S. Roudiez (New York: Columbia University Press, 1980), p. 140.

71. Gayatri C. Spivak, "Translator's Preface," in Jacques Derrida, *Of Grammatology*, p. xlvi. Cf. the quotation from Jameson on how modernism frustrates our detection of social content, at n. 62 above.

ultimately to deconstruct any possibility of establishing a theoretical framework for a modernist paradigm, or even of registering literary-historical paradigms at all.

On the other hand, one can argue that what makes modernism "different" is the way in which it is aware of and acts out the qualities of "différance." The emergence of a modernist paradigm could then be judged in terms of a break in the historical attitude toward language and communication as evinced in literary texts. According to another poststructuralist, Michel Foucault, literary modernism has a central place in demarcating historical paradigms, or "epistemes," as he calls them. When language, in the nineteenth century, had been thoroughly instrumentalized as an object and vehicle of knowledge, Foucault sees it "reconstituting itself elsewhere, in an independent form, difficult of access, folded back upon the emigma of its own origin and existing wholly in reference to the pure act of writing."[72] Questions concerning the very nature of language and literature "were made possible by the fact that, at the beginning of the nineteenth century, the law of discourse having been detached from representation, the being of language itself became, as it were, fragmented; but they became inevitable when, with Nietzsche and Mallarmé, thought was brought back, and violently so, towards language itself, towards its unique and difficult being" (306).

It is appropriate to end this chapter on such a note, for modernism does, after all, seek a break with tradition, a fact that is emphasized in varying degrees (or at least tacitly assumed) by all the different constructions of the modernist paradigm discussed above. This basic characteristic needs to be more comprehensively pursued in the light of the continuity of history that modernism sets out to explode. The next chapter, therefore, undertakes a critical examination of how modernism has been positioned in the context of literary history and how it has fared in the ceaseless process of canonization.

72. Michel Foucault, *The Order of Things: An Archaeology of the Human Sciences* (New York: Vintage Books, 1973), p. 300.

2

Modernism in
Literary History

In the wake of multitudinous structuralist, poststructuralist, and latter-day New Critical activities there appears to have been a gradual realization that literary history has not had its share of scholarly and critical attention. Literary history has been neglected and underrated as a field of literary study (as opposed to documentation), and this is so not least because it has been discredited as an area of theoretical inquiry. Tzvetan Todorov, for instance, in discussing the relation between poetics and literary history, concludes that "literary history today figures as a poor relation: historical poetics is the least elaborated sector of poetics."[1]

True and timely as this recognition may be, what is often not realized is the extent to which every discussion of an author or a literary work is an act of literary history: any approach to a particular work is bound to involve its implicit placement, its inscription, into literary history. Even a brief note directing the reader's attention to a certain book or author becomes a pointer toward literary history as a category and context that the reader is expected to supply as he or she receives the critical text. This in itself would seem ample justification for making literary

---

1. Tzvetan Todorov, *Introduction to Poetics*, trans. Richard Howard (Minneapolis: University of Minnesota Press, 1981), p. 63.

history a prominent and highly self-conscious discipline within literary studies.

If discussing and thus "placing" individual works is an implicit act of literary historiography, this is true on a more general and self-conscious level in the case of concepts such as "modernism"—terms that serve the function of calling forth a critical context for a whole range of works and hence for a major strand in literary history. Using the term is an immediate act of classification. Barbara Herrnstein Smith notes:

> Of particular significance for the value of "works of art" and "literature" is the interactive relation between the *classification* of an entity and the functions it is expected or desired to perform. In perceiving an object or artifact in terms of some category—*as*, for example, "a clock," "a dictionary," "a doorstep," "a curio"—we implicitly isolate and foreground certain of its possible functions and typically refer its value to the extent to which it performs those functions more or less effectively.[2]

Using a concept like "modernism" therefore actually invokes a *preclassification*, and as Smith notes, "preclassification is itself a form of pre-evaluation, for the labels or category names under which we encounter objects not only . . . foreground certain of their possible functions but also operate as signs—in effect, as culturally certified endorsements—of their more or less effective performance of those functions" (27).

We saw in chapter 1 that there are those who believe that the category name "modernism" is by now an unambiguous sign of a past literary period with its specific aesthetic and sociocultural characteristics. But such an agreement as to the meaning of the "sign," or of the changes in the literary system it is made to signify, does not exist. Indeed, the space of that meaning is rather a scene of aesthetic, cultural, and ideological conflict. One could of course argue that this is the case with any literary concept—after all, the use of such concepts always signals an appropriation of the past that reflects interests of the present. But the fact that this is such a crucial issue in the case of

2. Barbara Herrnstein Smith, "Contingencies of Value," in Robert von Hallberg, ed., *Canons* (Chicago: University of Chicago Press, 1984), p. 17.

modernism springs from our awareness that through the concept we are "constructing" our immediate past, we are creating a paradigm that we are not even certain we have surpassed, not to mention properly gauged and understood.

In the next chapter we shall look at examples of critical approaches that evince a great eagerness to "close off" modernism as a critical sign in order to stabilize and seek an "end" to it as an effective literary-historical practice, that is, to see it as a practice whose "effective performance," to use Smith's phrase, lies securely in the past. Of course chapter 1 was already indirectly about such construction of literary history, as was evident from the examples we encountered of critics of modernism who, in Smith's words, "isolate and foreground certain of its possible functions and typically refer its value to the extent to which it performs those functions more or less effectively." The present chapter does not seek to advocate or to delineate consistently a specific theory of modernism as a literary-historical category. My aim is rather to examine critically, and to some extent clarify, the context in which modernism is inserted into history on the basis of functions that are judged to be dominant in the modernist enterprise. Hence, I will skeptically trace what I see as the major roles and positions postulated for modernism in literary history.

On Forgetting Tradition

There is a certain paradox involved in "writing into" literary history, which inevitably assumes a certain continuity, a paradigm that appears bent on exploding precisely such a historical succession. For the self-conscious break with tradition must, I think, be seen as the hallmark of modernism, the one feature that seems capable of lending the concept a critical coherence that most of us can agree on, however we may choose to approach and interpret it. Wilhelm Emrich, one of Germany's chief authorities on modernist literature, notes that the "literary revolution" from 1910 on seems to be "a chaotic maze of antagonistic currents, emotions, ideas and forms of expression. There appears to be no uniting, mutual element, unless it be in the negation: in the break with tradition. But even that is not very accurate. There were also ties being established with traditions."[3]

It is a commonplace among critics to mention the break with, or negation of, tradition as a central characteristic of modernism, only to discard it as far too general an approach. Of course no one can, strictly speaking, write without tradition. As Edward Shils notes, a writer can have a good deal to say as to which traditions he adopts: "What he cannot do is become a writer without any tradition at all."[4] But Emrich's actual approach to modernism shows that he does need the notion of negation in order for his concept of "literary revolution" to make sense. It seems to me decisive that we are dealing with a negation of prevalent traditions, a process of becoming critically aware of the tradition that constitutes a writer's immediate background and environment, that is, the history out of which he or she emerges. Those traditions, at least during the early stages of modernism, were conceived and fostered by the social, political, and cultural forces of the nineteenth century. Before the heyday of modernism, that heritage had already been under severe attack from one of modernism's most important precursors, Friedrich Nietzsche.

John Burt Forster, Jr., sees Nietzsche's legacy for modernism consisting primarily in various portrayals of an "overwhelming sense of a break with the recent past."[5] Even though Forster fails to relate this tradition-breaking quality to Nietzsche's radical ideas about language (which Forster sees as mostly a different strand of Nietzschean thought, to be picked up later by poststructuralism), his emphasis is to the point. The one work of Nietzsche's that elucidates his "modernist" ideology of negation in the most compressed and elucidating manner is probably his second *Unzeitgemäße Betrachtung*, entitled *Vom Nutzen und Nachteil der Historie für das Leben*. It is a key text for modernist studies.

Nietzsche opens his topic by stating what he is later to

3. Wilhelm Emrich, *Protest und Verheißung: Studien zur klassischen und modernen Dichtung*, 2d ed. (Frankfurt and Bonn: Athenäum, 1963), p. 148 (my translation).
4. Edward Shils, *Tradition* (Chicago: University of Chicago Press, 1981), p. 160.
5. John Burt Forster, Jr., *Heirs to Dionysus: A Nietzschean Current in Literary Modernism* (Princeton, N.J.: Princeton University Press, 1981), p. 417.

develop as a central paradox in the essay: "Certainly we need history," he says, but we need it "for life and action," which he then proceeds to unfold as the very opposite of historical knowledge.[6] "Life" and "action" involve an "unhistorical" stance and a "power to forget" (9) that counteract the paralysis caused by the burden of the past, by historical consciousness constantly sorting out the facts and figures of what has gone by, laboring to understand and keep track of it. Man is ever more inundated by historical knowledge from every direction (24) and in the process of assimilating the various aspects of the past, education becomes lifeless and petrifying: "Historical education really is a kind of inborn grayheadedness" (44). On the whole Nietzsche is calling for a sudden break with nineteenth-century culture, its positivism and scientific ideology. This gesture of a rupture with the past is of course variously echoed in a great many manifestos and critical writings of modernist artists and writers, and in their aesthetic creations they can be seen attempting to put this gesture into immediate practice.

I am not here going to concern myself with Nietzsche's elitism, the way he thinks *only strong personalities can endure history*" (30), the way he dreams of a timeless gathering of the geniuses of history (53), or his theory that "modern man suffers from a weakened personality" (28). The reason this work of his retains its importance lies in his wielding of the paradox mentioned above: the manner in which he upholds the need for history while valorizing that which is directed against history.

Paul de Man argues that while Nietzsche seeks in this work to oppose art to history, the rudiments of that opposition, "life and action"—or "modernity," as de Man calls them—actually point beyond both art and language and display a nostalgia for immediacy.[7] As soon as we want to make this moment of spontaneous experience serve the function of art, de Man claims, it is bound to become an element of the respective historical discourse. Consequently, de Man seeks to deconstruct and collapse Nietzsche's dual categories:

6. Friedrich Nietzsche, *On the Advantage and Disadvantage of History for Life*, trans. Peter Preuss (Indianapolis, Ind.: Hackett, 1980), p. 7.

7. Paul de Man, "Literary History and Literary Modernity," *Blindness and Insight: Essays in the Rhetoric of Contemporary Criticism* (New York: Oxford University Press, 1971), pp. 158–59.

Modernity and history relate to each other in a curiously contradictory way that goes beyond antithesis or opposition. If history is
not to become sheer regression or paralysis, it depends on modernity for its duration and renewal; but modernity cannot assert
itself without being at once swallowed up and reintegrated into a
regressive historical process. Nietzsche offers no real escape out
of a predicament in which we readily recognize the mood of our
own modernity. Modernity and history seem condemned to being
linked together in a self-destroying union that threatens the survival of both. (151)

But to throw the concept of modernity back into a "regressive
historical process" hardly does justice to Nietzsche's dialectical approach to the problem. In his contradictory kind of rhetoric, Nietzsche is seeking to make the notion of "life and
action" a part of a *criticism* of history. The concept of criticism
is pivotal in this context; inevitably bolstered by the historical
and scientific developments of the nineteenth century, "criticism" seems to run counter to the notion of "life and action."
In de Man's view, "Nietzsche's ruthless forgetting, the blindness with which he throws himself into an action lightened of
all previous experience, captures the authentic spirit of modernity" (147). This "authentic spirit of modernity" may be something de Man is led to on the basis of Nietzsche's other writings, but in the context of this particular work it strikes me as a
blindly forced interpretation; even a cursory reading of Nietzsche's essay reveals that forgetting (as an act of modernity) is
repeatedly counteracted by its necessary opposite (i.e., the critical act, which Nietzsche also calls "modern" [58]). In the opening section Nietzsche states that being able to "remember at
the right time" is as important as forgetting "at the right time":
*"the unhistorical and the historical are equally necessary for
the health of an individual, a people and a culture"* (10). And
one of the three kinds of history Nietzsche finds essential is the
critical consideration of the past, which enables one "to shatter
and dissolve something to enable him to live" (21). Nietzsche
does not try to hide the paradox: memory is called upon in the
critical service of "forgetting." At one point, in his somewhat
precipitous valorizing of "youth" and in blasting "hopeless
sceptical infinity," Nietzsche even attacks the very work he is

writing for its "excess of criticism" (58). But earlier he has
stated that the "new age" is no specter without genesis, and the
origin of its enemy, historical education, "*must* itself in turn be
historically understood, history *must* itself dissolve the problem of history, knowledge *must* turn its sting against itself"
(45).

What we are witnessing, then, is a dialectic in which the
notion of "life and action" is used as an unspecified opposite to
a reigning historical paradigm, taking the place of its "other," of
that-which-is-not, and thus constantly threatening to dismantle the stability of the paradigm, its past heritage, in the service
of the present. Any such dismantling, however, requires the *use*
of history and a mode of reflection that inevitably is shaped by
the past. It is hardly a coincidence that Nietzsche, in the closing paragraph, states that one "must organize the chaos within
himself by reflecting on his genuine needs" (64). The past is
inevitably used when determining the "genuine needs" of the
present. We can discern the same kind of dialectics in Baudelaire's terms, "representation of the present" and "memory of
the present," both of which de Man also seeks to deconstruct.

Spreading Modernism Thin

From a literary point of view, Nietzsche can be seen as delv-
ing into the problematics and paradoxes of what we have come
to call intertextuality. He admits that everything we say or do is
"always already" there, inherited from past practices, but at the
same time he holds that a critical revolt against this burden can
yield something of an immediate impact for the present moment. We see why the essay is significant for an understanding
of modernism. This "action" can be observed in the revolt that
modernism, to some extent even riding on the impetus on
Nietzsche's writings, undertook against those traditions which
were the shaping forces of literary production. In the experimental formal endeavors of modernism we see how forgetting
is indeed a form of memory, how negation is a mode of critical
acknowledgment. If we then consider the historical juncture at
which Nietzsche's work is written, we seem to be moving
toward an understanding of the historical nature of modernism.

This is precisely what de Man chooses *not* to do. Instead he twists Nietzsche's historical dualism into an "ambivalence of writing" that "is such that it can be considered both an act and an interpretive process that follows after an act with which it cannot coincide." And thus de Man can suggest that the "appeal of modernity haunts all literature" (152), and that "modernity turns out to be indeed one of the concepts by means of which the distinctive nature of literature can be revealed in all its intricacy" (161). De Man is actually using Nietzsche's text to present literature as a privileged and isolated category of writing, deriving its specificity from the notion of modernity, "which is fundamentally a falling away from literature and a rejection of history," while it "also acts as the principle that gives literature duration and historical existence" (162).

The notion of "historical existence" here is of course blatantly ahistorical, a form of repetition that barely seems to need the concept of history: "The continuous appeal of modernity, the desire to break out of literature toward the reality of the moment, prevails and, in its turn, folding back upon itself, engenders the repetition and the continuation of literature" (162). Terry Eagleton notes that, according to de Man, to write "is to disrupt a tradition which depends upon such disruption for its very self-reproduction. We are all, simultaneously and inextricably, modernists and traditionalists, terms which for de Man designate neither cultural movements nor aesthetic ideologies but the very structure of that duplicitous phenomenon, always in and out of time simultaneously, named literature, where this common dilemma figures itself with rhetorical self-consciousness."[8] According to this logic, any radical human action "will always prove self-defeating, will always be incorporated by a history which has foreseen them and seized upon them as ruses for its own self-perpetuation" (137). Emancipatory inclinations in the face of tradition are sheer illusions, elements of a mode of blindness whose moments of insights sink in rapid succession back into blindness. Literary history becomes a monotonous succession of works that are born in a moment of modernity and then automatically swallowed up by the autonomous discourse and tradition of literature. As a prac-

8. Eagleton, "Capitalism, Modernism and Postmodernism," *Against the Grain*, pp. 136–37.

tice born of a historical crisis escalating in the late nineteenth century, a practice characterized by a cultural negation such as we see foregrounded most radically by Adorno, modernism has simply been erased.

Hence, de Man actually carries out what we saw, toward the end of chapter 1, as a latent deconstructive move, ultimately questioning or even discarding the notion of a theoretical framework for not only a modernist paradigm, but perhaps for *any* literary-historical paradigm. This tendency is also recognizable in other poststructuralist critics. According to Harold Bloom's poetics of anxiety, poetic history is "indistinguishable from poetic influence, since strong poets make that history by misreading one another, so as to clear imaginative space for themselves."[9] Unlike the New Critics, who argued that the meaning of a poem was the poem itself,[10] Bloom claims that "the meaning of a poem can only be a poem, but *another poem—a poem not itself*" (70). But this kind of intertextuality is still severely reductive, limiting the poem to other poems, preserving poetry as an uncontaminated category. Moreover, this poetic influence takes the form of a struggle of individuals, not of different aesthetic practices: "That Tennyson triumphed in his long, hidden contest with Keats, no one can assert absolutely, but his clear superiority over Arnold, Hopkins, and Rossetti is due to his relative victory or at least holding of his own in contrast to their partial defeats" (12). Thus, as in the case of de Man, literary history cannot account for the rise and development of aesthetic paradigms, for it primarily consists of a linear succession of individual writers busily misreading their forebears in order to survive as legitimate poets themselves. No wonder, then, that Bloom can state that "modernism in literature has not passed; rather, it has been exposed as never having been there."[11]

A similar picture of a literary sequence is drawn by one of Bloom's own critical forebears, whose theory of "Tradition and

9. Harold Bloom, *The Anxiety of Influence: A Theory of Poetry* (New York: Oxford University Press, 1973), p. 5.

10. See Cleanth Brooks, "The Heresy of Paraphrase," *The Well Wrought Urn* (New York: Harcourt, Brace & World, 1975), pp. 192–214.

11. Harold Bloom, "The Dialectics of Literary Tradition," *Boundary 2* 2 (Spring 1974): 529.

the Individual Talent" has been extremely influential in Anglo-American criticism and scholarship. T. S. Eliot states that "if the only form of tradition, of handing down, consisted in following the ways of the immediate generation before us in a blind or timid adherence to its successes, 'tradition' should positively be discouraged."[12] Since the modernist revolt against tradition was directed primarily against the most immediate literary heritage, this seems to me a distinctively modernist attitude. The several debates over modernism can actually be seen to center around this problem. The important expressionist controversy in *Das Wort*, as Hans-Jürgen Schmitt points out, centered on "establishing the right ties with the literary heritage."[13] As soon as there is a fairly widespread awareness that the prevalent mode of discourse is by no means necessarily the legitimate one, that discourse enters a state of crisis.

This revolt against tradition was to some extent prefigured by the *Querelle des anciens et des modernes*, in which the authority of the ancient tradition was called into question. With modernism, however, the target is no longer the sacrosanct texts of classical literature, but the very textual environment out of which the mutinous literature grows, and from which it can only "free" itself in the negative manner proclaimed by Nietzsche. The next step, again, would seem to be to examine the social implications and means of representation within that textual environment, in order to come closer to an understanding of the modernist revolt.

But this is where Eliot, like de Man albeit in a different fashion, veers away from an inquiry that would lead to a historical positioning of his topic. Tradition, Eliot says, "cannot be inherited"—as if the reigning textual order were not bound to shape our attitudes, be they ones of assent or revolt—and "if you want it you must obtain it by great labour" (4). But here he apparently no longer has in mind a struggle with tradition as a dominant historical paradigm, as becomes clear when he proceeds to present his oft-quoted definition of literary tradition:

12. Eliot, "Tradition and the Individual Talent," *Selected Essays, 1917–1932*, p. 4.
13. Hans-Jürgen Schmitt, "Einleitung," in Schmitt, ed., *Die Expressionismusdebatte*, p. 7.

The necessity that he [the poet] shall conform, that he shall cohere, is not onesided; what happens when a new work of art is created is something that happens simultaneously to all the works of art which preceded it. The existing monuments form an ideal order among themselves, which is modified by the introduction of the new (the really new) work of art among them. The existing order is complete before the new work arrives; for order to persist after the supervention of novelty, the *whole* existing order must be, if ever so slightly, altered; and so the relations, proportions, values of each work of art toward the whole are readjusted; and this is conformity between the old and the new. (5)

Eliot's insight, radical in itself, that new works change the order of old ones has earned him much critical praise, but as in the cases of Bloom and de Man, literature is judged as an isolated mode of writing, and, as Robert Weimann objects, "the acquisition and revaluation of past literature was quite divorced from other modes of consciousness and the cultural process in history. Consequently, the question of tradition became quite narrow; it was reduced to some finer concern of the individual artist."[14] The focus is clearly on what that individual does to tradition, the latter being an "ideal order" that does not seem to allow for any internal strife. And the end result is a "conformity between the old and the new," hardly a conclusion one would expect from someone at the forefront of modernist literary activity. In fact, I believe this amply demonstrates that we must not judge Eliot's poetry and his criticism as simply two forms of expressions of the same historical poetics. From the point of view of "Tradition and the Individual Talent" Eliot is hardly able to account for the historical significance of his own *Waste Land* as a major expression of a poetics that was seeking a break with prevailing traditions in poetry. His theory is unable to explain the emergence of new cultural paradigms; it could not, for instance, make any sense of Pound's view that "Eliot's *Waste Land* is I think the justification of the 'movement', of our modern experiment since 1900."[15]

14. Weimann, *Structure and Society in Literary History*, p. 75.
15. Ezra Pound, quoted in Stanley Sultan, Ulysses, The Waste Land, *and Modernism: A Jubilee Study* (Port Washington, N.Y.: Kennikat Press, 1977), p. 8.

Tradition and Literary History

The theories presented by such critics as de Man, Bloom, and Eliot indicate that the correlations between tradition and literary history are highly problematic. But these theories also suggest that the complexity of this correlation is apt to be slighted or overlooked.

For Lukács and the other critics who attacked expressionism in the thirties, literary tradition was firmly embedded in their conception of a bourgeois-humanist cultural heritage, whose continuity was to be ensured even while it had to be modified in order for it to suit a new century and meet social changes. We are familiar with a similar response among many traditional nonsocialist humanists, although they might want to steer that tradition in other directions. For such critics, literary realism often seems the only viable carrier of the tradition. Lukács, for instance, sought to establish a realist tradition extending from Goethe through Balzac (bypassing Flaubert as well as Zola and other naturalists), through such writers as Tolstoy, Gottfried Keller, and Romain Rolland, to a twentieth-century flowering in Thomas Mann (eventually he was to add Solzhenitsyn to this line). But while the critics discussed in the preceding section basically equate "tradition" with an ongoing current of "literary history" that is at best gradually modified in a retroactive manner, Lukács would not dream of collapsing the two concepts together. Indeed, much of his criticism constitutes a crusade against those (modernist) forces which he saw as totally diverging from "his" tradition, thus disrupting a desirable continuity of literary history. Whatever one may think of Lukács's theories and criticism, they do portray literary history as an arena of historical struggle—and also, therefore, of critical debate.

His concept of tradition, however, is sometimes open to the criticism of being a celebration of a sequence of "great figures," showing clear parallels to F. R. Leavis's method in *The Great Tradition*, as opposed to a critical inquiry into tradition as a mode of social textuality that allows for a continuity (and, at times, discontinuity) of literary practice. Incidentally, Weimann's criticism of Eliot and the New Critics, as well as more recent American critics, also centers on the failure to account for such a continuity. In calling for an alternative approach to tradition, Weimann outlines the issue in the following manner:

> In terms of the relationship of past writing and present reading (and new writing), tradition can be viewed as a concept that links the genesis and the structure of past creations to their present functions, origins to receptions. In more than one respect the study of both the process and the concept of tradition can trace not only the continuity but also the discontinuity and the crisis in the interrelationship of past values and present evaluations. (14)

Weimann criticizes a whole array of what he calls "modernist" critics for bringing about such a discontinuity and crisis. This is done, he argues, by recklessly imposing critical values of the present upon materials of the past without any regard for their historical continuity, instituting what he calls (probably borrowing the concept from Joseph Frank) the "spatial order" of the literary past (see 82–88) and an "*Ästhetisierung der Historie*" (29): "The function of art is not described and criticized in terms of the language of history; the function of history is described in terms of the language of art criticism" (26).

But while Weimann may be justified in his critique of the critics concerned, his own approach to "past significance" and "present meaning" (which easily helps to explain the continuity of, for instance, Lukács's realist tradition) leaves him unable to explain the disruptive practices of modernism with regard to tradition except as aberrations, blind deviations from historical continuity. It is noteworthy that while Weimann labels Eliot and the New Critics "modernist," he does not try to show how their supposedly misguided critical discontinuity with regard to the past is reflected in literary works of such modernists as Joyce, Kafka, or for that matter even Eliot.

But what is more interesting is that the "language of history" of someone whose Marxist background one would expect to keep him on the alert concerning radical historical changes and revolutions appears to rule out any negation of conventionalized dialogue with the past. I find the theory of tradition presented by Irving Howe in "The Culture of Modernism," heartily as I disagree with much he has to say in that essay, to yield a better understanding of how literary history can encompass both a tradition and its negation. Or, to put it differently, how it may concern itself with a literary system that, far from being an "ideal order," is also the scene of struggle and change: "At a given moment writers command an awareness of those past achievements which seem likely to serve them as models *to draw upon or deviate from*. That, surely, is part of what we mean by tradition: the shared assumptions among contemporaries as to which formal and thematic possibilities of the past are 'available' to them [emphasis added]."[16] Howe goes on to say that over an extended period "literary history must be affected by the larger history of which it is part," and that "it is when the inner dynamics of a literature and the large-scale pressures of history cross that there follows a new cultural style, in this case modernism" (14–15). Surely it is an illusion to think that the two only cross at certain isolated moments; rather, it is something that happens in the history of their constant relationship and intertexture that leads to the crisis of the dominant tradition as a model, and to the emergence of a (at least potentially) new paradigm.

But Howe does at least account for *deviation* as an integral element in the dynamics of literary history, and helps us avoid seeing tradition as simply an overpowering discourse that, even when we may succeed in slightly altering it, always keeps us subjugated and blind to other discourses (or discourses of the "other"). It is interesting, in this context, to counterbalance Weimann's Marxist concept of tradition with Raymond Williams's view in his *Marxism and Literature*:

The concept of tradition has been radically neglected in Marxist cultural thought. It is usually seen as at best a secondary factor, which may at most modify other and more decisive historical processes. This is not only because it is ordinarily diagnosed as superstructure, but also because "tradition" has been commonly understood as a relatively inert, historicized segment of a social structure: tradition as the surviving past. But this version of tradition is weak at the very point where the incorporating sense

16. Irving Howe, "The Culture of Modernism," *Decline of the New* (New York: Horizon Press, 1970), p. 14.

of tradition is strong: where it is seen, in fact, as an actively shaping force. For tradition is in practice the most evident expression of the dominant and hegemonic pressures and limits. It is always more than an inert historicized segment; indeed it is the most powerful practical means of incorporation. What we have to see is not just "a tradition" but a *selective tradition*: an intentionally selective version of a shaping past and a pre-shaped present, which is then powerfully operative in the process of social and cultural definition and identification.[17]

Literary tradition is like any other conventionalized social behavior in that it is closely tied to elements of ideological dominance and (actual or potential) cultural hegemony. Hence I would argue that any nonreactionary approach to modernism must allow for at least some degree of "negative" power of modernism as it faces tradition. Going so far as to say, as does Adorno at one point, that modernism negates tradition itself,[18] is, if understood literally, simply impossible. Whether it is true in another important sense is discussed in the next chapter.

Entering Literary History: Paradigms, Norms, Values

However strong we may want to emphasize the negative power of modernism, its dismantling of tradition, and the implicit critique of the social background of that tradition, in order to understand modernism as a force within literary history we must recuperate it in some sense. In other words, we need to place it within a historical context through which we seek to come to a better understanding of it, but with which we also risk "explaining away" some of its radical edge. The question at hand, then, is: How has modernism, as a signifying concept, entered historical understanding? I am thinking now of approaches that do not simply skirt or erase the issue, as we saw happening above. With a view to some of the issues discussed in the preceding chapter, this question will now be examined more explicitly in terms of literary history. But then

17. Raymond Williams, *Marxism and Literature* (Oxford: Oxford University Press, 1977), p. 115.
18. Adorno, *Ästhetische Theorie*, p. 38; *Aesthetic Theory*, p. 31.

we find another question intruding upon us: What guiding principles of literary historiography can be "reconstructed" when we observe the various uses of a concept like "modernism"? A minor theoretical digression is inevitable.

René Wellek, in the final chapter of his and Austin Warren's *Theory of Literature* (1949), utters what has become a familiar complaint: "Most leading histories of literature are either histories of civilization or collections of critical essays. One type is not a history of *art*; the other, not a *history* of art."[19] While his aversion to any kind of "extrinsic approaches" to literature (which could be related to "histories of civilization") is clearly reflected in *Theory of Literature*, it must have been obvious to him that the New Critics, with whom he shared theoretical (including professional and ideological) interests, were unable to transcend the latter limitation. Even when working with the concept of "tradition" and the notion of a break with aesthetic conventions, as in Cleanth Brooks's *Modern Poetry and the Tradition* (1939), their work tended to take the form of "collections of critical essays." Hence, Wellek argues, in order to "trace the evolution of literature as art" literary history must proceed "in comparative isolation from its social history, the biographies of authors, or the appreciation of individual works" (253–54). This last category is especially noteworthy, since it is precisely the New Critical close "appreciation of individual works" that *Theory of Literature* seeks to justify and facilitate.

The alternative, in Wellek's view, is a construction of literary history through the rigorous and theoretically grounded use of "period terms"; a logical conclusion in view of the fact that period terms are constantly being used, however loosely, in discussing the evolution of literature. The period, Wellek notes, "is not an ideal type or an abstract pattern or a series of class concepts, but a time section, dominated by a whole system of norms, which no work of art will ever realize in its entirety" (265). Wellek, of course, was to go on to write several definitions of such period terms; they are collected in his *Concepts of Criticism* and *Discriminations*. When arguing for the use of period terms and claiming that literature "must not be

19. René Wellek and Austin Warren, *Theory of Literature*, 3d ed. (Harmondsworth, Eng.: Penguin Books, 1963), p. 253.

conceived as being merely a passive reflection or copy of the political, social, or even intellectual development of mankind," Wellek may be right in the sense that there is no need to subjugate the body of texts we refer to as "literature" to some other, hierarchically dominant, signifying systems. But he is surely committing the reverse fallacy by concluding: "Thus the literary period should be established by purely literary criteria" (264).

This whole problem, highly relevant to the issue of "modernism" as a concept, was in fact more fruitfully dealt with earlier in the century by one of the Russian formalists, Jurij Tynjanov. "On Literary Evolution" starts with a critique, largely equivalent to that of Wellek, of previous tendencies in literary history. Tynjanov finds that "individualistic psychologism" has unjustifiably replaced "the problem of literature with the question of the author's psychology, while the problem of literary evolution becomes the problem of the genesis of literary phenomena." He also notes: "The theory of value in literary investigation has brought about the danger of studying major but isolated works and has changed the history of literature into a *history of generals.*"[20] Tynjanov holds that "the study of literary evolution or changeability" must make the *"mutation* of systems" its major concept (67), and he greatly reduces the unifying force generally attributed to tradition. Each system is characterized by the interrelationship of its formal elements and their functions. It is on the basis of this relationship that we, at any point in time, judge something as being "literary." But such judgment can never be based on literature alone:

> Even in contemporary literature, however, isolated study is impossible. The very existence of a fact as *literary* depends on its differential quality, that is, on its interrelationship with both literary and extraliterary orders. Thus, its existence depends on its function. What in one epoch would be a literary fact would in another be a common matter of social communication, and vice versa, depending on the whole literary system in which the given fact appears. (69)

20. Jurij Tynjanov, "On Literary Evolution," in L. Matejka and K. Pomorska, ed., *Readings in Russian Poetics: Formalist and Structuralist Views* (Ann Arbor: Michigan Slavic Publications, 1978), p. 66.

Although one could perhaps accuse Tynjanov of bad faith in using the concept "literary" in defining that very concept, his approach helps solve the main problem in Wellek's theory: namely, how to explain changes, that is, the mutations of the literary system as it is conceived at any point in history. In calling for an "internal history" of literature (253), Wellek ends up undermining his own theory by concluding that "literary change" is "a complex process varying from occasion to occasion; it is partly internal, caused by exhaustion and the desire for change, but also partly external, caused by social, intellectual, and all other cultural changes" (267). This would actually stand as a logical outcome of Tynjanov's arguments: "The very concept of a continuously evolving synchronic system is contradictory. A literary system is first of all a *system of the functions of the literary order which are in continual interrelationship with other orders.*"[21] A mutation of systems occurs because of changes in this relationship and never in isolation from that intertexture.

Tynjanov's theory remains to a surprising degree unsurpassed to this day. This is reflected, for instance, in Tzvetan Todorov's recent almost unmodified application of Tynjanov's basic arguments.[22] Yet Tynjanov's essay is marked by a formalist inclination that I view skeptically, namely, the urge to make literary study and the history of literature "become finally a science" that can "claim reliability" (66). Thus, while Tynjanov criticizes "theories of naive evaluation, which result from the confusion of points of observation, in which evaluation is carried over from one epoch or system into another," he believes that evaluation itself can be "freed from its subjective coloring, and the 'value' of a given literary phenomenon must be considered as having an 'evolutionary significance and character'" (67).

21. Ibid., p. 72 (emphasis in original).
22. See, for example, the entry on "History of Literature" in Oswald Ducrot, and Tzvetan Todorov, *Encyclopedic Dictionary of the Sciences of Language*, trans. Catherine Porter (Baltimore: Johns Hopkins University Press, 1979), pp. 144–49. In his *Introduction to Poetics*, however, Todorov questions Tynjanov's dismissal of genesis as an external phenomenon, for, as Todorov puts it: "As far back as we trace genesis, we find only other texts, other products of language; and it is difficult for us to conceive their apportionment. Must we exclude from the linguistic factors that preside over the genesis of a novel by Balzac the writings of those who were not poets but philosophers, moralists, memorialists, chroniclers of social life?" (60).

Wellek, who also aims for scientific reliability, feels that the evolution of literature has to be dissociated from the analogy with biological evolution: "The solution lies in relating the historical process to a value or norm. Only then can the apparently meaningless series of events be split into its essential and its unessential elements." But since he, like Tynjanov, yearns to eschew the "confusion of points of observation," he claims that "the series of developments will be constructed in reference to a scheme of values and norms, but these values themselves emerge only from the contemplation of this process. There is, one must admit, a logical circle here: the historical process has to be judged by values, while the scale of values is itself derived from history"; but this he finds necessary lest we be tempted to judge literature by something "extraneous to the process of literature" (257). Here Wellek appears to be using a "logical circle" in order to skirt the so-called hermeneutic circle, which entails, among other things, that our appraisal of the past cannot take place without an involvement of present interests.

As we shall see, Wellek cannot escape the interactive relation between, in Barbara Herrnstein Smith's formulation, "the *classification* of an entity and the functions it is expected or desired to perform."[23] Any differentiated reading of a historical continuum (and that is the only kind of reading there is) involves a preevaluation of that material, if only through its very classification.

We may derive from the above that in the context of twentieth-century literature, "modernism" is potentially a vital concept for any literary history that seeks to distance itself both from "a history of generals" and from the view of literature as simply an isolated progression of a certain category of texts labeled "literature." Such a reorientation might instead want to focus on the underlying intertextual systems that make possible and generate the production of certain kinds of texts during certain historical periods. Through "modernism" we are referring to the emergence of a major recent system that seeks to dismantle the prevalent ideas of what literature is and means. No wonder, then, that any reference to this system should be loaded with preconceptions, drawn not only from the reading

23. Smith, "Contingencies of Value," p. 17.

of representative literary works and authors but from criticism about that literature, and from dominant aspects of literary theories developed to some extent in response to this literature. We also need to be aware of and observe what happens to the literary system as a whole, as pictured in a literary history working with the concept of modernism.

Degrees of Modernism

If we look at Wellek's concept of modernism—which he, following Edmund Wilson and perhaps others, prefers to call "symbolism"—we note that, true to his theory in *Theory of Literature*, he seeks to pin down a systematic norm that can be seen to dominate the period, and then goes on to demarcate the period itself. In symbolist poetry, he says (and here, as in *Theory of Literature* and in most New Critical work, *poetry* is used as a paradigm for the whole of literature), "the image becomes 'thing.' The relation of tenor and vehicle in the metaphor is reversed. The utterance is divorced, we may add, from the situation: time and place, history and society, are played down."[24]

This notion of antirepresentational poetics appears to be in line with much criticism on modernism and thus may seem a workable thesis in tackling the concept, but when Wellek goes on to place the "movement" in historical terms, his concept as a whole becomes very weak. Wellek argues that symbolism is "clearly set off from the new avant-garde movements after 1914: futurism, cubism, surrealism, expressionism, and so on. There the faith in language has crumbled completely" (119). Hence, he is led to call "the period of European literature roughly between 1885 and 1914 'symbolism,' [and] to see it as an international movement which radiated originally from France but produced great writers and great poetry also elsewhere." But while his list of symbolist writers includes Eliot, Wallace Stevens, Crane, Joyce, Faulkner, O'Neill, and the "later

24. René Wellek, "The Term and Concept of Symbolism in Literary History," *Discriminations: Further Concepts of Criticism* (New Haven, Conn.: Yale University Press, 1970), p. 113.

Thomas Mann," most of these writers' significant works appeared in the twenties and thirties, that is, in a period allegedly dominated by a different poetic norm. In fact, the critical consensus seems to be that modernism was clearly not a dominant norm before World War I. This is a good example of how the conceptions of functional literary poetics and of the supposedly respective historical period simply do not coalesce. In this case it happens because of Wellek's desire to allow the concept of symbolism a narrow, "scientifically" reliable scope, partly in order for it to fit into his scheme of a clear succession of literary periods from the end of the Middle Ages to the present (see p. 91). What is even more striking is that Wellek is seriously suggesting that "new avant-garde movements" become the dominant literary norm after 1914, and that realist works that were appearing around the turn of the century are to be seen as struggling remnants of a realist period that had already been through its decline (90, 120). But as we shall see, Wellek is not alone in having problems with realism as part of a literary history based on a succession of period movements that supposedly are born, blossom, and then die.

For a more recent attempt to draw strict limits to modernism as a decisive moment in modern literary history, we can look to Douwe W. Fokkema's *Literary History, Modernism, and Postmodernism*. Fokkema argues, much as I have done above, that literary history must direct its attention to the "system of conventions that regulates the organization of a text," or in other words to the "code" that helps produce a certain kind of text at a certain historical juncture.[25] Like several other scholars, Fokkema works with "a basic difference between Realism on the one hand and Modernism on the other" (13), but he also tries to argue that symbolism and the various avant-gardes: futurism, expressionism, Dada, surrealism, and so forth, are all different from, and "compete" with, modernism. Fokkema has obvious problems isolating modernism in this manner. His basic definition of modernism rests on its "selection of hypothetical constructions expressing uncertainty and provision-

---

25. Douwe W. Fokkema, *Literary History, Modernism, and Postmodernism* (Harvard University Erasmus Lectures, Spring 1983 [Philadelphia: John Benjamins, 1984]), p. 5.

ality. It affects the relations between the text and other factors of the communication situation, as well as the organization of the text itself" (15). Modernism is to be seen as an art of provisional deliberations with preference for hypothesis, epistemological doubt, and metalingual commentary (14–18). This, Fokkema argues, clearly sets modernism, which celebrates intellectual freedom, movement, and antitotalitarianism, off from symbolism, according to which the ideal work is a crystal, a self-sufficient but immobile entity (19–20). Fokkema shows no awareness of the fact that highly influential interpretations of basic works that he calls "modernist" have actually judged them as autonomous crystalline entities in the symbolist tradition; or of the fact that the symbolist "crystals" can, if approached from a different angle, be seen as evincing all the qualities that he labels "modernist." What is Mallarmé's *Un coup de dés* if not a symbolist poem of "hypothetical construction," highlighting, not least on a metalingual level, provisionality, textual uncertainty, and epistemological doubt?

In the approaches discussed above we see how modernism, partly due to the effort of confining it within strictly definable lines that ensure an isolated field of study, is presented as an unaccountably narrow textual field. There is, however, no lack of studies that give rise to the opposite complaint. Sometimes "modernism" is used as such a broad concept that we are hard at task figuring out what is *not* modernism. One of the best-known examples of such an approach is Barthes's famous statement that in the wake of the decline of "transparent" classical writing around 1850 "the whole of Literature, from Flaubert to the present day, became the problematics of language."[26] Of course, to some extent this is simply a rhetorical move characteristic of Barthes in carving out the focus of his study, but as such it also reveals how decisive the "point of observation" is: Barthes is led to this generalization through his own critical interests in writing that in one way or another flaunts its status *as writing* and hence prevents us from reading it as a "transparent" text. His assertion may hold true in the case of any number of modernist works, but hardly when it comes to the

26. Roland Barthes, *Writing Degree Zero*, trans. Annette Lavers and Colin Smith (New York: Hill and Wang, 1968), p. 3.

works of Emile Zola, John Steinbeck, Halldór Laxness, or Heinrich Böll, to mention examples from fiction that falls within the period in question (unless, of course, Barthes's statement is also taken to signal a deconstructive reading of realistic strategies).

We saw how Marshall Berman also used modernism, although in a different manner, as a broad category, which (although this is certainly not Berman's intention) seems capable of encompassing almost every literary or aesthetic endeavor of our times—for it might be hard to refute the status of any modern text as a cultural counterpart of, or response to, social modernity. James M. Mellard, as mentioned earlier, draws a parallel between the scientific revolution and the aesthetic revolt of modernism, noting (to repeat an above quote) that when "the new science exploded the world, it exploded with it the novel as well." This analogy has not helped Mellard to use the concept of "exploded form" in order to focus on modernism as a separate textual project, for it seems that basically anything that happens after this "explosion" is modernist. Mellard's concept of modernism even covers writers like Saul Bellow, Bernard Malamud, John Updike, William Styron, and Ralph Ellison.[27] Used in this broad and unqualified manner, the concept has really become what some critics seriously wish it to be, namely useless.

However, even if we direct our attention to critics like Barthes, who in discussing modernism are focusing on more specific, nonrealistic practices, one notes that what a great many of them have in common is the silent (or not so silent) assumption that modernism is the *dominant* literary mode of the present century. This assumption parallels Wellek's notion of period terms as "names for systems of norms which dominate literature at a specific time of the historical process."[28] But to take such dominance for granted in the case of modernism seems exceedingly rash. We need only take a brief common-sense glance at the book and theater market at any point in the twentieth century to realize that nonmodernist practices are

27. Mellard, *The Exploded Form*, p. 16.
28. René Wellek, "The Concept of Romanticism in Literary History," *Concepts of Criticism*, ed. Stephen G. Nichols, Jr. (New Haven, Conn.: Yale University Press, 1963), p. 129.

well and thriving. That is to say, there is no slackening in the production of works that follow a conventional pattern often associated with nineteenth-century realism and naturalism—whereby we have to allow for some historical modification within what we call "convention" or "tradition." This is especially true if we include in such an overview every kind of "popular literature," which is frequently exiled from the privileged domain of Literature.

One kind of response that the notion of period dominance has called for is a typological approach, such as we find in David Lodge's mapping of modern literature. Lodge notes of Barthes's dictum quoted above: "The only modern writing which is authentic in this scheme is therefore writing which is conscious of its problematic status, the *scriptible* rather than the *lisible*."[29] One reason this issue is particularly relevant for Lodge, as he admits, is the fact that his own interests are tied not only to criticism and scholarship but to his status as a novelist "who has written several books of the kind that Roland Barthes says it is no longer possible to write, i.e. novels that are continuous in technique with 'classic realism' " (72). Lodge goes on: "What is needed, it has always seemed to me, is a way of mapping the literary history of the modern period which describes all the varieties of writing in it within a single conceptual scheme, without prejudging them" (72). Using Popper's critique of the kind of historicism that highlights the "emergence of a really new period" and the *"laws of historical development* which determine the transition from one period to another,"[30] Lodge argues that modernism as an aesthetic movement is historicist in precisely this "totalitarian" sense (70), claiming to usher in a radically new and different period.

Lodge seeks to counter notions of periodic dominance with a typological binary system that accounts for both modernism and realism (or antimodernism), basing it on Roman Jakobson's distinction between metaphor and metonymy: "I would suggest not only that these two kinds of writing, modernist and

29. David Lodge, "Historicism and Literary History: Mapping the Modern Period," *Working with Structuralism: Essays and Reviews on Nineteenth- and Twentieth-Century Literature* (London: Routledge and Kegan Paul, 1981), p. 71.

30. Karl Popper, *The Poverty of Historicism*, quoted in Lodge, *Working with Structuralism*, pp. 69–70.

antimodernist, persist throughout the modern period, but that we can map out alternating phases of dominance of one kind or another."[31] Actually, judging from Lodge's theoretical premises, which are presented and applied in his *Modes of Modern Writing*, his categories are so stringently structuralist in character that they appear divorced from *any* historical period: literary history becomes a repetitive cyclical motion from one pole to the other. This system "is not intolerant, exclusive, prescriptive. On the contrary, it is inclusive and evenhanded."[32]

Evenhanded and formalist as his system may be, Lodge's writing betrays an awareness of the presence of historical pressure when he tries to locate modernism as a moment of literary history. He nonchalantly summarizes the characteristics of modernism: "formal experiment, dislocation of conventional syntax, radical breaches of decorum, disturbance of chronology and spatial order, ambiguity, polysemy, obscurity, mythopoeic allusion, primitivism, irrationalism, structuring by symbol and motif rather than by narrative or argumentative logic, and so on" (71).

But these features are only activated as elements of literary history when charged with their broader historical significance. "It is easy to see how these strategies and themes reflect the sense that the modern period has a specific historic destiny, perhaps to abolish history itself," Lodge adds. Elsewhere he states that various modernists share "the view that God (at least the God of orthodox Christianity) was dead and that the world was a wasteland, a place of meaningless suffering, unsuccessful communication and shattered illusions."[33] This reading of modernist characteristics clearly implies that the above, more technical summary does indeed bear on a particular historical period. Furthermore, Lodge consistently uses the term "modern period," even though he feels impelled to conclude his essay "Historicism and Literary History" by stating: "If there is one modern period that begins some time in the late nine-

---

31. Lodge, "Modernism, Antimodernism and Postmodernism," *Working with Structuralism*, p. 7.

32. Lodge, "Historicism and Literary History," *Working with Structuralism*, p. 74.

33. David Lodge, *The Modes of Modern Writing: Metaphor, Metonymy, and the Typology of Modern Literature* (London: Edward Arnold, 1977), p. 157.

teenth century and still goes on, the terms of its definition must be sought beyond boundaries of the arts" (74–75).

I do not want simply to discard Lodge's attempt to replace "modernism" as a concept for a single dominant aesthetic practice in the modern "period" with an all-inclusive binary system. Despite his tendency to dehistoricize formal features, he provides us with an alternative view of modern literary history, different from those which assume that a "modern period" necessarily entails a single dominant modern style or poetic practice. We might want to ask, then, where such views have been functional. In other words, what historical background, in terms of literary criticism and scholarship, spurs Lodge's endeavor to set up his supposedly unprejudiced system?

Modernism and the Academy

The fact that someone is seeking to establish a system that is not prejudiced against realist writing is of course an indication that such a prejudice has been evident in the respective critical context, which in Lodge's case is Anglo-American criticism, more explicitly Anglo-American *academic* criticism. As an arena of critical discourse it is an appropriate example for us, since, for reasons hinted at below, "modernism" has been a particularly significant concept in the Anglo-American sphere. And it is primarily the academy, as a literary institution, that has engendered and fostered the norms and values determinant in "constructing" paradigms of modernism.

If we observe the critical enterprise within the Anglo-American academy, we note an obvious predilection for modernist as opposed to nonmodernist writers, as witnessed by the voluminous criticism on writers such as, to name but a few, Joyce, Eliot, Beckett, Woolf, and Stein. Here, within the confines of the modern academy, we no longer have to doubt that modernism has indeed been a "dominant" literary discourse. Which is not to say that it has been powerless in other spheres, for instance among writers as a social group (a case that is further complicated by the increasing immigration of writers into the universities, especially in the United States).

How do we explain the "popularity" of modernism among

academic critics? One possible answer is given by Bradbury and McFarlane: "Modernism is our art; it is the one art that responds to the scenario of our modern chaos."[34] Our value judgment would then be drawn from a broad consideration of the modern "human condition." This would be an appropriate rejoinder to some critics of modernism, such as Francis Russell, who ponder why it is that "chaos, dissonance and obscurity draw so much emotional response from the modern mind."[35] We might want to note that, as demonstrated in chapter 1, chaos and dissonance are actually *not* what many critics find to be predominant characteristics of modernism, even when such critics acknowledge the "obscurity" of individual works. This last point links up with another conceivable explanation: modernist works tend to be notoriously "difficult" as literary works go, that is, they tend to resist immediate understanding and thus often call for arduous interpretation, which is a central task of serious criticism. But this answer also clearly connects with other professional reasons for the central position of modernism (or, rather, of certain modernist writers and works) in the academic canon of modern literature.

The fact that modernism was gaining significant ground at a time when literature was becoming a "respectable" field of academic study is salient in this context. Terry Eagleton has surveyed how, through the radical endeavor of I. A. Richards, F. R. Leavis, and their followers, English was turned into a serious, even a privileged, discipline. As Eagleton puts it, in his humorous manner: "In the early 1920s it was desperately unclear why English was worth studying at all; by the early 1930s it had become a question of why it was worth wasting your time on anything else."[36] One of the pioneers of this new "movement" was of course T. S. Eliot, who, while not a practicing academic, had immense influence on academic criticism. The close textual scrutiny of these people was later to be echoed in

34. Bradbury and McFarlane, "The Name and Nature of Modernism," in Bradbury and McFarlane, ed., *Modernism, 1890–1930*, p. 27.

35. Francis Russell, *Three Studies in 20th Century Obscurity* (Chester Springs, Pa.: Dufour Editions, 1961), p. 18.

36. Terry Eagleton, *Literary Theory: An Introduction* (Minneapolis: University of Minnesota Press, 1983), p. 31.

much American criticism. Emphasizing the negative aspect of "close reading" (without which, however, it is hard to imagine literary or any other textual studies today), Eagleton claims that it signaled the "beginnings of a 'reification' of the literary work, the treatment of it as an object in itself, which was to be triumphantly consummated in the American New Criticism" (44). The rise of close reading, furthermore, relates to the fact that New Criticism "evolved in the years when literary criticism in North America was struggling to become 'professionalized', acceptable as a respectable academic discipline. Its battery of critical instruments was a way of competing with the hard sciences on their own terms, in a society where such science was the dominant criterion of knowledge" (49).

How does the "professionalization" of literary criticism (as opposed to philology, which was of course a classical profession) relate to the status and reception of modernism? When Foucault states that "in the modern age, literature is that which compensates for (and not that which confirms) the signifying function of language,"[37] we may sense in his notion of "compensation" a double-edged quality that seems to me crucial in answering this question. On the one hand it refers us to modernism's revolt against the rationalized, hegemonic signifying power of the language of social communication, but on the other it brings to mind the critical attempts, so prevalent in this century, to isolate and elevate literary uses of language. This latter point ties in with the vested professional interests of those whose careers are felt to be dependent upon literature as an autonomous field of study. By securing the autonomy of literature, preventing it from being overly "polluted" or even swallowed up by "other" modes of social discourse, literary criticism is also protecting its vulnerable specificity and justifying its existence as an area of significant cultural inquiry.

There is little doubt that eminent modernist works have been produced, as Richard Poirier states, as "an attempt to perpetuate the power of literature as a privileged form of discourse."[38] But this in itself says nothing about the social func-

37. Foucault, *The Order of Things*, p. 44.
38. Poirier, "The Difficulties of Modernism and the Modernism of Difficulty," p. 126.

tion of that discourse. Those who see an obvious or "natural" parallel between modernist literature and prevalent modern types of criticism frequently point to the coexistence, mentioned above, of futurist literature and formalist studies in Russia, where the two seem to have carried out parallel projects. But we have already seen the ambivalence of the formalist endeavor as reflected in their theory of "defamiliarization," an ambivalence that echoes that of Foucault's "compensation." However, the more criticism and literary theory have become specialized disciplines, the more it has seemed that a literature of "modernist" complexity is the natural aesthetic counterpart of their inquiry (even while in actuality prominent studies of formalist, structuralist, and New Critical cast are frequently aimed at traditional and nonmodernist literary productions). When literature is seen as an autonomous discourse, criticism of formalist-aestheticist bent tends to elaborate on the less representational aspects of language. This appears to be precisely what modernist literature itself does; this seems indeed to constitute the very source of its complexity.

Hence, literary studies that make it their business to study not just literature but, in Roman Jakobson's term, more explicitly "literariness" would seem bound to evince a clear preference for modernism as opposed to more conventional modes of literary discourse. Indeed, since modernist works by Proust or Pound appear readily to live up to theories of "literariness," be it in the guise of "defamiliarization," New Critical "tension" or "ambiguity," or other relevant concepts, they may as a result seem more "literary" than works by Heinrich Mann or Philip Larkin. According to the same principle, we ought to be able to create a scale based on structural complexity, according to which modernism points toward one pole and works of highly conventional and predictable literary structure toward the other.

This has indeed been done. My example comes not from an advocate of modernism, as could perhaps be expected, but from a specialist on popular literature. John G. Cawelti notes that "all cultural products contain a mixture of two elements: conventions and inventions."[39] Popular forms such as the Western

39. John G. Cawelti, *The Six-Gun Mystique* (Bowling Green, Ohio: Bowling Green University Popular Press, n.d.), p. 27.

and the spy novel rely on a great deal of shared convention among their readership, whereas several modern works try to shatter such "agreement" through a heightened level of invention. Thus, Cawelti proceeds to correlate the distinction between convention and invention to that between "formula and structure," which

> can be best envisaged as a continuum between two poles; one pole is that of a completely conventional structure of conventions—an episode of the Lone Ranger or one of the Tarzan books comes close to this pole; the other end of the continuum is a completely original structure which orders inventions—*Finnegans Wake* is perhaps the ultimate example of this, though one might also cite such examples as Resnais' film *Last Year at Marienbad*, T. S. Eliot's poem *The Waste Land*, or Beckett's play *Waiting for Godot*. (29)

The second pole, as we see from Cawelti's examples, is obviously of a modernist nature. It has of course often been argued that modernism was and is largely a reaction to the cultural configurations that have caused the Western world to be flooded with totally conventionalized popular material calling for passive "consumption." One is reminded of Adorno's remark that modernism and popular culture are two halves of a freedom that do not add up to a whole.[40] Others stress modernism's complicity in initiating this gap. Jameson argues that, beginning with Flaubert, the two "levels" of the narrative text, style and narrative, "begin to drift apart and acquire their own relative autonomy." He states: "The plotless art novel and the styleless bestseller can then be seen as the end products of this tendency, which corresponds to the antithesis between . . . the *molecular* and the *molar* impulses in modern form-production no less than in contemporary social life itself."[41]

40. Theodor W. Adorno, *Über Walter Benjamin*, ed. Rolf Tiedemann (Frankfurt: Suhrkamp, 1970), p. 129.

41. Fredric Jameson, *Fables of Aggression: Wyndham Lewis, the Modernist as Fascist* (Berkeley: University of California Press, 1979), pp. 7–8. Other critics, perhaps most notably Daniel Bell, have directly blamed modernism for the chaotic and hedonistic state of modern popular culture. See Daniel Bell, *The Cultural Contradictions of Capitalism* (New York: Basic, 1976) and "Beyond Culture, Beyond Self," *The Winding Passage*, pp. 275–302.

Turning the scale into a blatantly dualistic and oppositional system, as Jameson does, is not the only risk involved in the use of such a continuum based on structural complexity. Cawelti, of course, emphasizes "that the distinction between invented structure and formula . . . is a descriptive rather than a qualitative one" (29), but when we think of this scale in terms of structural elaboration, it is easy to see that value judgments will often automatically favor "invented structure." This is obviously what has happened in the academic study of modern literature, whereby the respective formal analyses often take scant notice of where the structural complexities of modernist writing stand in relation to other modes of social form-production.

I have emphasized the dominant academic "construction" of modernism since, as I shall explain, it plays a decisive role in locating modernism in a historical understanding of twentieth-century literature. Charles Newman actually conflates the modernist "revolution" with the criticism that has accumulated around it—which he calls the "second revolution": "Modernism is transmitted through criticism, to the extent that the two revolutions have become indistinguishable." He goes on to say that "when we talk about the Modern, we are at this point talking about Interpretation—how literature enters the social context."[42] Paradoxically, while we might think that Newman is here equating "Interpretation" with reading—for it is surely already at that point that literature enters the social context—he has in mind some center of critical authority that not only interprets modernist literature, but also has an "interest in making Modernism the reigning cultural orthodoxy. Without this 'managerial revolution,' Modernism would not play the major role in our consciousness that it does" (32).

Newman makes at least two highly questionable assumptions. First, he takes criticism on modernism to be a monolithic phenomenon, and even states that "the Second Revolution comes to exemplify a profusion of methodologies without a *methodenstreit* (a conflict of rival methodologies)" (34). While one can, especially in the Anglo-American context,

42. Charles Newman, *The Post-Modern Aura: The Act of Fiction in an Age of Inflation* (Evanston, Ill.: Northwestern University Press, 1985), p. 27.

speak of a dominance of formalistic constructions of a modernist paradigm, this is an odd comment for someone who also quotes such major authorities on modernism as Adorno and Benjamin. Second, Newman's claim that "the triumph of Modernist orthodoxy is complete—to use *Time* magazine's words, 'Modernism *is* our institutional culture!'" (34) calls for a good deal of skepticism. The fact that *Time* may accept modernism as our "institutional culture" says very little about its status with regard to dominant modes of textual production and understanding. If modernist forms were indeed hegemonic in such production in society as a whole, then we could speak of "modernist orthodoxy."

But in *whose* consciousness does modernism play a "major role"? Where is it taken for granted as a "natural" sociocultural mode of production? In other words, on what scale or level can we conceive of an "interpretive community," to use Stanley Fish's concept,[43] for which modernism is an intelligible discourse shared by enough members to be considered a "natural" mode of communication? This is certainly what it takes for a discourse to play a major role in our consciousness, and this is also related to the whole issue of "tradition," which remains insistent even for a literary history that seeks to dismantle any notion of the compulsory stronghold of a single tradition.

We can also discuss this topic in terms of the "institution of literature" or "literary competence," which Jonathan Culler has placed at the center of the inquiry into systems that make it possible for us to read and understand literary texts. But Culler's approach also shows how dangerous these concepts are. True enough, we can only read and understand a poem because there exists a convention of reading poetry, and the same holds true for other literary genres: "Such conventions are the constituents of the institution of literature."[44] Culler therefore argues that each text is to be placed against the background of convention and studied intertextually, which then immediately involves us in questions about the basic operations of discourse within the literary system. To approach this

43. Stanley Fish, *Is There a Text in This Class?: The Authority of Interpretive Communities* (Cambridge, Mass.: Harvard University Press, 1980).

44. Jonathan Culler, *Structuralist Poetics: Structuralism, Linguistics and the Study of Literature* (London: Routledge and Kegan Paul, 1975), p. 116.

system, Culler posits an ideal reader: "The question is not what actual readers happen to do but what an ideal reader must know implicitly in order to read and interpret works in ways which we consider acceptable, in accordance with the institution of literature" (123–24). These acceptable ways, then, constitute "literary competence."

Again, a number of objections are in order. What does "institution of literature" mean? Does it mean the total scene of literary "consumption" in society—and does *that* really constitute a *single* mode of "competence"? It seems that Culler is rather thinking of the "Scene of Instruction" that Harold Bloom finds so crucial as a medium of literary tradition.[45] In other words, Culler is focusing on the academic study of literature, which has of course established conventions to deal with modernist works. Thus, he is able to state that "*The Waste Land* or *Ulysses* once seemed strange and now seems intelligible" (123), whereas we know that for a great majority of readers in any society *Ulysses* is still a very strange book indeed.

This indicates that "literary competence" is not really applicable as a general, unified concept, for texts meet with various "competences," depending on when and by whom they are read. It could be argued, however, that within the academy—which wields a certain social authority and as such exerts some influence on the "outside world," as we may gather from the *Time* quotation—modernism has become a "tradition," that is, a conventionalized discourse for a limited interpretive community. But even here it may be hard, or at least misleading, to speak of a single literary competence, for we have seen the severely conflicting notions of the very meaning and function of modernist discourse. Are Adorno's theory of modernism and his readings of modernist works "acceptable" for, or "in accordance with," the very influential conventions that judge modernism as primarily a formalist endeavor?

Needless to say, such questions weigh heavily in contemplating the role that is accorded modernism in modern literary history. Is it to be portrayed as a broad cultural movement that has been in a position of hegemony with regard to other aesthetic and literary traditions for most of the twentieth century,

45. Bloom, "The Dialectics of Literary Tradition," p. 533.

or as an oppositional discourse that however became a significant object of study for literary criticism? It should be evident that my own position lies somewhere close to the second answer, but among the factors that complicate the issue is the fact that it is not modernism in its conceptual totality (which as we shall see is charged with important contradictions) that has made up this "object of study," but what Raymond Williams might have called "selective traditions" of modernism, established and shaped by various branches of the critical establishment.

Modernist Canons

The great majority of studies in modernism is composed of investigations into a limited number of individual writers, that is, into specific canons. If I am right in saying that any discussion of a writer is an implicit inscription into literary history, then this obviously holds true for canons as well. Any mention of a work rests on the assumption that it is exemplary in one way or another, and thus in a sense involves its canonization. If we think of canonization in this broad sense (which is a necessary criterion for the narrower sense), we realize that the only act of "noncanonization" is complete silence. The recently escalating questioning within the academy of existing canons, which, as Robert von Hallberg puts it, often judges canons as something that "other people, once powerful, have made and what should now be opened up, demystified, or eliminated altogether,"[46] bears within it an affirmation of the power of the canons that are to be dismantled.

The mere act of challenging a particular canon, however, need be little more than an exhibition of a shallow kind of "liberalism," which furthermore can lead one to ignore the critical process of canonization. I have no quarrel with the simple insistence that Joyce and Kafka are among the most important writers of the twentieth century—but I may be in fierce disagreement as to *why* they should hold that position, and of course we cannot be certain that they always will. Bar-

46. Hallberg, introduction, in Hallberg, ed., *Canons*, p. 1.

bara Herrnstein Smith puts the matter succinctly: "At a given time and under the contemporary conditions of available materials, technology, and techniques, a particular object—let us say a verbal artifact or text—may perform certain desired/able functions quite well for some set of subjects. It will do so by virtue of certain of its 'properties.'"[47] These properties are not, as Stanley Fish would have it, constituted solely by the receiving methodology and interests of the interpretive community; they are, as Smith goes on to say, products of the interaction of the subject with the variously highlighted structural elements of the work. We should be able to understand, by examining the works in question and the context of their reception, why certain critics might be more interested in analyzing the products of Joyce or Kafka than those of, say, Zola or Theodore Dreiser.

Hence, it often seems to me that what should be resisted is not so much the "preservation" of certain writers as the "innocent" maintenance of critical and interpretive models used in "reading" the writers in question. The latter kind of resistance, however, fully legitimates a thorough inquiry into prevalent canons, as the case of feminist criticism amply testifies. Interpretive models are frequently coterminous with an approach to a specific writer or group of writers, while the contingency of the approach might quickly come to light if brought to bear on someone outside the respective canon.

In an effort to counter the questioning of canons with strategies of assent, Charles Altieri argues: "Given our need for memory and the manifest power of various canonical works to transcend any single structure of social interest, I think it is possible to recover some of the force in classical ideals of a canon. Through that effort, we recover modes of thought about value and human agency sorely lacking in the dominant critical attitudes fostered by the hermeneutics of suspicion."[48] What Altieri plays down, in his emphasis on canons as "central stories that unify society," is the fact, so obvious in the case of modernism, that while canonical works may transcend any

47. Smith, "Contingencies of Value," p. 30.
48. Charles Altieri, "An Idea and Ideal of a Literary Canon," in Hallberg, ed., *Canons*, p. 42.

narrowly conceived social interest, the violently conflicting interpretations of the meaning of their practices clearly links up with broader ideological views of meaning-production in society at large.

It is the fact that such practices *can* be examined as semiotic processes in a social context, and not just as the mode of expression of individual writers, that makes such paradigmatic concepts as "modernism" so important. According to Altieri, however, we do not even "want dialogue with texts; we want to encounter the full force of what the author imagined, in the terms the author chose to present it." Authority is at all costs to be kept "within the imaginative processes of a dialogue with great minds" (61). This appears to be an unequivocal endorsement of Hirschian intentionality, which, when combined with the elitist notion of "great minds," shows the arbitrariness of the very canon-formation that it is supposed to legitimate. For how can the construction or the reception of a literary canon take place without the synthesizing power of the interpretive moment, which then clearly compromises the sovereignty of the individual "great minds"?

In the case of modernism we need, instead, a concept that retains its facility for historical interpretation while allowing for the arbitrariness of the canon that in each case will be constructed by the respective literary historian. Such construction is a selective moment that literary history cannot escape, which it can only try to make as self-conscious as possible, in order to prevent canonization in literary history from creating, in Tynjanov's terms, "a history of generals." This is perhaps nowhere more imperative than in the Anglo-American sphere, where the elevation of a number of *individual* modernists seems to have been greatly enhanced by the lack of prominent avant-garde groups practicing in the English language. One might, to use a paradoxical expression, argue that there is no "avant-garde tradition" in Britain and the United States, whereas critical discourse around modernism in, say, the German-speaking countries and France is heavily influenced by the presence of avant-garde movements like surrealism, Dada, and expressionism, and is therefore less likely to be shaped by the shadows of iconic individuals. The presence of such groups appears to make it more feasible to discuss modernism as a historical-aesthetic practice and not just as the endeavor of a number of "superwriters," the way Joyce, Eliot, and Pound are frequently treated in the Anglo-American context.

It is not hard to demonstrate that canon formation has been both highly arbitrary and of prime significance in Anglo-American modernist studies. In one of the first books to use the concept, *A Survey of Modernist Poetry*, Laura Riding and Robert Graves make E. E. Cummings their representative modernist, but the "movement" appears to include both Eliot and Hemingway, whereas Williams and Pound (and all the Imagists) are aggressively banished without any logically presented reason.[49]

Canon formation sometimes takes the form of an observable power play within the critical institution. Marjorie Perloff has demonstrated how two groups of critics have carried on an argument as to whether the modernist period is the "Pound era" or the "Stevens era."[50] Once a single writer is elevated in this manner, the issues involved will necessarily be streamlined accordingly. But the choice is never obvious; Perloff concludes by hinting that we can perhaps tell quite a different tale by calling "the first half of the century the Eliot Era" (506).

Sometimes one notices a tricky link between a strictly limited canon formation and the focus of the respective study. Kermode's severe formal-ideological critique of modernism in *The Sense of an Ending* is a good example. In arguing how the totalitarian use of form in modernist writing reflects that of the "closed authoritarian society" and leads the writers to lose hold of reality, Kermode draws on Pound, Eliot, Yeats, Lawrence, and Lewis. It may appear that he has a sound canon under his belt; he clearly feels he can dismiss Virginia Woolf (at least he does not mention her), who would complicate the issue for him. But bypassing Joyce would probably be too blatant an omission. Kermode therefore has to go into an awkward explanation of how Joyce is "a realist"[51] (not that he is alone in trying to "save"

49. Laura Riding and Robert Graves, *A Survey of Modernist Poetry*, 2d ed. (London: Heinemann, 1929 [first pub. 1927]).

50. Marjorie Perloff, "Pound/Stevens: Whose Era?" *New Literary History* 13 (Spring 1982): 485–510.

51. Kermode, *The Sense of an Ending*, p. 113.

Joyce from the "hell" of modernism[52]. Even more striking, since Kermode is presenting a highly significant and ideologically charged theory of modernism, is the fact that he completely restricts himself to the British literary scene, never even asking, for instance, whether his theory of modernist form would be at all applicable to modernism on the European continent.

A very different but perhaps more typical creation of a modernist canon comes to light in a recent book by Ricardo Quinones. He has few qualms about outlining "his" modernist canon: "As is apparent, the focus of this study will rest on the 'high' or 'classical' Modernists, whom tradition tends to group in by now familiar litanies: Proust, Mann, Pound, Eliot, Stevens, Joyce, Virginia Woolf, D. H. Lawrence, Kafka."[53] Quinones does not hesitate to isolate some "Modernist masterpieces of twentieth-century literature" (6) and to dissociate them from the various avant-gardes, for, he argues, "in the final achieved masterpieces of the twenties and thirties, the major Modernists went beyond their earlier associations with the avant-garde and brought to their works a sense of personal appropriation that resulted in fuller aesthetic experience" (19). Quinones is here enforcing a historical split that will be discussed in a later chapter (versions of which we have already seen in Wellek and Fokkema), but it should be obvious how vacuous his criteria are—how can "personal appropriation" and "fuller aesthetic experience" be judged as integral features of the works in question? The central argument of Quinones's book further foregrounds the arbitrariness of his canonization. He wants to see modernism developing, directly *advancing*, from its original negative critical attitudes and toward the "evocative mythic dimensions of Greek tragedy" (8), the fulfillment of which is allegedly to be found in *Four Quartets, Joseph and His Brothers*, and *Finnegans Wake*. In spite of the wide scope he grants such a development (as we can infer from his examples), his canon has little use for even some of the enlisted

52. See Fredric Jameson, "Ulysses in History," in W. J. McCormack and Alister Stead, ed., *James Joyce and Modern Literature* (London: Routledge and Kegan Paul, 1982), pp. 126–41.

53. Ricardo Quinones, *Mapping Literary Modernism: Time and Development* (Princeton, N.J.: Princeton University Press, 1985), p. 18.

"high" modernists, notably Kafka, who is barely mentioned in the book.

A better-known, in fact highly influential, canonizing venture within modernist studies is the work of Hugh Kenner. His magnum opus, the fascinating *Pound Era*, is a flagrantly subjective construction of the modernist project, with Ezra Pound massively centered and elevated and a few other figures moving gracefully around him. Kenner frankly notes that a canon is "not a list but a narrative of some intricacy," in fact it is "the story I have been elaborating for 35 years."[54] It is a tale of a "supranational movement called International Modernism" (53), the central characters being Pound, Eliot, Joyce, Marianne Moore, Wyndham Lewis, and Beckett. These are of course the writers Kenner has spent his career working on, and most of them he has known personally. Writers like Woolf, Faulkner, or Wallace Stevens are not a part of this "International Modernism"; each is a "provincial" writer, apparently belonging only to a "Homemade World," to quote the title of Kenner's book on American modernism—once Kenner actually appears to make a false step, placing William Carlos Williams both in the province and in "International Modernism" (56, 57).

The arbitrariness of Kenner's use of that concept is everywhere visible. He states that modernism "flourished for some forty years. Its last masterpiece was *Waiting for Godot*" (54), to which we can only respond: Is *Endgame* not a "masterpiece" or not a "modernist" work? Kenner notes that while one might have expected modernism's "literary language to be French" (53), it turned out to be English, and its works were either written in or disseminated from London, while the writers were Americans and Irishmen living in "exile." Kenner solves the problem of Wyndham Lewis by pointing out that he was born "near a dock at Amherst, Nova Scotia, on his American father's yacht" (55).

While it is easy to react playfully to certain quirks characterizing Kenner's "story" of modernism, I want to make two serious objections. First, Kenner's unabashed Anglocentrism is unfortunately a hallmark of a great deal of modernist studies.

54. Hugh Kenner, "The Making of the Modernist Canon," *Chicago Review* 34 (Spring 1984): 59–60.

While everyone seems to agree that as a phenomenon modernism is radically "international" (although admittedly in the limited Western sense of that word), constantly cutting across national boundaries, this quality is certainly not reflected in the majority of critical studies of modernism. Such studies are mostly restricted to the very national categories modernism is calling into question, or they are confined to the (only slightly wider) Anglo-American sphere. Peter Faulkner's monograph *Modernism*, published in the Methuen *Critical Idiom* series,[55] is symptomatic. In outlining the concept of modernism it touches briefly on James and Yeats, then dwells exclusively on Eliot, Woolf, Pound, Joyce, and Lawrence. The urge to "secure" works, writers, and canons within the boundaries of national literatures does not originate in the present century, but in the case of modernism it does come strikingly to the fore. There are exceptions, of course, the most notable of which is fortunately widely read: Bradbury and McFarlane's *Modernism* anthology. Partly because it is written by several different people (and despite the varying quality of the contributions), that symposium gives a sense of the chaos and contingency of the concept without letting it run completely out of bounds.

Modernism and Feminism

If Hugh Kenner's claim that English is the language of modernism is in step with much that goes on in modernist studies, his account also typifies another striking characteristic of modernist (as well as other) canonizations, namely the small number of canonized women—only one in "International Modernism"! Is "woman" a marginal element in modernism?

Here, as elsewhere, it may be tempting recklessly to conflate modernist practices and critical projections of modernist canons. Obviously women have been submerged in the historical documentation of modernist culture. This is now being corrected—not least in American criticism—and women are surfacing, thanks to the endeavors of scholars who not only are calling attention to neglected writers but are also asking ques-

55. Peter Faulkner, *Modernism* (London: Methuen, 1977).

tions different from those raised in the past. This process may include broadening the scope of literary study to include the cultural environment of modernist practices.

A case in point is Shari Benstock's *Women of the Left Bank*, which charts, not least through sociobiographical studies, various cultural configurations that fostered modernist achievements in the early twentieth century. Observing literary history as a kind of palimpsest, Benstock retraces a "female subtext" that exposes that which "Modernism has repressed, put aside, or attempted to deny."[56] Leaving aside the question of what "Modernism" exactly stands for in such context, we can certainly appreciate the way in which Benstock changes the historical face of modernism. Analyzing the publication and promotion of modernist literature (editorial work, business matters, the small magazines, publishing companies, bookstores, artistic saloons), Benstock refuses to forget women active in "literary midwifery," whose "contributions differed little from those of Ezra Pound, who is remembered for similar efforts on behalf of Modernism" (21).

Through a different kind of palimpsest deciphering, Benstock's work also highlights the more specifically literary achievements of women modernists. This involves revising the modernist canon, centering figures who have been only marginally present in literary history. In this respect Benstock's work is part of an expanding "feminization" of the modernist paradigm noticable in recent years. The position of, for instance, Gertrude Stein in the modernist canon has radically shifted in the past decade. Until recently, as Benstock points out, Stein's "literary reputation rested on anecdotal (and often incorrect) information about her life in Paris" (20). True enough, Edmund Wilson was audacious enough to include her in the canon in *Axel's Castle* as early as 1930, but it is telling that in commenting on Wilson's book forty years later, René Wellek feels thàt we "might only deplore the inclusion of Gertrude Stein."[57]

A revaluation of Stein's work in the seventies is signaled for

56. Shari Benstock, *Women of the Left Bank: Paris, 1900–1940* (Austin: University of Texas Press, 1986), p. x.

57. Wellek, "The Term and Concept of Symbolism in Literary History," *Discriminations*, p. 101.

instance by Michael J. Hoffman's appraisal in 1976, placing her squarely in the center of modernism: "to reject Stein any longer is to reject Modernism."[58] It is easy to agree with Marianne DeKoven that as a whole Stein's work "fits neatly nowhere."[59] But quite aside from the fact that this could be said of most major writers, we can object that in order for us to discuss her as a modernist writer, we have to "fit" her into a canon. The recently surging Stein criticism, much of it feminist and post-structuralist, has found her to be representative for an aesthetic or literary relation to modernity.[60] As a central figure of modernism, Stein is bound to become, in a sense, typical of what modernism is about. The same holds true for other women writers who in recent years have been strongly foregrounded in Anglo-American criticism, in particular Virginia Woolf, but also for example H. D. and Djuna Barnes.

To return to a question implicit in previous comments, what bearing does the issue of canonization have on the problematics of modernist practices? How will the pronounced presence of women writers change our view of more "established" texts generally taken to manifest the poetics of modernism? When Benstock states that she wishes to unearth a subtext that "exposes all that Modernism has repressed, put aside, or attempted to deny" (x), we cannot be sure whether "Modernism" refers to the forces at work in constructing a dominant modernist paradigm or to a repressive faculty in the textual activities of canonized modernists.

From a certain feminist standpoint it may seem desirable to project male dominance directly onto a linguistic level. Benstock is in fact pulled in this direction in certain parts of her

58. Michael J. Hoffman, *Gertrude Stein* (Boston: Twayne Publishers, 1976), p. 134.

59. Marianne DeKoven, "Gertrude Stein and the Modernist Canon," in Shirley Neuman and Ira B. Nadel, ed., *Gertrude Stein and the Making of Literature* (Boston: Northeastern University Press, 1988), p. 14.

60. See for instance Marianne DeKoven, *A Different Language: Gertrude Stein's Experimental Writing* (Madison: University of Wisconsin Press, 1983); Jayne L. Walker, *The Making of a Modernist: Gertrude Stein from* Three Lives *to* Tender Buttons (Amherst: University of Massachusetts Press, 1984); Neuman and Nadel, ed., *Gertrude Stein and the Making of Literature*. See also recent essays published in Michael J. Hoffman, ed., *Critical Essays on Gertrude Stein* (Boston: G. K. Hall, 1986), esp. Catharine R. Stimpson, "The Somagrams of Gertrude Stein," pp. 183–95, and Lisa Ruddick, "A Rosy Charm: Gertrude Stein and the Repressed Feminine," pp. 225–39.

study, especially when contrasting women's endeavors in modernism with those of the "Modernist fathers." In Gertrude Stein's "investigation into language, she placed herself not with the signified (semantic content), that which is usually privileged in literature." She "discovered that the equation between sign and substance, between form and meaning, on which Modernism staked its claim was not sacred" (186). Against the background of a conservative, even apparently classical-realist, model for the "Modernist fathers," Stein becomes the deconstructive angel, mother of the "wandering signifier."

To a degree male modernists may certainly have functioned as a part of—in some cases even a strong confirmation of—a general partriarchal tradition that female modernists felt they were up against. This is reflected for instance in H. D.'s dual struggle with mythic patterns of her classical sources and the "fatherly" presence of Ezra Pound (and Sigmund Freud, for that matter).[61] It may be fruitful to observe the differences between her poetics and Pound's, or to attend to how H. D.'s treatment of classical material diverges from male travels through past history and mythology, for example in the case of Pound, Joyce, and Eliot, the focus being no longer on Odysseus or the Fisher King but on displaced women of classical narratives.

This aspect of cultural reappropriation, however, needs to be viewed in conjunction with other structural qualities, in particular, I believe, with language and the subject in language. After noting that "in or about December, 1910, human character changed,"[62] Virginia Woolf related the change both to a modern shift in human relations and to a revolt against the realist novel in terms of the language of fiction and the mediation of the individual life of the mind. While she is critical of James Joyce—somewhat prudishly reproaching him for possessing the "calculated indecency of a desperate man" (334)—she feels that he and other male modernists are as involved in this revolt as she is. Some contemporary feminists have devel-

---

61. See Benstock, *Women of the Left Bank*, pp. 311–56. For H. D.'s "re-vision" of classical material and her radical appropriation of women-centered myths, as well as for her relationship with Freud, see esp. Susan Stanford Friedman, *Psyche Reborn: The Emergence of H. D.* (Bloomington: Indiana University Press, 1981).

62. Virginia Woolf, "Mr. Bennett and Mrs. Brown," *Collected Essays*, vol. 1 (London: Hogarth Press, 1966), p. 320.

oped a different perspective on the gender of modernism, for instance Catharine R. Stimpson: "By 1910, of course, the modern counterreformation in support of patriarchal laws had also begun. Among its most powerful popes amd priests were otherwise avant-garde male modernists. As Sandra M. Gilbert has written: 'For the male modernist . . . gender is most often an ultimate reality, while for the female modernists an ultimate reality exists only if one journeys beyond gender.' "[63]

How do male modernists support patriarchal laws, and how are they at the same time "otherwise avant-garde"? Are some of them perhaps torn between deep-rooted and patriarchal social habits, still guiding their individual lives, and a radical new view of human subjectivity expressed through language or whatever their artistic medium might be? If such were the case, we might come to the conclusion that whatever their individual positions as social beings, their literary discourse works to disrupt patriarchal structures. It is interesting to note that much of Sandra Gilbert and Susan Gubar's energy in the first volume of their trilogy in progress, *No Man's Land*, is taken up with forestalling precisely this approach to the question of gender in modernism. They "attempt to theorize about the ways in which modernism, because of the distinctive social and cultural changes to which it responds, is differently inflected for male and female writers," and they claim that it is "for men as much as for women a product of the sexual battle that we are describing here, as are the linguistic experiments usually attributed to the revolutionary poetics of the so-called avant-garde."[64] Shrugging off recent challenges to historical narrativity and the questioning of authorship as determinate for textual meaning (see p. xiv), Gilbert and Gubar proceed to construct their sociological narrative of the battle of the sexes in a way that, amazingly, appears to make male modernism the prototype of men's negative response to the "New Woman."

63. Stimpson, "Gertrude Stein and the Transposition of Gender," in Nancy K. Miller, ed., *The Poetics of Gender* (New York: Columbia University Press, 1986), p. 2. The quote from Gilbert comes from her essay "Costumes of the Mind: Transvestism as Metaphor in Modern Literature," in Elizabeth Abel, ed., *Writing and Sexual Difference* (Chicago: University of Chicago Press, 1982), p. 196.

64. Sandra Gilbert and Susan Gubar, *No Man's Land: The Place of the Woman Writer in the Twentieth Century*, vol. 1—*The War of the Words* (New Haven, Conn.: Yale University Press, 1988), p. xii.

Gilbert and Gubar are conspicuously less comfortable as they move into the twentieth century than they were in theorizing about the woman writer in the nineteenth[65]—not least, perhaps, because they confront a maze of issues regarding modernism without ever coming to terms with the concept itself. Thus, while "modernism" is initially used to denote revolutionary poetics, it slides at times into serving as an indistinct period term. In this latter guise it is used as a frame for highly literalist readings of various male texts, where for example violence perpetrated against women in a novel can be translated in a disturbingly direct manner as a misogynistic attribute of the text.[66] Also, by means of a reading strategy whose lucidity is not matched by fruitful provocation, Gilbert and Gubar consistently polarize parallel features in male and female texts, so that for instance the description of female assertiveness in texts by women is a laudable feminist gesture while female assertiveness and vitality in texts by men is shown to be an element of a male chauvinist agonistic reaction to "ladies of letters," or other threatening modern women on the rise.

On the whole, Gilbert and Gubar's reading of women's literature is more sophisticated than their approach to men's texts, and more attentive to issues of language. At the same time, however, their polarizing method is doubled at this level. Arguing that male writers suffer from an anxiety induced by the vernacular "mother tongue"—and this is backed up with reference to Tennyson's Merlin in *The Idylls of the King*—they claim that men seek to regain their linguistic privilege by retaining through metalingual comment the charm of a lost "father tongue." Lucky's use of Latin words in Beckett's *Waiting for Godot* serves as an example of how male writers imply

65. I am referring, of course, to Sandra Gilbert and Susan Gubar, *The Madwoman in the Attic: The Woman Writer and the Nineteenth-Century Literary Imagination* (New Haven, Conn.: Yale University Press, 1979).

66. See, for example, Gilbert and Gubar's reaction to the "disturbing depictions of female sexuality and aggression" and male reactions in Faulkner's *Light in August* and West's *Miss Lonelyhearts* (*The War of the Words*, 41). They are disturbed in the same way, however, by Richard Wright's descriptions of femicides in *A Native Son* (49), which makes one wonder about the usefulness of the concept of "modernism" as employed by Gilbert and Gubar as a frame of reference or as a category of modern texts. Their reading of male texts, incidentally, is strikingly reminiscent of Kate Millett's challenging but often naive reading methods in the third section of her *Sexual Politics* (New York: Avon Books, 1971), pp. 315–472.

that such language "can be used *in partibus* to distinguish their work from what Thoreau called the 'brutish . . . mother tongue'" (257).

They note further: "Such a transformation of the comment into the charm is most notably accomplished in a number of different ways by the most radical, even avant-garde fantasists of language, men who, from Mallarmé to Joyce to Derrida, repossess the ancient strength of the *patrius sermo* through the creation of a literature of 'comment, densest condensation, hard. . . .'" Evidence is even found in Hugo Ball's sound poetry and the most radical Dadaist devastation of language, such as Kurt Schwitters's "priimiitittiii," understood (literally?) as "liturgical chanting" (258). "In just about every case, that is, these linguistic revolutionaries became latter-day Merlins seeking, through 'densest condensation,' to regain the mastery lost when male artists were forced by history to operate within the confines of the vernacular mother tongue" (258–59).

The story of female modernism is naturally quite different: "It seems clear that women's imaginary languages, unlike men's, are for the most part founded on a celebration of the primacy both of the mother tongue and the tongue of the mother. . . . Women from Dickinson to Woolf and her descendants subversively transform classical languages into female native tongues and praise matriarchal witchcraft. For these artists, the lure of the mother's lore always takes precedence over what Lacan calls the 'Law of the Father'" (262).

Gilbert and Gubar's approach to the sexual politics of modernism is thus characterized by an insistence on a gender-bound dichotomy of textual qualities. This form of equation mark between gender and the function of linguistic experiments makes one wonder if it is not bound to be reproduced at the level of *reading*—in fact its alleged appearance in writing must be preconditioned by a gender-oriented reading of tradition. Gilbert and Gubar's own reading strategies, however, would seem to undermine such dichotomy. Their feminist approach to male modernism is a stiff reading, quite in line with conservative approaches already discussed in this study. Their rigorous separation of genders, the very line they draw between the modernist sexes, is the phallic Law of the Father. Maleness is reconstituted as a monolithic, logocentric foundation of meaning—even though this move is admittedly made in order to enhance the subversive elements of women's writing.

I have discussed Gilbert and Gubar's book at some length because I am aware of its potential influence in the wake of their previous work. I do not want to give the impression, however, that they are uniformly representative for feminism in this area of study. Confronting modernism has brought out significant differences within feminism and this helps us avoid rigidly confining its discourse to a single file. Above I quoted Catharine Stimpson's statement on male modernists as popes of patriarchal laws. Stimpson's concluding words in "The Somagrams of Gertrude Stein" seem to imply that this need not hold true in matters of actual literary discourse. Having discussed Stein's power struggle with language, which involves a radical deconstruction of gender boundaries, Stimpson notes that she may be called "a visionary of the 'post-post-Oedipal.'"

> If we do so, however, we must limit our Oedipal vocabulary to a way of talking about historical experience and various social uses of language. Stein's texts warn us against going on to genderize grammar itself. Her literary language was neither "female," nor an unmediated return to signifiers freely wheeling in maternal space. It was instead an American English, with some French twists and a deep structure as genderless as an atom of platinum. It could bend to patriarchal pressures, or, lash against them. It could label and curse monsters, or, finally, respond to a monster's stubborn and transforming will.[67]

Describing how "Stein is utterly impure: linear as well as pluri-dimensional; 'male' as well as 'female;' the fountain as well as the womb," Stimpson points out that "one might argue that Stein clinches the case for Kristeva," for like *male* avant-garde writers (whose texts are a source of many of Kristeva's examples of the maternal process of "signifiance"), Stein shows "how the semiotic and the symbolic—play off and against each other" (193). From this perspective, the "lure of the mother" consists in a tendency among male as well as female writers to rupture the signifying chains of the patriarchal symbolic order and create what we shall call the nonorganic text.

67. Stimpson, "The Somagrams of Gertrude Stein," p. 194.

This feminization of modernism is completely different from that reflected in Gilbert and Gubar's exclusion of men from the subversive power of modernist discourse. The erasure of the classical subject evident in the radicalized structures of modernist texts is a gesture toward an "other modernity," toward a space not charted by the Law of the Father or its manifestations in the master narratives of Western cosmology. This space, as Alice Jardine notes, "has been coded as *feminine*, as *woman*." The movement toward it she terms "*gynesis*—the putting into discourse of 'woman' as that *process* diagnosed in France as intrinsic to the condition of modernity," or in other words "the transformation of woman and the feminine into verbs at the interior of those narratives that are today experiencing a crisis in legitimation."[68]

While "woman" as a textual force may thus speak the crisis of master narratives, it can no longer be taken to reflect, realistically, an empirical female subject. In fact, one of its subversive moves is precisely the unsettling of gender distinctions. Jardine notes, for instance, that "to assume that the two sexes and their imaginations can somehow be separated" is incompatible "with the major challenges of modernity's fiction" (40–41).

The Burden of Tradition

If we accept the deconstruction of gender boundaries as a vital part of the subversive powers of modernism, are we to see criticism based on gender separation as simply a burdensome aspect of patriarchal heritage? Hardly, for then we risk being subjugated in a different way by that heritage, for instance because there would seem to be no need for canon revision on behalf of women's literature, and various challenges linked with the issue of gender would be eradicated.

Important as it seems not to make differences within modernism completely dependent upon gender separation, it may be fruitful to observe how crises in modernist signification relate to trafficking across the boundaries of gender. Perhaps

68. Alice Jardine, *Gynesis: Configurations of Woman and Modernity* (Ithaca, N.Y.: Cornell University Press, 1985), p. 25.

Gilbert and Gubar are correct in detecting a "sexual crisis that underlies modernism" (162), although it may not function in quite the "ideal" or clearcut way they describe. They find it "significant that modernist formulations of societal breakdown consistently employed imagery that was specifically sexual and, even more specifically, imagery of male impotence and female potency."[69] Similarly, Jardine suggests that "gynesis at work in the male text is rooted in male paranoia" (263). Male impotence is indeed a prominent feature of much modernist literature; we need only think of Kafka or Beckett. But does it not often function as something very different from chauvinism or misogyny? It seems to me that by undermining classical images and traditional linguistic vehicles of male power, such writing may contribute to creating a space for "other" discourses, a space inhabited, among other things, by a ghostly female subject, or by what Adorno terms the "negativity of the subject." This other subject may often take "shape" as an "abject," a "weight of meaninglessness," a force that holds one in abeyance and uncertainty between the place of the subject and the nature of the object.[70]

Writing that embodies such discourse raises some very important questions about the interrelations of gender and subject as projected by language. Nancy K. Miller laments that the "death of the author" called for by Roland Barthes and other poststructuralist critics has had the side effect of "deligitimating other discussions of the writing (and reading) subject."[71] She argues convincingly that this state of affairs helps facilitate a masculine recuperation of the feminine, while it also leads to the failure of male critics to "meet the female" in the text (282). Miller's difficulty, however, lies in being unable—or perhaps unwilling—to argue how a female subject is to be reconstituted

---

69. Sandra Gilbert and Susan Gubar, "Tradition and the Female Talent," in Herbert L. Sussman, ed., *Literary History: Theory and Practice. Proceedings of the Northwestern University Center for Literary Studies*, vol. 2, 1984, p. 21. This sentence has been cut from the essay as it appears in the first volume of *No Man's Land*.

70. Julia Kristeva, *Powers of Horror: An Essay on Abjection*, trans. Leon S. Roudiez (New York: Columbia University Press, 1982), p. 2.

71. Nancy K. Miller, "Arachnologies: The Woman, the Text and the Critic," in Nancy K. Miller, ed., *The Poetics of Gender*, p. 271.

without being caught in the web of the symbolic order and its patriarchal social codes.

But while literary texts by themselves may offer "no infallible signs, no fail-safe technique by which to determine the gender of an author,"[72] gender is still bound to be one of the determining factors in the subject's positioning in language. This alone would be sufficient justification for questioning the canon, for the pressure of women's literature keeps us on edge regarding the relationship of gender, identity, and text. Such reassessment need not occur only through the use of gender as a mode of inclusion and exclusion; it can also come about through the deployment of gender as a challenge to texts that seem to have become "classic," that is, as a way of aggravating their internal conflicts, for instance by reading Stein next to Joyce, H. D. on a level with Pound, Djuna Barnes with Eliot. This strategy should not in any capacity subordinate female modernism. On the contrary, female modernism will prove its strength all the more by subverting and radicalizing the (presumably) desirable male presence.

I have emphasized the issue of canonization not because I find "canon" as such the most relevant concept in approaching literature, but because it is to such a vital extent immediately correlative with both tradition and literary history.

To begin with, if canons can be shown to be subject both to violently conflicting interpretations and to significant revisions, then tradition can hardly be an omnipotent form of textuality that automatically determines our reception of texts, old or new. The hermeneutic circle does allow room for "suspicion" and critique, and the fact that critical concepts may come to us through another form of the circle need not discourage us, as long as we are able to pursue a self-conscious dialectic criticism.[73]

At the same time, however, our criticism also operates in the

---

72. Nancy K. Miller, "Emphasis Added: Plots and Possibilities in Women's Fiction," *PMLA* 96 (January 1981): 38.

73. I am thinking here in terms of Gadamer and Habermas's debate over the status of skepticism and critique in the hermeneutic circle. See Karl-Otto Apel et al., ed., *Hermeneutik und Ideologiekritik* (Frankfurt: Suhrkamp, 1971). A more detailed discussion would lead us astray at this juncture, but the subject will be broached again later.

hermeneutic context of previous criticism. We have seen what an urgent issue this is in the case of modernist studies, in which it sometimes seems hard to disentangle modernist literature from the salient forms of its "institutionalization." Fredric Jameson has remarked that "the classics of high modernism are now part of the so-called canon and are taught in schools and universities—which at once empties them of any of their older subversive power."[74] Jameson is either saying that *anything* that gets taught in schools is immediately robbed of its subversive potential—a rather bleak hegemonic notion that would of course also cover everything that he, as a Marxist professor, has recourse to in teaching; or he is implying that there is some kind of dominant mechanism at work that effects this voiding process in the case of modernism. The latter implication is prominent when Jameson talks elsewhere about the "liberal or modernist establishment thought,"[75] apparently assuming, as does Alan Wilde, that "modernist literature is by now virtually inextricable from the shape modernist criticism has impressed upon it."[76] But if "modernist criticism"—a term used with astounding carelessness by numerous critics—means criticism dealing with modernist writing (rather than criticism that itself uses modernist techniques), then we have seen that it is far from being all shaped by a uniform mold.

Even when we are facing a kind of "modernist criticism" felt to be overpowering in a certain critical context, the very notion that it has "impressed" a "shape" upon modernist discourse implies that this shape can be dislodged. It is interesting that our predicament, then, runs parallel with the historical impetus of modernism: in both cases we are asking if, and then how, it is possible to revolt against traditional and dominant discursive practices. But while we may succeed in calling dominant critical approaches into question, this does not mean that modernism is going to be disclosed to us as it "really is," in all its glory, as it were. It must be reiterated that "modernism" is not a concept that emanates directly from literary texts; it is a construct created by the critical inquiry into a certain kind of texts.

74. Jameson, "Postmodernism and Consumer Society," p. 124.
75. Jameson, *Fables of Aggression*, p. 23.
76. Wilde, *Horizons of Assent*, p. 20.

As I see it, it is necessary to work critically through the various uses of the concept in order to begin establishing another understanding of what modernism is. Hence, in line with my above reading of Nietzsche (which is of course also partly my "construct"), I am calling upon memory in the critical service of "forgetting."

This chapter has not presented a rounded theory of modernism's place in literary history. Rather, I have attempted to pursue skeptically some of the frames of reference used in facilitating such a placement. My criticism of the various roles assumed for modernism in literary history is generated by the importance I accord to modernism's "negative" power in the face of traditional discourse. Purposely, however, I have so far not clearly distinguished between the two uses or meanings implicit in the concept of literary "tradition," for the two overlap in a most pregnant fashion that is of great consequence to any understanding of modernism and its place in (literary) history. We use "tradition" for a sequential order of writers or their artifacts, an order based on various kinds of affinity. This is the use reflected in our canon formations. Tradition, in this sense, is always a very *selective* affair, as Raymond Williams has stressed, but it is an inescapable part of literary history. Also, in this sense, we can talk about not only a realist tradition but also a modernist tradition, or an avant-garde tradition, without the slightest note of contradiction.

But why, then, do we (at least some of us) sense a contradiction in the concept of "avant-garde tradition"? I think it is not so much because we know that the avant-garde constantly strives to transcend tradition, but because literature as "a whole" is no isolated tradition in society. Hence, avant-garde practices still stand in marked contrast to dominant modes of social discourse. As long as we do not judge a piece of writing as an isolated aesthetic artifact (which, however, can easily happen once we acquire the kind of institutional "literary competence" discussed above), our understanding of it will be heavily conditioned by prominent modes of social signification. In fact, I believe that however "aestheticized" we may be, on some level we are bound to judge literary works in their relation to dominant modes of social textuality and meaning production. In other words, our reaction to them is always significantly related to our view of the social and symbolic order. *Tradition*, in this sense, relates to conventionalized modes of behavior and communication according to which society "functions," and our use of the term is frequently loaded with this perception.

It is on this ground that I wish to proceed toward a clearer conception of modernism as a mode of modern practice, as a broad but certainly not all-inclusive poetics at work in modern literature. The present project can only be a gesture toward an outline of this poetics, a gesture, however, that cannot skirt an inquiry into other concepts that form the critical context essential in making "modernism" a meaningful term. The first of these, at the present moment of literary criticism, is necessarily "postmodernism."

3

Reading Modernism
through Postmodernism

IN GREGORY BENFORD'S SCIENCE FICTION NOVEL *In the Ocean of Night* the following exchange takes place between the couple Nigel and Alexandria:

> "Shirley's coming over after supper tonight," Alexandria said.
> "Good. You finish that novel she gave you?"
> Alexandria sniffed elegantly. "Nope. It was mostly the usual wallowing in postmodernist angst, with technicolor side shows."[1]

Inasmuch as the novel was published in 1971, it seems likely that this interesting use of the concept of postmodernism was instigated by the recent "invention" of the term: "postmodernism" did not effectively enter the critical jargon until the latter half of the 1960s. On the other hand, the reader inevitably understands the concept in the context of the novel's portrayal of a future period, since the action takes place in 1999. The novel's setting looks "postmodern" in a very real sense—the "modern era" appears to have come to an end, the Western capitalist sphere of economic expansion and general technological progress has floundered, the world has seen major catastrophes, warfare, and devastating civil strife. The only area in

---

1. Gregory Benford, *In the Ocean of Night* (New York: Dell, 1977), p. 46.

which there has been significant development is space travel, while planet Earth is reminiscent of the postapocalyptic world we know, for instance, from some of Doris Lessing's novels.

But although the use of the concepts "postmodern" and "postmodernism" occasionally shows prophetic traces of an imminent annihilation of our present type of society, that is, of late-twentieth-century modernity, the term is in fact far more often applied specifically in relation to literary and aesthetic modernism, usually for that which comes, in a significant manner, "after" modernism. At the same time "postmodernism," by including the name of the "father" concept, highlights its intertextual dependence on the predecessor. In other words, by using the concept of postmodernism we immediately invoke that of modernism, and the use of the former almost always carries with it a preconditioned "reading" of the latter. Only in this sense does the present chapter seek to cope with the problem as to what postmodernism ultimately is: I am primarily interested in how concepts of modernism can be read through theories of postmodernism.

Theorists of postmodernism have provided ample evidence for those who believe in cyclical motions of literary history, for like the former adherents of modernism, they have been eager to sign the death certificate of what is felt to be, paradoxically, both an overpowering and a lifeless tradition. "Death" is the unmistakable catchword here. In the early decades of the century, avant-garde spokesmen relentlessly declared prevalent and dominant forms of literature and art to be dead and buried. In his futurist manifesto of 1909, Marinetti says that museums can be visited once a year, "just as one goes to the graveyard on All Souls' Day," and he states that "admiring an old painting is the same as pouring our sensibility into a funerary urn, instead of hurling it far off, in violent spasms of action and creation."[2] Even Virginia Woolf, a considerably less radical modernist who retained a good deal of traditional features in most of her works, noted of the prominent devices of realist narrative that "for us those conventions are ruin, those tools are death."[3]

2. F. T. Marinetti, "The Founding and Manifesto of Futurism 1909," in Umbro Apollonio, ed., *Futurist Manifestos* (New York: Viking, 1973), pp. 22–23.
3. Woolf, "Mr. Bennett and Mrs. Brown," *Collected Essays* I, p. 330.

This rhetoric is being recapitulated today, but now frequently with modernism as the target. In noting how modernism has been "largely absorbed," Hal Foster concludes that it is "dominant but dead."[4] An even more militant gravedigger is Leslie Fiedler, who states: "The kind of literature which had arrogated to itself the name Modern (with the presumption that it represented the ultimate advance in sensibility and form, that beyond it newness was not possible), and whose moment of triumph lasted from a point just before the First World War until just after the Second World War, is *dead*, i.e., belongs to history not actuality."[5]

One cannot help noting the Nietzschean distinction between "history" and "actuality," which of course comes right out of the modernist arsenal, whether Fiedler is aware of that or not. But even if we allow for the demise of modernism, what do we see as following in its wake? Even here the death metaphor has been found useful; Franco Moretti, for instance, claims that the modernist masterpieces "constituted the last *literary season* of Western culture. Within a few years European literature gave its utmost and seemed on the verge of opening new and boundless horizons: instead, it died. A few isolated icebergs, and many imitators: but nothing comparable to the past."[6] This sentiment has probably found its most famous expression in Harry Levin's essay "What Was Modernism?" In the belief that "the modernistic movement comprises one of the most remarkable constellations of genius in the history of the West,"[7] Levin judges postmodernism primarily as a fall from grace and a loss of "the giant race" (278), producing literature that "shows little concern for the life of the mind" (273), finding virtue, instead, in "stupidity" and the "defence of ignorance" (292). Levin's essay, influential though it has been, has little to say about what has actually happened "after" modernism, al-

4. Foster, "Postmodernism: A Preface," in Foster, ed., *The Anti-Aesthetic*, p. ix.
5. Leslie A. Fiedler, "Cross the Border—Close That Gap: Post-Modernism," in Marcus Cunliffe, ed., *American Literature since 1900, History of Literature in the English Language*, vol. 9 (London: Barrie and Jenkins, 1975), p. 344.
6. Franco Moretti, "From *The Waste Land* to the Artificial Paradise," *Signs Taken for Wonders: Essays in the Sociology of Literary Forms*, trans. Susan Fischer, David Forgacs, and David Miller (London: Verso, 1983), p. 209.
7. Harry Levin, "What Was Modernism?" *Refractions: Essays in Comparative Literature*, p. 284.

though its title clearly declares his wish to find a closure for the celebrated period, partly so as not to contaminate it with what has happened in the interim. Levin's value judgments serve to preclude any analytical or historical inquiry into the literary mutation he is postulating. While I cannot claim "objectivity" to be my aim in what follows, I shall seek to avoid the traps of nostalgia as well as those of the facile discarding of the past. It may therefore serve us well to begin this inquiry by examining approaches that do *not* allow for a break or schism between modernism and postmodernism.

Neomodernism?

Frank Kermode has proposed that we adopt "a useful rough distinction between two phases of modernism, and call them paleo- and neo-modernism; they are equally devoted to the theme of crisis, equally apocalyptic; but although they have this and other things in common, they have differences which might, with some research, be defined, and found not to be of a degree that prevents our calling both 'modernist.' "[8] Kermode's words can be read as a response to revolutionary claims of 1960s art and criticism, whose activities have come to be termed "postmodernist." In *The Sense of an Ending*, Kermode concedes that in the later phase the "schismatic . . . has gained in power," but also points to Beckett "as a link between the two stages, and as illustrating the shift towards schism" (114–15). Paleomodernism sought to rewrite its past, while neomodernism is more blatantly antihistorical and nihilistic (122). Kermode finds the latter less accessible than earlier modernism: "That the new modernism should be hard to talk about is a sign that there is a gap between the elect and the rest, and that is only another of its apocalyptic aspects" (114–15). We shall see that this is in direct opposition to some other prominent theories of postmodernism. Kermode's approach to modernism, as noted in the preceding chapter, is undermined by the narrowness of his focus, which allows him to make some preposterous generalizations: "Early modernism tended towards fascism,

8. Frank Kermode, *Continuities* (New York: Random House, 1968), p. 8.

later modernism towards anarchism."[9] Despite such differences, however, Kermode wants to uphold "the truth that there has been only one Modernist Revolution, and that it happened a long time ago. So far as I can see there has been little radical change in modernist thinking since then. More muddle, certainly, and almost certainly more jokes, but no revolution, and much less talent" (24).

Julia Kristeva appears largely to agree with Kermode's non-schismatic reconstruction, although her approach is sympathetic toward the more recent developments within modernism. Modern experimental literature, which she terms "writing-as-experience-of-limits," is expressive of how "the biological reservoir threatens the symbolic system, the speaking being reveals itself capable of unimaginable restructuring in language or discourse of its crises or breakdowns."[10] The move from modernism to postmodernism she sees as a modification rather than a radical shift:

> The question is whether or not this borderline writing has changed in aspect and economy since Mallarmé and Joyce, who together reflect that contemporary radical quality of borderline writing which in other civilizations and times had analogies in the mystical tradition. If we take Artaud and Burroughs as examples, it becomes clear that this writing confronts more directly than did its predecessors the *asymbolicity* peculiar to psychosis or the logical and phonetic drifting that pulverizes and multiplies meaning while pretending to play with it or flee from it. (139)

Jean-François Lyotard argues for a different kind of continuity, a perpetual nascent state, in which the postmodern is always a part of the modern. Indeed, "a work can become modern only if it is first postmodern."[11] And the postmodern is the experimental utterance, in "writing itself, in the signifier," of

9. Ibid., p. 23.
10. Julia Kristeva, "Postmodernism?" in Harry R. Garvin, ed., *Romanticism, Modernism, Postmodernism* (*Bucknell Review* 25, no. 2; Lewisburg, Pa.: Bucknell University Press, 1980), p. 137.
11. Jean-François Lyotard, "Answering the Question: What Is Postmodernism?" trans. Regis Durand, pub. as an appendix in *The Postmodern Condition: A Report on Knowledge*, trans. Geoff Bennington and Brian Massumi (Minneapolis: University of Minnesota Press, 1984), p. 79.

the unpresentable. Hence, it is "that which, in the modern, puts forward the unrepresentable in presentation itself; that which denies itself the solace of good forms, the consensus of a taste which would make it possible to share collectively the nostalgia for the unattainable" (81). The celebration of experimentalism ties in with Lyotard's general notion of the "postmodern condition," characterized by a breakdown of Western master narratives and the withering of their historical codes and explanatory power. In aesthetic terms his theory may seem to imply an elitist program, but through the rejection of a collectively shared nostalgia, Lyotard may also be seeking to forestall any kind of fascist appropriation threatening those who explore the boundaries, or search for the unpresentable. Such a reading would bring him, in this matter, close to Kristeva, who is very much aware of the ideological ambivalence of "writing-as-experience-of-limits" (for there are always forces ready to salvage us from chaos). But both Kristeva and Lyotard are adamant in advocating the continuity of the poetic revolution.

Most of those who do see a continuity between the two "modernisms," however, do so on the basis of their negative view of the whole development. Gerald Graff's criticism is a case in point; in *Literature against Itself* he argues that the whole trajectory of literature from romanticism through modernism to postmodernism, as well as a great deal of modern literary theory, is one massive attack not only on literary realism but on any possibility of securing an "objective" hold on reality. He challenges "the standard description of postmodernism as an overturning of romantic and modernist traditions," arguing that postmodernism should be seen "rather as a logical culmination of the premises of these earlier movements, premises not always clearly defined in discussions of these issues."[12] While I am tempted to say the same of Graff's own premises concerning the continuity between romanticism and modernism, he does argue forcefully against the severance of postmodernism from modernism. He points out, for instance, that while a postmodernist such as Barthelme may intend to break

12. Gerald Graff, *Literature against Itself: Literary Ideas in Modern Society* (Chicago: University of Chicago Press, 1979), p. 32.

with the modernist "tradition" by "conceding the arbitrary and artificial nature of his creation" (53), this self-conscious undermining (which Graff finds deplorable) of the objective legitimacy of the work is actually an integral part of modernist poetics.

Metaliterature

The whole notion of the self-consciousness of literary artifacts, complex as it is, would indeed seem to be one of the chief links between the two "modernisms." In *Partial Magic*, Robert Alter sees modernism effecting a revival of self-conscious fiction after its eclipse in the nineteenth century, a revival that was to lead to its ultimate flowering in postmodernism. Interestingly, Alter sees the modernists as "transitional" figures, arguing that their greatness "can be traced to their transitional character," since "for all the affirmation of artifice in the classic modern novelists, they retain a residue of belief in the large possibility of capturing reality in fiction, however much they may be troubled by a sense of things collapsing historically."[13] In postmodernism, Alter claims, the intricacies of the flaunted artifice become more pervasive and the interplay of reality and fiction more self-conscious still. Later in this chapter we shall see how Alter's theory clashes with that of other prominent theorists of postmodernism.

Charles Russell provides us with a typical appraisal of the metaliterary aspect of the postmodern enterprise when he notes how the work of representative postmodernists

is characterized by an emphatic self-reflexiveness. It presents itself as a direct manifestation of aesthetic language investigating itself *as language*; that is, the text or artwork points to itself as a particular expression of a specific meaning system, as a construct that explicitly says something about the process of creating meaning. Instead of presuming and attempting to speak about or

13. Robert Alter, *Partial Magic: The Novel as a Self-Conscious Genre* (Berkeley: University of California Press, 1975), p. 153.

illustrate the phenomenal world, the artwork regards itself as the primary reality.[14]

Patricia Waugh argues that such metafictional writing "is clearly emerging as the dominant characteristic of the contemporary novel *as a whole*."[15] The problems Waugh has in the theoretical and critical application of her central concept are very telling for the difficulties of pinpointing self-consciousness in modern literature, or in language in general. According to her initial definition, metafiction "is a term given to fictional writing which self-consciously and systematically draws attention to its status as an artifact in order to pose questions about the relationship between fiction and reality." Waugh further states that "over the last twenty years, novelists have tended to become much more aware of the theoretical issues involved in constructing fictions. In consequence, their novels have tended to embody dimensions of self-reflexivity and formal uncertainty" (2).

I spot at least three problems here. First, how can Waugh limit the term to "fictional writing" if the very relationship between "reality" and "fiction" is being problematized in such writing? Second, to say that such writing draws attention to its fabricated reality "in order to pose questions" about this relationship makes the issue hinge on intentionality, which may have nothing to do with the "self-consciousness" of the text as it is received by the reader. But most important, the very notion of a "systematic" metafiction cannot simply be assumed to coincide with that of "formal uncertainty." Indeed, Waugh's examples of metafiction are frequently works that I do not find to have a high degree of formal uncertainty, such as Fowles's *French Lieutenant's Woman* or Lessing's *Golden Notebook*. Lessing's multilayered presentation of a "chaotic" female identity is certainly an example of a metafictional interplay of fabrication and reality, and so is Fowles's twentieth-century narrator, who does not try to hide his temporal distance from the novel's Victorian setting but frankly admits that the "char-

14. Charles Russell, "The Context of the Concept," in Harry R. Garvin, ed. *Romanticism, Modernism, Postmodernism*, p. 183.
15. Patricia Waugh, *Metafiction: The Theory and Practice of Self-Conscious Fiction* (London: Methuen, 1984), p. 68 (emphasis in original).

acters I create never existed outside my own mind,"[16] and later presents us with three different endings for the novel. But while they do violate the code of the "suspension of disbelief," so important for most realist writing, these novels do not go against the kind of linguistic referentiality integral to realist discourse. The same holds true for the self-conscious inter-twining of autobiography and fiction writing that prominent contemporary writers have practiced, for instance Günter Grass in *Kopfgeburten oder Die Deutschen sterben aus* or Max Frisch in *Montauk*. I find this to be so even in the case of John Barth's admittedly "wilder" self-exploratory usurpation of "ex-hausted" forms, in which we come across niceties such as: "The reader! You, dogged, uninsultable, print-oriented bastard, it's you I'm addressing, who else, from inside this monstrous fiction."[17] Actually, once the reader agrees to play Barth's game, it is not too often that he or she is really "lost" in the funhouse.

It turns out that Waugh finds the orderly, "civilizing" (41) features of metafiction to be salient in demarcating the con-cept. In order to make it all the more manageable, she repeat-edly plays down the "formal uncertainty" she had initially foregrounded. Some of her statements actually point to a good deal of formal certainty: "Metafiction explicitly lays bare the conventions of realism; it does not ignore or abandon them" (18). She further contends that "redundancy" in literary texts is only provided for "through the presence of familiar conven-tion," whereby she means that such conventions have to be made explicit in the text itself. "Experimental fiction of the aleatory variety eschews such redundancy by simply ignoring the conventions of literary tradition. Such texts set out to resist the normal processes of reading, memory and understanding, but without redundancy, texts are read and forgotten. They cannot unite to form a literary 'movement' because they exist only at the moment of reading" (12). Hence, metafiction "very deliberately undermines a system, unlike, say, aleatory or Dadaist art which attempts to embrace randomness or 'illinx'. In a novel like Brautigan's *Trout Fishing in America*, there is

16. John Fowles, *The French Lieutenant's Woman* (Frogmore, England: Triad/Panther, 1977), p. 85.

17. John Barth, "Life-Story," *Lost in the Funhouse* (New York: Bantam Books, 1969), p. 123.

playfulness but none of the systematic flaunting characteristic of metafiction" (43). This is also how Waugh proposes to distinguish between modernism and metafiction, for modernist self-consciousness (and here Waugh draws on Alter's theory), "though it may draw attention to the aesthetic construction of the text, does *not* 'systematically flaunt its own condition of artifice' . . . in the manner of contemporary metafiction" (21).

I do not find that this distinction yields much critical insight. There has been far too little skepticism among critics concerning the disruptive power of such "systematic" flaunting of artifice. We need to ask ourselves to what extent a realist discourse is able to "swallow up" the effects of explicit or "confessional" revelations of a text's fictional nature in cases where the referentiality of the linguistic discourse itself is not otherwise undermined. It is noteworthy that we find Thackeray's *Vanity Fair* and Trollope's novels "realistic," despite the narrators' repeated affirmation of the artificiality of their character-puppets. Furthermore, one must ask how such cases of explicit flaunting relate to the general structure of the work. Although Waugh admits that Joyce uses many self-conscious devices in *Ulysses*, she claims that the "only strictly metafictional line is Molly's 'Oh Jamesy let me up out of this Pooh'" (25). This statement can only make one wonder about the usefulness of distinguishing between "metafiction" and other instances of the text's self-awareness of its means of production. For one thing, Waugh has missed other well-known metafictional moments in *Ulysses*.[18] But more important, she has not realized how other, wider-ranging motifs function as metafictional "pointers," for instance how the crucial word "metempsychosis" is self-consciously related to the various maneuvers and metamorphoses that the text as well as the characters undergo in the process of the textual fabrication.

"Metafiction," according to Waugh's "strict" definition, would not cover what I find one of the most powerful instances of metafictional passages in modern literature, the church

18. Such as when, to name two examples from the "Oxen of the Sun" chapter, we are told that the "establishment" had never "listened to a language so encyclopaedic," or when Theodore Purefoy is declared "the remarkablest progenitor barring none in this chaffering allincluding most farraginous chronicle." James Joyce, *Ulysses* (New York: Vintage Books, 1961), pp. 417, 423.

scene in *Der Prozeß* (1925), when the priest alternately presents and refutes interpretations of the story of the man from the country; a story that in turn might be (although we cannot be sure) an allegory of K's "process" or trial. But while the scene has important implications for Kafka's novel as a whole (or the unfinished and fragmented "whole" that it is), it is not an element of a systematic flaunting of the novel as a fabricated artifice. The same is true for this striking passage from Rilke's *Aufzeichnungen des Malte Laurids Brigge* (1910): "For a while yet I can write all this down and express it. But there will come a day when my hand will be far from me, and when I bid it write, it will write words I do not mean. The time of that other interpretation will dawn, when not one word will remain upon another, and all meaning will dissolve like clouds and fall down like rain."[19] This self-referential passage is all the more powerful and disturbing for not being an obvious element in a systematic metafictional network. The first section of William Carlos Williams's *Great American Novel* (1923) is yet another striking example: "If there is progress then there is a novel. Without progress there is nothing." "To progress from word to word is to suck a nipple." "Progress is to get. But how can words get.—Let them get drunk. Bah. . . . Words cannot progress. There cannot be a novel. Break the words."[20] We would be hard put to prove that the novel is systematically metafictional, but the opening section does take us into the intrigues of production, acquisition, and desire (with regard to words, things, and people) that harass us throughout the novel, blowing conventional narrative structures to pieces.

The issue of self-consciousness is pivotal, since, as Waugh points out, it relates to the very possibility of becoming aware of the social process of operating communication and generating meaning. It may well be that one can distinguish between modernist self-consciousness and the kind of systematic metafiction that some find dominant in postmodernism, but I doubt that the latter is necessarily more productive in probing the

19. Rainer Maria Rilke, *The Notebooks of Malte Laurids Brigge*, trans. M. D. Herter Norton (New York: Norton, 1964), p. 52.

20. William Carlos Williams, *Imaginations* (New York: New Directions, 1970), pp. 158–60.

social "fabrication" of reality. If we take William Burroughs's *Naked Lunch* (1959) as an example (without trying to determine whether it is modernist or postmodernist), we read the following "strictly" metafictional comment toward the end of the book: "This book spills off the page in all directions, kaleidoscope of vistas, medley of tunes and street noises, farts and riots yipes and the slamming steel shutters of commerce, screams of pain and pathos and screams plain pathic, copulating cats and outraged squawk of the displaced bull head."[21] This particular passage is written in fairly "normal" diction compared to most of the book, whose language is constantly fragmented by the strain of horrors, obsessions, obscenities, and absurdities that it is seeking to communicate. Reading such writing-as-the-experience-of-limits, because of the demands it makes on the reader, seems to me more likely to activate his or her awareness of the means of text production than does a message literally reminding us that we are reading a text and not experiencing the "real" thing.

In short, the text's mode of speaking of its own fabrication may only fully reveal the texture and "fabric" of its language if this language is itself turned against its traditional referential function. Here is one of Gertrude Stein's curious "definitions" in *Tender Buttons* (1914):

MILK
  Climb up in sight climb in the whole utter needles and a guess a whole guess is hanging. Hanging hanging.[22]

When words are forced out of their habitualized contexts in this manner, the result is bound to be a heightened consciousness of our "normalized" use of language—immediately we are involved in questions having to do with the arbitrary relations of words and reality, even if this does not happen in a "strictly" metafictional manner. This is not the least so in the case of words that themselves seem to be utter nonsense, *if* they are delivered in a context that we know is supposed to yield mean-

---

21. William Burroughs, *Naked Lunch* (New York: Grove Press, 1966), p. 229.
22. Gertrude Stein, *Selected Writings of Gertrude Stein*, ed. Carl Van Vechten (New York: Vintage Books, 1972), p. 487.

ingful utterances. If we were told that the following words were the recorded gibberish of a child, we might find them quite a natural "product," but to hear them recited by a poet makes for a radically different context:

> gadji beri bimba glandridi laula lonni cadori
> gadjama gramma berida bimbala glandri galassassa laulitalomini
> gadji beri bin blassa glassala laula lonni cadorsu sassala bim[23]

Admittedly, when we push the concept of "self-consciousness" to the limit, as I may seem to be doing by bringing it to bear on this "sound poem" by Hugo Ball, we note that it turns out to possess the same ambivalence as the concept of "defamiliarization"—oscillating between liberation from meaning and an inquiry into the very production of meaning. And of course the two concepts are intimately related, both pointing, at best, to a shattering of our automatized view of reality, indicating a process of becoming aware that conventionalized relations between reality and received modes of communication are by no means "natural" and inevitable. It seems, therefore, that while we may talk of certain modifications and developments, a break between modernism and postmodernism on these grounds is inconceivable.

Crossing Borders—Closing Gaps

In spite of this conclusion, Patricia Waugh's attempt to delimit the concept of metafiction to writing that does not stray too far from the traditions of realism does link up with other prominent tendencies in the construction of postmodernism as a category antagonistic to its modernist predecessor. In "The Literature of Exhaustion," John Barth argues that "the used-upness of certain forms or exhaustion of certain possibilities"[24] in the realm of fiction should be used, "with ironic intent," to the benefit of contemporary fiction, which could "rediscover

23. Hugo Ball, "Gadji Beri Bimba," in Mel Gordon, ed., *Dada Performance* (New York: PAJ Publications, 1987), p. 41.
24. John Barth, "The Literature of Exhaustion," *Atlantic Monthly* (August 1967): 29.

validly the artifices of language and literature—such farout notions as grammar, punctuation . . . even characterization! Even *plot!*" (31). Thirteen years later, aware that as a postmodernist (and partly because of this essay) he has been strongly associated with metafiction, and that this makes him an heir of modernism rather than its opponent, Barth sought to redefine postmodernism in a manner that would legitimately disentangle it from earlier modernism. "The proper program for postmodernism," he says, "is neither a mere extension of the modernist program . . . nor a mere intensification of certain aspects of modernism," but rather "the synthesis or transcension of these antitheses, which may be summed up as premodernist and modernist modes of writing. My ideal postmodernist author neither merely repudiates nor merely imitates either his twentieth-century modernist parents or his nineteenth-century premodernist grandparents."[25]

This "program" of synthesis and historical reconciliation, which appears to reflect the sentiment among a great many writers and critics as to what postmodernism is all about, was recently endorsed by semiotician and novelist Umberto Eco. In his *Postscript to The Name of the Rose*, Eco quotes Barth at length, and also notes, much as Barth has, that the modernist destruction of the past must be reverted; now "the past, since it cannot really be destroyed, because its destruction leads to silence, must be revisited: but with irony, not innocently."[26] It is interesting to note what Eco has to say about the cultural politics of modernism, whose adherents he clearly finds responsible for an elitist disapproval of popularity in the past: "If a novel was popular, this was because it said nothing new and gave the public only what the public was already expecting." Hence, "the successful book was identified with the escape novel, and the escape novel with the plot novel; while experimental works, novels that caused scandal and were rejected by the mass audience, were praised." Eco declares that he has "always thought that, no matter what, a novel must also—especially—amuse through its plot" (60–61). He elaborates on the reemergence of "enjoyability" in fiction, and mentions how

25. John Barth, "The Literature of Replenishment," pp. 69–70.
26. Umberto Eco, *Postscript to The Name of the Rose*, trans. William Weaver (New York: Harcourt Brace Jovanovich, 1984), p. 67.

he was once faced with the question, "Could there be a novel that was not escapist and, nevertheless, still enjoyable?" (65). The assumption behind this seems to be—and this is astounding for someone who is a specialist in Joyce—that modernist or avant-garde nonescapist novels were traditionally *not enjoyable*. Even more astounding, however, is Eco's positioning of Joyce in this literary-historical scheme, especially since he is celebrating the return of the plot and the marriage of realism and modernism: "The *Portrait* is the story of an attempt at the modern. *Dubliners*, even if it comes before, is more modern than *Portrait*. *Ulysses* is on the borderline. *Finnegans Wake* is already postmodern, or at least it initiates the postmodern discourse: it demands, in order to be understood, not the negation of the already said, but its ironic rethinking" (68). Thus, according to Eco, Joyce's career progresses from his modern *Dubliners* through the less modern *Portrait* and the borderline *Ulysses* to the postmodern *Wake*. Needless to say, critics have generally read Joyce's career as a fiction writer quite differently, finding the early work still significantly dependent upon realist modes, while these are powerfully dismantled in *Ulysses*, and for most readers *Finnegans Wake* signals a far more radical "negation" of traditional literary discourse of the past than any other of Joyce's works. (It is, incidentally, one of Barth's prime examples of modernism.) Eco, brilliant thinker that he is, may of course be able to locate some kind of "plot" in the *Wake*,[27] but it is hardly the kind of plot he is advocating in the *Postscript*, which clearly has more to do with the traditional mode of plot that he plays with in *The Name of the Rose*.

The notion of a coalescence of modernism and realism, called for by Barth and Eco, is in fact far from an original idea. In *Axel's Castle* (1931), where Edmund Wilson works with the polar categories of "symbolism" and "naturalism," he notes that "the literary history of our time is to a great extent that of the development of Symbolism and of its fusion or conflict with Naturalism."[28] I find it rather odd that so many critics,

27. See for instance Eco's interesting discussion of *Finnegans Wake* in the second chapter of *The Role of the Reader* (Bloomington: Indiana University Press, 1979), pp. 67–78.

28. Edmund Wilson, *Axel's Castle: A Study in the Imaginative Literature of 1870–1930* (New York: Norton, 1984), p. 25.

especially the detractors of modernism and recent experimental literature, have lately been celebrating either the "reemergence of story"[29] or the sophisticated intermingling of realism and modernism. Realist fiction, seeking to adapt itself to "modern" times, was being written all the time, although this tends to be forgotten because critical and theoretical interests have inclined toward more innovatory forms of fiction. And important works were being written and celebrated that, at least from our contemporary vantage point, can be seen to carry out the synthesis of modernism and realism that Wilson saw in the making and that some critics are propagating today. Works like Conrad's *Heart of Darkness*, Henry James's *Ambassadors*, Ford's *Good Soldier*, Mann's *Zauberberg*, Malraux's *Condition humaine*, Sartre's *Nausée*, and major works by Hesse, Hemingway, and D. H. Lawrence are often referred to as "modernist," but they serve well as examples of such a synthesis (and its many variants). We might even include Joyce's *Portrait of the Artist as a Young Man*, which, because of the aesthetic ideology it is taken to present, is consistently discussed as a representative modernist novel, often without the slightest regard for its actual modes of representation.

If postmodernism is to designate the marriage of realism and modernism, it clearly makes a great deal more sense to look at Eco's *Name of the Rose*, rather than *Finnegans Wake*, as an example of the postmodernism he and others are outlining. At the same time, it is hard not to read Eco's *Postscript* as a form of apology for having written a "popular" novel, indeed, a bestseller. Some may find that with *The Name of the Rose*, Eco has actually lived up to the program that Leslie Fiedler and others have envisioned for postmodernism, that is, not only the marriage of modernism and realism, but a total closing of the gap between "elitist" or "high" culture (often associated with modernism) and mass or popular culture. Considering the deep chasm we sometimes sense between the two, the project of bridging it may seem to be an attempt at solving one of the greatest cultural dilemmas of our time. But as the arguments of Leslie Fiedler make clear, this may involve risking the loss of

29. Andreas Huyssen, "The Search for Tradition: Avant-Garde and Postmodernism in the 1970s," *New German Critique*, no. 22 (Winter 1981): 37.

any critical stance for judging cultural phenomena. Stating that "a closing of the gap between elite and mass culture is precisely the function of the novel now," Fiedler notes of "young Americans" pursuing this function that "it is not compromise by the market-place they fear; on the contrary, they choose the genre most associated with exploitation by the mass media: notably, the Western, Science Fiction and Pornography."[30]

Similarly, Calinescu, while maintaining a critical attitude, distinguishes between modernism and postmodernism on the issue of "popularity," contrasting "postmodernism's taste for public acclaim" with modernist "minority culture," defining itself through its opposition to a "dominant culture."[31] But how do we then distinguish between postmodernism and the products of popular culture? Bridging the gap hardly means simply creating another piece of mass culture. In order for them to straddle the border, there has to be some perceptible *difference* between such "postmodernist" works and the reigning popular forms. *Irony* may provide the key. Just as Barth and Eco talk about visiting the past with ironic intent, so many critics argue that popular modes can be "redeemed" by processing them through irony or parody. Perhaps no one has done this more consistently than Thomas Berger. Several of his novels are celebrations as well as parodies (with distancing effects) of different popular genres—*Arthur Rex* of the Arthurian legend, *Little Big Man* of the classic Western, *Who Is Teddy Villanova?* of the private-eye novel, *Killing Time* of the police novel. Likewise, in his use of the thriller form and evocations of Hollywood films in novels like *The Buenos Aires Affair* and *Kiss of the Spider Woman*, Manuel Puig reenacts these tropes of entertainment with a vengeance.

The most obvious hunting ground for such practitioners of parody has been the detective novel. Its preoccupation with criminal enigmas and gradual development toward a "solution," making everything fall into place and thus achieving a firm narrative closure, is ideally prone to subversion by those who believe the "crime" is always with us—the puzzle is never

30. Fiedler, "Cross the Border—Close That Gap," p. 351.
31. Calinescu, "Avant-Garde, Neo-Avant-Garde, Post Modernism: The Culture of Crisis," *Clio* 4 (1975): 328–29.

really solved. We see an example of this game in Paul Auster's *New York Trilogy*.

But if we judge the ironic recycling of popular culture to be a major element of postmodernism, does this help us to distinguish it from earlier modernism? And if so, what kind of perspective does it lend us with regard to modernist writing? Michael Holquist, drawing on the detective issue, has no qualms about drawing the line, arguing that "what the structural and philosophical presuppositions of myth and depth psychology were to Modernism (Mann, Joyce, Woolfe [*sic*], etc.), the detective story is to Post-Modernism (Robbe-Grillet, Borges, Nabokov etc.)."[32] It is easy to see how this argument immediately puts modernism at an ideological disadvantage. While postmodernism is taken to use the detective format in a highly self-conscious and subversive manner, modernism supposedly—and here the ghost of Eliot's essay on Joyce is ever present—accepts myth "innocently" as a structural paradigm. And "myth," as the concept is used here, has of course none of the subtleties and richness that modern anthropology has shown it to possess, but is rather a rigid, "totalitarian" structure that the modernist work is deemed to be emulating. Also inherent in this widely accepted characterization of modernism, one might assume, is the pejorative sense of myth as a "lie" or an "illusion."

If the works of Kafka were more prominent in Anglo-American studies in modernism, Holquist might have been less likely to make such a blunt distinction. For as Adorno notes of Kafka's novels: "The large works are rather like detective novels in which the criminal fails to be exposed."[33] Using Kafka as a paradigmatic figure, and bearing in mind modernist obsessive explorations of the individual consciousness (the "private eye," so to speak), it is probably not too difficult to demonstrate how the modernist hero is frequently in the role of the detective who never solves the crime, for he is of course also the guilt-ridden criminal. There are other, more general characteristics of modernism that would seem to point toward popular cul-

---

32. Michael Holquist, "Whodunit and Other Questions: Metaphysical Detective Stories in Post-War Fiction," *New Literary History* 3 (Autumn 1971): 135.
33. Adorno, "Notes on Kafka," *Prisms*, p. 265.

ture. In view of the fact that *Ulysses* is consistently at the center of critical inquiry into modernist writing, it is surprising how often modernism is accused of "purity" with regard to popular culture. Joyce's novel is seething with popular culture: popular songs and music, bits and pieces out of newspapers, religious pamphlets (which may also be one of Joyce's ironic gestures toward art as religion), advertisements, shop windows, brothels, pub talk, reverberations from popular novels. We could draw on other writers for similar evidence, such as Döblin, Musil, William Carlos Williams, Mayakovksy, and Brecht.

Such examples and objections could be met as follows: modernist works, through the "thickness" of their referential texture, establish a radical distance between themselves and such products of popular culture that we perceive in the background. Postmodernism, on the other hand, self-consciously working with the desires involved in the production and consumption of such products, seeks to seduce its audience into compliance with the work before setting about to reveal the sources of its illusion. In that case the romance would seem as appropriate a form as the detective novel. In *The French Lieutenant's Woman*, John Fowles can be seen performing this play, involving the reader in Charles and Sarah's love affair only to refuse us the closure (both of the affair and of the novel) we have been led to desire. As Peter Conradi says: "The story therefore seduces and betrays us exactly as Sarah seduces and then betrays Charles—after which we, like him, face an inconclusive ending and suffer our freedom together."[34] This also holds true for the way the novel makes us participate in the reconstruction of a realistic historical past, while also making us face the fictional status of that narrative.

Perhaps one can sense in this double-edged preoccupation with both popular forms and history some traces of a properly postmodern sensibility.[35] This makes one wonder about the

34. Peter Conradi, *John Fowles* (London: Methuen, 1982), pp. 67–68.
35. In *A Poetics of Postmodernism: History, Theory, Fiction* (London: Routledge, 1988), Linda Hutcheon sees the interplay of history and self-conscious fiction, or "historiographic metafiction," as a basic characteristic of a postmodernism that rejects "the naïveté of modernism's ideologically and aesthetically motivated rejection of the past" and "its inability to deal with ambiguity and irony" (30). Quite apart from my disagreement with Hutcheon concerning the nature of mod-

extent to which literature and art parallel other cultural tendencies. One of the chief features of Western culture at present is no doubt nostalgia. At the same time, much literature, most obviously fiction, can be seen as flirting—in varying degrees of irony and critical self-consciousness—with both nostalgia and historical restitution. In novels as different as Eco's *Name of the Rose*, Fowles's *French Lieutenant's Woman*, Patrick Süßkind's *Parfüm*, Graham Swift's *Waterland*, and Thor Vilhjálmsson's *Grámosinn glóir* (*The Gray Moss Glows*), the narrative is "seduced" by realistic scenes from a historical past, whereupon it undertakes to circumscribe a place of the "epic self" and to hold it up against the predicament of present history and subjectivity. Whatever the intricacies of the relationship between modernism and this brand of postmodernism, its view of the past seems to have a stronger affinity with a Proustian search for lost time than with the explosive historical excavations of, for instance, Joyce or Pound.

In Search of Contingency

We have observed how postmodernism is frequently judged as at least a partial return to realist writing. In certain places the reaction against modernism has indeed very much harked back to realist discourse. This is perhaps nowhere more evident than in Britain, where the post–World War II period saw a strong resurgance of realism in fiction. Writers like Kingsley Amis, John Braine, and John Wain became prominent,[36] flanked by older writers like C. P. Snow, Graham Greene, and Evelyn Waugh. Many of these writers are adamant opponents of modernism. The most sophisticated writer in this category is Iris Murdoch, who in her essays has been an outspoken anti-modernist. In "The Sublime and the Beautiful Revisited," she

---

ernism, I find her theory of postmodernism marred by the way in which it seems to embrace just about every branch of fiction in the past few decades, as witnessed by her numerous examples. She pays too little attention to boundaries other than the one she erects between modernism and postmodernism.

36. For a general account of this generation of British writers see William Van O'Connor, *The New University Wits and the End of Modernism* (Carbondale: Southern Illinois University Press, 1963).

begins by outlining two philosophical traditions which dominate our understanding of the human condition, namely linguistic empiricism and existentialism: "What we take ourselves to be like is, I think, successfully portrayed by Ordinary
Language Man on the one hand, and Totalitarian Man on the
other. And I shall argue presently that this regrettable situation
is to be intimately connected, both as cause and effect, with the
decline of our prose literature."[37] It turns out to be primarily
our preoccupation with the Sartrean "Totalitarian Man" that
she finds instrumental in this recession, which is a decline
from "the great novelists" of the nineteenth century, "Scott,
Jane Austen, George Eliot, Tolstoy, especially Tolstoy" (257).
The Totalitarian Man is "also Hegel's man who abhors the
contingent and the accidental"; and "according to Sartre, a
desire for our lives to have the form and clarity of something
necessary, and not accidental, is a fundamental human urge"
(255). Now Murdoch proceeds to link this existentialist urge to
symbolism, which she, like Edmund Wilson, uses as a general
term for modernism. Despite the fact that she is discussing the
decline of fiction, Murdoch chooses T. S. Eliot as the representative symbolist, arguing that the self-bounded Symbol is what
such writing is striving after: "What is feared is history, real
beings, and real change, whatever is contingent, messy, boundless, infinitely particular, and endlessly still to be explained;
what is desired is the timeless non-discursive whole which has
its significance completely contained in itself" (260). At this
point we hardly need to point out the kind of "reading" of
modernism involved here; I have already discussed both positive and negative renderings of it in some detail. Typically,
Murdoch draws primarily on the critical writings of Eliot and
Hulme, and barely mentions examples of the respective practice in poetry or fiction, although she touches on "*The Stranger*
of Camus, which is a small, compact, crystalline, self-contained myth about the human condition" (265).

In a more recent essay seeking a consensus of attitudes
among contemporary writers, Richard Wasson draws on Murdoch's essay, as well as on the essays of Robbe-Grillet and "only

37. Iris Murdoch, "The Sublime and the Beautiful Revisited," *Yale Review* 49
(December 1959): 256.

the ideological features of Barth's *The End of the Road* and Pynchon's *V.*"[38] By curiously isolating these "ideological features," Wasson can proceed to recreate a mutual "new sensibility" for this group of writers, some of whose novels seem worlds apart. What unites them is the opposition to the "mythic" method of modernism. Wasson's central example and theoretical source is, not surprisingly, Eliot's essay on Joyce the usurper of myth. We are reminded of the impact that Eliot's essay has made on criticism and reception of modernist works—an impact that is truly astounding in view of Eliot's narrow perspective. For besides neglecting the problem that, as an epic, the *Odyssey* is *not* a myth in the general sense of the word, Eliot is working with a shallow notion of myth as a "narrative" grid that provides structural support for the modern work. Critics are untiring in replaying his argument and using the essay as a kind of model or program for the modernist work. And as such the essay becomes a particularly convenient text to draw on for those arguing for a militant reaction against modernism.

This strategy allows Wasson to bring under the same umbrella writers like Murdoch, whose effort as a novelist and critic is geared toward a revitalization of realism, and Robbe-Grillet, a fierce opponent of the realist tradition. "Robbe-Grillet and Murdoch, Barth and Pynchon share the feeling that the modernist consensus over the nature of myth and metaphor and the centrality of both to literature led to false and disastrous views of the world" (476). "The work of art," Wasson quotes Murdoch, becomes "the analogue of the lonely self-contained individual purged of contingency," and he states that "Totalitarian Man rules out of existence everything which cannot be given symbolic significance in his consciousness" (465, 464).

The notion of a modernist self-isolation of both the individual and the aesthetic object has been very much highlighted in recent theories of how postmodernism makes a "deconstructive" move beyond the "formalism" or "symbolism" of modernism. It is representative of this approach to claim, like Craig Owens, that

38. Richard Wasson, "Notes on a New Sensibility," *Partisan Review* 36 (1969): 463.

[A] deconstructive impulse is characteristic of postmodernist art in general and must be distinguished from the self-critical tendency of modernism. Modernist theory presupposes that mimesis, the adequation of an image to a referent, can be bracketed or suspended, and that the art object itself can be substituted (metaphorically) for its referent. This is the rhetorical strategy of self-reference upon which modernism is based, and from Kant onwards it is identified as the source of aesthetic pleasure. For reasons that are beyond the scope of this essay, this fiction has become increasingly difficult to maintain. Postmodernism neither brackets nor suspends the referent but works instead to problematize the activity of reference.[39]

It is striking to note what happens to modernism in the course of this argument. Owens posits a specific "modernist theory," which in itself is highly questionable; but even if we grant him that nonreferential autonomy is indeed the "presupposition" of a good number of modernist writers and artists, as well as of many critics of modernism, we find him moving in a short-circuit fashion from presupposition to actuality. At the conclusion of the argument we are, it seems, faced with a modernism that apparently "succeeds" in bracketing and suspending reference. We are still at a loss as to precisely how such suspension takes place; indeed, is it at all possible? The potential argument that modernist works at least strive in that direction is self-defeating, for what is that but a way of problematizing the act of reference?

On the whole, the theory that modernism produces self-sustained, internally balanced, crystalline objects only makes sense for those who *set out to read in precisely that way*, either because they have adopted that approach to reading and interpretation or because they have come to assume that it is the proper way to approach works associated with modernism. Since Murdoch finds that modernism will have no part in con-

39. Craig Owens, "The Allegorical Impulse: Toward a Theory of Postmodernism. Part 2," *October*, no. 13 (Summer 1980): 79–80. Here, at the conclusion of his useful essay, Owens ignores the implications of his insight in the first part of the essay, when he notes in discussing Benjamin's reading of Baudelaire, how it "suggests the previously foreclosed possibility of an alternate reading of modernist works. . . . These examples suggest that, in practice at least, modernism and allegory are *not* antithetical, that it is in theory alone that the allegorical impulse has been repressed." *October*, no. 12 (Spring 1980): 80.

tingency, in the "messiness" of life, we can probably foresee her response to these lines from Eliot's *Waste Land*:

> A rat crept softly through the vegetation
> Dragging its slimy belly on the bank
> While I was fishing in the dull canal

Aware that they were written by Eliot (who is known to have been repelled by the "messiness" of modern society), Murdoch is likely to argue, as Denis Donoghue does in discussing these and subsequent lines, that they are typical of symbolist poetry, which "yearns for a world in which the governing laws and conditions would be those of Pure Poetry; purely internal laws, marking internal relations between one word and another. In such a world, time would be replaced by prosody. In the passage from 'The Fire Sermon' no effect is allowed to escape from the words, to leave the medium of language."[40] It is, however, not hard to imagine readers who, not being equipped with prevalent theories of the "holy language of modernism," would be jolted out of a "poetic" response to the work at this point, precisely because they would feel themselves flooded with "messiness" not traditionally associated with the experience of poetry. Their "literary competence," to use Culler's term, would not facilitate a neat packaging of such semantic referents into self-bounded verbal constructs.

Another dimension of this reader-response problem is highlighted by Auerbach in his essay on Virginia Woolf and modernism. As Woolf explores the layers of consciousness in her characters, he notes, she submits "to the random contingency of real phenomena."[41] The text registers the various objects of the characters' world, but in the way they are "processed" there is little or confused awareness of their temporal or spatial order and their place in a conventional hierarcy of values. This, it seems to me, is one of the chief characteristics of modernism. It takes on various forms: we find it in Joyce's stream of consciousness, perhaps most obviously in the way various nor-

---

40. Denis Donoghue, "The Holy Language of Modernism," in George Watson, ed., *Literary English since Shakespeare* (London: Oxford University Press, 1970), p. 397.
41. Auerbach, *Mimesis*, p. 538.

mally insignificant details are perceived by Leopold Bloom in *Ulysses*, entering his ruminations with great allusive weight; we see it in Stein's lengthy descriptions in *The Making of Americans*, where rhythm and ceaseless repetition are used to confer an elusive significance on mundane objects; we are particularly struck by it in Kafka's writing, where the sheer weight of such dehierarchized details plays no small role in shattering the secure worlds of Josef K. and other Kafka heroes. Critics have found the same characteristic in Flaubert's treatment of the objective world. To mention more recent literature, it seems to me a basic element of Beckett's works, and a highly aggressive one in those of Robbe-Grillet. This leveling of the relative hierarchy of thoughts and objects can be judged to express a process of reification, but, as I shall discuss later, it can also be seen as an effort to dissolve that very reification.

But how does this mode of "contingency" relate to what Murdoch finds missing in modernist writing? It seems to me that her contingency, which Wasson mistakenly also attributes to writers like Robbe-Grillet, is much closer to what Roland Barthes calls "the reality effect" in traditional realist writing, details that are not there for any specific symbolic reason, but simply serve to naturalize the environment and present the message: this is mundane "reality," this is "life."[42]

The Rage for Disorder

Actually, a major characteristic of theories of postmodernism is the contention that modernism fails to signal the message "this is life," or that this is occluded by the message "this is art." In such cases the modernist referential contingency and crisis discussed above is ignored—a formalist concept of modernism is of course a great deal more convenient if one wants to argue for postmodernism as a groundbreaking antiformalist paradigm. Wasson's stance is quite telling in this respect, for he concludes that "the moderns sought an Apollonian unity where contemporaries cautiously celebrate Dionysian contin-

42. See Roland Barthes, "The Reality Effect," in *The Rustle of Language*, trans. Richard Howard (New York: Hill and Wang, 1986), pp. 141–48.

gency" (476). Similarly, Alan Wilde has argued that through the "suspensive irony" of postmodernism "the world in all its disorder is simply (or not so simply) accepted,"[43] and that postmodernism thus bodes a return to an "affirmation of the Lebenswelt" (49), which makes "tolerating the anxiety" a "reasonable, if not complete, definition of the postmodern, in any case of its ironic wing" (45). A writer such as Ivy Compton-Burnett, in moving from modernism toward postmodernism, comes closer to "an acceptance of life as it is" than do the modernists, who impose on the world "a form, a frame, that resembles the mediating order of art, thereby confirming their estrangement from the life they seek" (118). The assumption here seems to be that "life" is without form, an assumption shared by Murdoch when she (almost reluctantly) concedes that, despite the desirable contingency of art, it "has *got* to have form, whereas life need not."[44] One cannot but suspect an ideological naiveté behind such celebratory revolt against modernism in the name of "life."

Wilde's work also exemplifies a critical practice noticeable in several studies of postmodernism. Having gradually painted modernism as a rather conservative aesthetic project, he can proceed to use terms such as "fragmentation," "disruption," and "disintegration of form" to characterize postmodernism (43–45), terms that generally have been brought to bear on modernism but are now being recycled to illustrate the reaction against it. This tendency is even more striking in the case of Fokkema, who discusses modernism in terms of "constructions expressing uncertainty and provisionality." When he comes to talk about postmodernism, however, we see a very different picture of modernism, for now he can speak with "certitude" of its hypothetical constructions, how "the Modernist aimed at providing a valid, authentic, though strictly personal view of the world in which he lived," for instance by keeping up a "standard of well-connected sentences, paragraphs, and chapters."[45] Needless to say, postmodernism is taken to have shattered all of this.

43. Wilde, *Horizons of Assent*, p. 9.
44. Murdoch, "The Sublime and the Beautiful Revisited," p. 271.
45. Fokkema, *Literary History, Modernism, and Postmodernism*, pp. 15, 37, 40, 44.

Perhaps the most extreme case of how modernism is recast in a staunchly "conservative" mold is the classificatory criticism of Ihab Hassan, an adamant spokesman for and model maker of postmodernism. Through books like *The Literature of Silence*, *The Dismemberment of Orpheus*, and *Paracriticisms*, Hassan has sustained an elaborate argument regarding the literary development toward silence, "silence" meaning basically the silencing of conventional language. Modernism, in its creation of aesthetic authority, is not the least of the sirens that postmodernism, tending toward aesthetic anarchy, seeks to silence.[46] Hassan even sets up a considerable list of items that are to show the basic contrasts between modernism and postmodernism. A few specimens should give a rough idea of Hassan's categorization (modernism is on the left, of course):[47]

Form	vs.	Antiform
(conjunctive/closed)		(disjunctive/open)
Purpose	vs.	Play
Design	vs.	Chance
Hierarchy	vs.	Anarchy
Creation/Totalization	vs.	Decreation/Deconstruction
Centering	vs.	Dispersal
Signified	vs.	Signifier
Lisible (readerly)	vs.	Scriptible (writerly)
Narrative	vs.	Anti-narrative

It may come as a surprise to some that the modernist features are those usually reserved for traditional, especially realist, literature, against which modernism was supposedly revolting. It may be tempting at this point, on the behalf of criticism, to fall back upon Harold Bloom's theory of misprision and argue that "reductiveness," the "kind of misprision that is a radical misinterpretation in which the precursor is regarded as an over-idealizer,"[48] is a matter of cyclical recurrence, so that if theories of postmodernism now portray modernism as an amaz-

---

46. Ihab Hassan, *Paracriticisms: Seven Speculations of the Times* (Urbana: University of Illinois Press, 1975), p. 59.

47. Ihab Hassan, *The Dismemberment of Orpheus: Toward a Postmodern Literature*, 2d ed. (Madison: University of Wisconsin Press, 1982), p. 267.

48. Bloom, *The Anxiety of Influence*, p. 69.

ingly tame and regressive project, the very same would probably hold true for "modernist" readings of realism. But such an inquiry, I believe, would have to take us into questions of social referentiality and how it relates to both realism and antirealist forms. Hassan, however, simply ignores realism, and "solves" the problem of historical development (since he finds so much "disjunctive," "anarchic," "deconstructive" literature in the "modernist" period) by arguing that modernism and postmodernism are not successive forms but are actually simultaneous—an argument one is beginning to hear with increasing frequency in current criticism. Sade, Kafka, a number of avant-garde groups, Hemingway, Genet, and Beckett are all in the postmodern trajectory, whereas Eliot, Faulkner, and early Joyce belong to modernism (the later Joyce of *Finnegans Wake* must of course be salvaged for postmodernism). Despite the arbitrariness of Hassan's distinctions, I shall not discuss them further here, since they are very much akin to those between modernism and the avant-garde discussed in the next chapter.

Hassan's modernism sums up the "conservative" features one finds bestowed on modernism in numerous other works on postmodernism. "The Age of T. S. Eliot," writes Leslie Fiedler, gave us "a literature dedicated, in avowed intent, to analysis, rationality, anti-Romantic dialect—and consequently aimed at eventual respectability, gentility, even, at last, academicism."[49] Wilde holds that the modernists, in their formal practices, were actually the true heirs of the Western Aristotelean tradition.[50] But such views are frequently tied to narrow modernist canons, such as I have already discussed, canons that are, moreover, restricted to a single language. Nothing obliges us to accept this form of modernism. A striking example of its rejection can be found in an interesting interview that William Spanos had with the poet, anthologist, and enthnopoetician Jerome Rothenberg. Spanos, an adamant theorist of postmodernism, claims that it counteracts "the spatializing impulse of the Western literary tradition, which begins with Aristotle's teleological understanding of a poem and 'ends,' i.e. reaches its fulfillment in the Modernism of Hulme, Joyce, Woolf, Eliot, etc. and, above all, in

49. Fiedler, "Cross the Border—Close That Gap," p. 345.
50. Wilde, *Horizons of Assent*, p. 40.

the American New Criticism."[51] Not surprisingly, Spanos gives Rothenberg a list of poets—"T. S. Eliot, W. B. Yeats, W. H. Auden, John Crowe Ransom, Allen Tate, Randall Jarrell, Robert Lowell"—whom Rothenberg had not included in his anthology *Technicians of the Sacred,* and asks: "Does this mean that you do, in fact, distinguish between a Modern and a Postmodern American Poetry? If so, why do you think early Modernism has run its course or arrived at a dead end?"[52] Rothenberg begins by asserting that "we're working on two very different sets of assumptions," and after commenting on the canon set up by Spanos, goes on to say:

> Now, if there were only Eliot's criticism & that of the New Critics to define the "classic" modern poem, I would write off modernism as the dead end you mention. But, as I said, we must be talking about two different things to start with, & for me all that tasteful, middle-ground retrenchment is almost wholly opposed to what I would see as early modernism (Stein, Williams, Cummings, Pound, Duchamp, the Dadaists, Surrealists, Objectivists, & so on)—work that stands in germinal relationship to the poetry that's been developed in my own generation. (521)

Rothenberg's response constitutes a pertinent illustration of some of my arguments above, in particular of how the notion of modernism is dependent upon the intrigues of canonization, as well as upon the authority of certain critical practices in the reception of modernist works and within the critical institution in general. Rothenberg, unlike so many critics of modernism, is fully aware that his "modernism" is a "construct," one that he is able to account for in terms of his own views of poetic functions, and in placing it he notes that it "explodes circa 1914 in a series of transformative moves, then continues UNBROKEN to our own time" (528).

A great many of Rothenberg's contemporaries, however, are eager to see a decisive break in the place of such unbroken development, and the formalist, conservative construction of

51. William Spanos, quoted in Michael Kohler, " 'Postmoderismus': Ein begriffs-geschichtlicher Überblick," *Amerikastudien* 22 (1977): 15.

52. Jerome Rothenberg, "A Dialogue on Oral Poetry with William Spanos," *Boundary 2* 3 (Spring 1975): 520.

modernism is a great deal more "useful" for those arguing for a major historical shift between the two modernisms. Some of them see the 1960s as a period of changes that make modernism obsolete. David Antin argues: "We have seen since 1968 the collapse of virtually every necessity to which modernism bravely responded. There is no coercive dominion of reason over our other faculties. . . . We have no measure of how constraining conventionalized discourse is, because we hardly know what discourse is, or representation, or narration, and what roles they play in the real human psychic economy and transactions. . . . I would like to suggest that this cheerful chaotic ignorance is the postmodern condition."[53]

This hypothesis is indicative of a distinction sometimes made between modernism and postmodernism on the basis of "uncertainty," to raise again an issue I discussed in the context of metafiction. David Lodge argues that in postmodernism the ordering principles of modernism are "displaced by a growing insistence that there is no order, no shape or significance to be found anywhere."[54] Even in the case of "Finnegans Wake (to take the most extreme product of the modernist literary imagination) . . . we persist in trying to read it in the faith that it is ultimately susceptible of being understood—that we shall, eventually, be able to unpack all the meanings that Joyce put into it, and that these meanings will cohere into a unity. Postmodernism subverts that faith" (226). Susan Sontag has presented a similar argument: "The unintelligible in Finnegans Wake not only is decipherable, with effort, but is meant to be deciphered. The unintelligible parts of Artaud's late writings are supposed to remain obscure—to be directly apprehended as sound."[55] Lodge maintains that "the difficulty, for the reader, of postmodernist writing is not so much a matter of obscurity, which might be cleared up, as of uncertainty, which is endemic."[56]

This distinction elicits, I find, a confusion between textual

53. David Antin, "Is There a Postmodernism?" in Garvin, ed., Romanticism, Modernism, Postmodernism, p. 134.

54. Lodge, The Modes of Modern Writing, p. 223.

55. Susan Sontag, "Approaching Artaud," Under the Sign of Saturn (New York: Vintage Books, 1981), p. 62.

56. Lodge, Working with Structuralism, p. 12.

structures and functions on the one hand, and the writer's intentions as well as the reader's knowledge thereof on the other. Not only could it be contested that textual meanings or obscurities are as a rule actually "cleared up," but the history of recent criticism indicates that, in their "openness," modernist works call for particularly multivarious interpretive approaches. Kafka's work is a prime example of this richness in generating interpretations, and so is *Finnegans Wake*. As Gerald Bruns has pointed out, *Finnegans Wake* performs an elaborate free-play not just of words, but of *contexts*.[57] Because of its radical displacement of syntagmatic contexts, it seems capable of inviting almost anything as its hermeneutic circumscription, that is, as a context to stop its playful signifiers from "floating." In this, *Finnegans Wake* is symptomatic for modernism in general, although it takes such context-crisis to the boundaries of what most nonprofessional readers conceive of as non-sense.

On the whole, to map the distinction between modernism and postmodernism onto the binary opposition of "obscurity" and "uncertainty" is, as I see it, to create a false difference. Actually, by making our preregistered knowledge of such an opposition between modernist and postmodernist categories an integral element of the reading experience, one could argue for the reverse effect of "uncertainty." A reader who knows that he or she is reading a postmodernist text that the author intended to be an unresolvable network of signifiers is definitely less prone to experience formal uncertainty than the reader struggling with an obscure text in the knowledge that its author meant it to be deciphered. But what kind of reader would approach a text with the certitude that it does not possess a "meaningful," socially preestablished matrix of references? Is there a "postmodern reader"?

One cannot help feel that a postmodernism associated with textual uncertainty and characterized in various ways by a celebration of disorder is a far cry from the postmodernism represented by Barth, Eco, and Murdoch, despite the link we may see in the emphasis on the contingency of "real life." The

57. Gerald L. Bruns, *Modern Poetry and the Idea of Language: A Critical and Historical Study* (New Haven: Yale University Press, 1974), pp. 158–63.

latter is one in which literature is seen to renegotiate a "democratic" contract with the reader, in contrast with the "difficult," and often hermetic, disruptive project of modernism.
The former, on the other hand, emphasizes a whole new paradigm of disruptive practices in the face of a modernism taken to
be (or to have become) sedate and conservative. This brand of
postmodernism obviously has strong ties with recent critical
practices, especially poststructuralist theories and criticism,
which in their way are also celebrating "disorder" in the form of
uncertainty and indeterminacy. The Derridean notion of "différance" is used as a tool to dismantle referential authority,
either that which a certain text is itself taken to assume or that
of prevalent interpretations or critical assumptions. Analogously, perhaps especially in the United States, such criticism
frequently sees its task in the revelation of the deconstruction
inherent in "the text itself"; a task often far removed from the
intertextual implications of Derrida's own work. But whether
this criticism is practiced in a "properly" Derridean manner or
in a "corrupted" form, it has clearly become a mode of *reread-
ing* the entire canon of literature. As such it also becomes a
mode of discovering "postmodernism" (in the form of indeterminacy, referential uncertainty, slipping signifiers, etc.)
throughout the entire history of world literature. Works of the
formula "X and the Postmodern (Spirit)" and "Postmodernism
in X" have been so prevalent in recent years that one no longer
raises an eyebrow when finding a paper on "The Postmodernism of Childe Harold" announced in the program for the MLA
convention.[58] A paper on the postmodernism of *Njal's Saga* or
the *Niebelungenlied* would probably be no more surprising.

The question is whether the term "postmodernism" should
be used in such cases, where it mostly serves as a sounding
board for a poststructuralist approach to the work in question,
that is, where it really signals a certain method of reading or
interpretation. But the two "post" concepts have come to be
strongly associated with one another, not only because the
literature some call postmodernist seems to be carrying out the
chaotic play of signifiers foregrounded by poststructuralism,
but also because the latter has itself sought to act out the

58. *PMLA* 101 (November 1986): 1069.

promiscuity of the signifying agents. In critical debates the two are sometimes completely conflated, especially if both are under attack. But the parallelism between their practices may blind us to the historical development of the antirealist poetics prevalent in both. Arguing that "post-war literary criticism is intimately bound up with literary modernism," Ronald Schleifer, drawing on *Madame Bovary*, maintains that it is actually modernism that has taught us to read in the manner prominent in this criticism.[59] And in analyzing the aesthetics and ideology of "textuality" as it is promulgated in recent theory and criticism, Fredric Jameson discusses Jonathan Culler's book on Flaubert, *The Uses of Uncertainty*, as being representative for this critical approach, not the least because it focuses on a writer who can be seen to usher in the kind of reading practiced by many poststructuralists: "Flaubert is in any case the historical fountainhead of an aesthetics of textuality, and, unlike the Balzac of Barthes, may be said for Culler to represent the first genuinely *scriptible* novelist in terms of which the older 'legible' and traditional ones are explicitly or implicitly condemned."[60]

According to these critics, then, the "postmodern reader," the reader who cuts through texts with full awareness of the uncertainty of textuality, might be more aptly called the "modernist reader." As long as "uncertainty" is not made synonymous with New Critical "ambiguity," this reader is potentially very different from the formalist reader so often constructed for modernism. But it is important not simply to conflate text and reader. If the notion of uncertainty does not profit from a reader who is capable of "solving" all uncertainties, it neither seems feasible to hypothesize a reader constantly willing to accept and even reproduce uncertainty, for that would make uncertainty the "normal," and thus "certain," state of affairs. "Uncertainty" can only be the characteristic of a textual practice found to induce referential instability against the background of prevalent, largely stable, social production of texts. This is an inevitable feature in the definition of modernism, and as such

59. Ronald Schleifer, "The Poison of Ink: Modernism and Post-War Literary Criticism," *New Orleans Review* 8 (Fall 1981): 241.
60. Fredric Jameson, "The Ideology of the Text," *Salmagundi*, no. 31–32 (Fall 1975–Winter 1976): 226.

is totally misleading as a means of distinguishing between modernism and postmodernism.

The Age of Pluralism?

This chapter has not sought to answer the question, "What is postmodernism?" Rather, I have tried to probe the nexus between modernism and postmodernism that comes to light in the various theories of postmodernism. Although I see no reason to join those asserting the death of modernism, it seems evident that the period of its most iconoclastic outburst in the face of tradition lies in the past, in the period 1910–1935 in most Western countries, although somewhat later in the Nordic countries. I do not see, however, why we should restrict the use of the concept of "modernism" to the period of its most energetic or concentrated outpouring, nor do I believe that we should assume the traditions it revolted against to have simply evaporated. But whatever the achievement of modernism, it seems to me, again, intimately tied to the concept and function of "tradition," and this may help us gain a new angle of approach to "postmodernism."

The notions and theories of postmodernism surveyed in this chapter may seem overwhelmingly contradictory. It is not only, as in the case of modernism, that we find diverging interpretations of a central "event" (the historical revolt against tradition), but also antithetical ideas about what consolidations have actually emerged in the wake of modernism to assume the leading edge of literary practice. It is tempting to think that the central feature of the recent development lies in the fact that while we have a postmodern era, there may be no postmodernism. Its nonexistence may in fact be a key characteristic of the postmodern era.

The various uses of the term "postmodern" clearly indicate that it threatens to become an omnibus concept for anything that has happened since World War II; perhaps it already serves that broad function. This is not to say that it is necessarily a placatory term. It carries with it some sense of crisis, which is also to be perceived in recent criticism, for, as Jameson points out, "the crisis in modern criticism is surely closely linked to that more fundamental crisis in modern literature and art which is the proliferation of styles and private languages."[61] Similarly, Geoffrey Hartman notes that "the modern problem is not a lack of exemplary forms but a surfeit of outmoded forms refusing to die completely: they bounce back like defeated Titans. To displace or disconfirm them is just another way of acknowledging their presence."[62]

If criticism is living an era of deconstruction and decentering, literature is going through a similar period of stylistic dispersal and perhaps a phase of increasing "entropy," to use a currently fashionable term. It is hard not to judge modernism as being to a considerable degree "responsible" for the eclecticism perceived in current aesthetic (as well as critical) productivity. After all, the major achievement of modernism may have been its subversion of the *authority* of tradition, creating a situation in which the attitude toward the various traditions of the past becomes to an increasing degree a matter of self-conscious choice and adaptation—and in this sense Adorno may be right in stating that modernism negated not only traditional literature but *tradition itself*. The erosion of the authority of tradition leads to a situation that can and has been described as "pluralism": the writer or artist has various traditions at his or her disposal and can sift out, revaluate, and rework whatever proves useful and appropriate for the work in question. No approach or method can be claimed to be more "authentic" than others. Thus, ironically, modernism may also have helped, indirectly, to legitimize the classical modes of writing it set out to oust from respectability.

Such pluralism does not in itself prevent cohesive literary activity with a critical edge, as the case of the Gruppe 47 in West Germany shows. This group has been one of the most significant forces in post–World War II European literature, and has spanned a great variety of literary forms, from traditional realist fiction to highly experimental writing.

There is little doubt, however, that recent pluralism has also

61. Ibid., p. 208.
62. Geoffrey H. Hartman, "The Maze of Modernism: Reflections on Louis MacNeice, Robert Graves, A. D. Hope, Robert Lowell, and Others," *Beyond Formalism: Literary Essays 1958–1970* (New Haven and London: Yale University Press, 1970), p. 270.

resulted in a slackening of critical faculties among many "producers" of contemporary literature and art. It sometimes seems that we are living in an era of "anything goes," to use another fashionable expression. Again, it could be argued that this is one result of the modernist dehierarchization of textual material. It was the distrust of any preestablished order that led many modernists, as Mann so powerfully illustrates in *Doktor Faustus*, to find parody the preeminent form of aesthetic expression. According to some critics, modernist parody, in moving into postmodernism, has abated into pastiche. Like parody, Jameson notes, pastiche is "the imitation of a peculiar or unique style, the wearing of a stylistic mask, speech in a dead language: but it is a neutral practice of such mimicry."[63] He goes on to relate this to the postmodern sense of the "used-upness" of styles and inventions, causing reworkings of existing modes and devices to take on cynical guises of mimicry, mannerism, and self-indulgent stylization, often with a heady air of nostalgia. Taking a cue from Jameson, Terry Eagleton also finds the production of pastiche characteristic of the postmodern condition, but as his discussion makes clear, it is far from being a "neutral practice." Eagleton argues that the pastiche of postmodernism is a sardonic double parody of the critical parody of the earlier avant-gardes, dumping aesthetic practice right into the matrix of capitalist commodification:

> Postmodernism is thus a grisly parody of socialist utopia, having abolished all alienation at a stroke. By raising alienation to the second power, alienating us even from our own alienation, it persuades us to recognize that utopia not as some remote *telos* but, amazingly, as nothing less than the present itself, replete as it is in its own brute positivity and scarred through with not the slightest trace of lack. Reification, once it has extended its empire across the whole of social reality, effaces the very criteria by which it can be recognized for what it is and so triumphantly abolishes itself, returning everything to normality.[64]

If this is an accurate depiction of the postmodern condition, then it appears that the cultural nightmare implicit in Adorno's

63. Jameson, "Postmodernism and Consumer Society," p. 114.
64. Eagleton, "Capitalism, Modernism and Postmodernism," *Against the Grain*, p. 132.

work has actually come true. In *Ästhetische Theorie*, Adorno points out how dissonance itself, the hallmark of modernism, runs the risk of solidifying into indifferent material, creating a form of immediacy without cultural memory.[65]

Some recent critics of postmodernism, in highlighting its "strategies of forgetting"[66] or its congelation in forms of "hyperreality," have expanded the field of inquiry beyond a scope that has its point of departure in modernist aesthetics. In describing postmodernism—and we see this also in Jameson and Eagleton—they tend to ignore any dividing lines between art and other cultural fields. They do so, apparently, in an effort to define the "aesthetics" of the zeitgeist, to diagnose the spiritual symptoms of contemporary history, and this has resulted in some overwhelmingly pessimistic appraisals. Jean Baudrillard finds that the signs of our reality are inevitably "simulacra," whose seductive surfaces are always already reproduced: "Never again will the real have to be produced. . . . A hyperreal henceforth sheltered from the imaginary, and from any distinction between the real and the imaginary, leaving room only for the orbital recurrence of models and the simulated generation of difference."[67] Some critics see this as a more appropriate description of the "postmodern condition" than the more "optimistic" one we saw in Lyotard. For instance, Arthur Kroker and David Cook, under the influence of Adorno and Baudrillard, describe, in glaringly apocalyptic terms, the "postmodern scene" as that of "excremental culture," as a floating empire of reprocessed and bewildered signifiers.[68]

We may recognize, in recent literature, figures traveling in this kind of hyperreality—I am thinking for instance of Kathy Acker's *Don Quixote* (1986)—but we may also ask whether this pessimism is fully warranted in the case of literature. Does literature not present us with examples of how it is still possible to sustain a critical space within the postmodern scene? It is interesting that while both Eagleton and Jameson have referred

65. Adorno, *Ästhetische Theorie*, p. 31; *Aesthetic Theory*, pp. 21–22.

66. See Burghart Schmidt, *Postmoderne—Strategien des Vergessens* (Darmstadt and Neuwied: Luchterhand, 1986).

67. Jean Baudrillard, *Simulations*, trans. Paul Foss, Paul Patton, and Philip Beitchman (New York: Semiotext[e], 1983), p. 4.

68. Arthur Kroker and David Cook, *The Postmodern Scene: Excremental Culture and Hyper-Aesthetics* (New York: St. Martin's Press, 1986).

us to Deleuze and Guattari's *Anti-Oedipus* for the theoretical implications of this cultural situation, neither literary theorist draws on convincing examples of literature as a vehicle of a totalized reification. Whether this is because literature is considered radically decentered and marginalized in postmodern practice remains unclear. Jameson's most pointed examples are films, such as *Body Heat*. A better example of the postmodern pastiche, it seems to me, is Brian de Palma's *Body Double*, in its grotesque, manneristic reworking of Hitchcockean cinematography and its aggressive awareness of its own fictionality, while at the same time preserving a gratuitous play with visual desire that ultimately swallows up the critical space of self-reflexivity. In its self-conscious attempt to function on several levels the film commits a kind of pluralistic suicide.

It must be stressed again that there is in itself nothing objectionable about a culture that is aware of a plurality of available modes of expression. What is worrisome is the possibility of pluralism becoming a blissful ideology. In *Has Modernism Failed?* Suzi Gablik argues—and this would seem to support Eagleton's diatribe quoted above—that such pluralistic awareness in the visual arts has led to the evaporation of a critical stance with regard to capitalist society.[69] Aesthetic pluralism can easily take on the appearance of both a reflection and a logical consequence of a pluralistic society. The ideology of social and cultural pluralism (which of course has a particularly strong tradition in the United States) has come powerfully to the fore in some recent criticism of both modernism and postmodernism. I will only mention it briefly here, drawing on the work of two critics, Charles Newman and Gerald Graff. Their criticism, which has drawn a good deal of attention, is remarkable in that, while each purports to be aggressively critical of contemporary capitalist culture, both acquiesce in its pluralistic ideology.

Both Newman and Graff argue that the antirealist practices of modernism and postmodernism have become quixotic in today's society, since the centralized social order that was the target of such aesthetics no longer exists. Graff notes that while

69. Suzi Gablik, *Has Modernism Failed?* (New York: Thames and Hudson, 1984), pp. 55–87. For another good critique of pluralism, see Hal Foster, "The Problem of Pluralism," *Art in America* (January 1982): 9–15.

"Gide, Kafka, Musil, and other writers of the modernist generation had the advantage of being able to take for granted *what it
was they were opposed to*,"[70] this is no longer so in the center-
less society of today. There may have been writers who took
social order for granted, but this is certainly not the case for the
writers Graff mentions. Their predicament, expressed for instance through the displacement of the traditional bourgeois-
capitalist subject, consists not least in the desperate search for
a social order they can only describe in its negativity, as they
battle with the illusion that it has disappeared even while
retaining its grip on the life of the individual. Modernism (and
certainly not only its postmodern variants) is arguably to a
considerable extent a response to the retreat of social power
into subtler and more dispersed, but no less hegemonic, forms,
hard as they may be to pinpoint.

One of Newman's premises in *The Postmodern Aura* is that
"the pluralism of contemporary art parallels the increasingly
sectarian divisions of society" (9). Newman senses no contradiction in talking of a "system" that is "unstructured" (10), or
of "the hyperpluralism of the social order" (33); or in stating
first that modern capitalism is pluralistic, not monolithic (52),
and later that "the problem with our pluralistic culture is that
it is not very pluralistic" (135). "What is 'real' about Post-
Modernism," Newman says, "is its reflection of a society
which is no longer centered in any sense, much less capital
centered" (58). This declaration is only an updating of Lukács's
argument that the textual chaos of modernist writing is not a
response to, but an accurate reflection of, capitalist society;
except here it is presented in a totally defeatist context. It is no
surprise, after the reiterated depiction of a society that no
longer has any center, to find Newman informing us not only
that postmodernism is "a revolution without an enemy" (192),
but that we (he seems to be thinking primarily of the United
States) live in "a relatively classless society" (197).

The end result of Graff's and Newman's criticism is the other
side of the coin that Daniel Bell presents us with. They call for
the end of adversary modes of aesthetic production in the form
of experimentation and antimimetic endeavors; in their case

---

70. Graff, *Literature against Itself*, p. 214 (emphasis in original).

not because of its destructive effect on modern culture, but because of its uselessness in the face of a society that cannot be identified as an adversary in any sense. This is the one situation in which modernism, in whatever form, would be truly dead, but by endorsing its undoing in this way, Graff and Newman have also succumbed to a powerful ideological force, namely the illusion that capitalism has no ideological center.

It should not be ignored, however, that precisely this ideology may be instrumental for the function, including cooptation, of modernism in capitalist society, which is an issue to which I shall return in my final chapter. It is this ideology, moreover, that makes such critics as Alan Wilde perceive of a postmodernist revolt against modernism on the premise that "a world in need of mending is superseded by one beyond repair."[71] This construction of postmodernism, at any rate, ought to be rejected.

71. Wilde, *Horizons of Assent*, pp. 131–32.

4

The Avant-Garde
as/or Modernism?

THE TERMS "avant-garde" and "modernism" both became
prominent concepts of Anglo-American criticism during the
1960s.[1] While they are not considered exactly synonymous,
they are usually assumed to be intimately related. Most frequently, "avant-garde" is taken to be the subordinate term,
which at the same time illustrates a central characteristic of
modernism.

Although I agree to a large extent with this general understanding of the use of the two concepts, we cannot, for a number of reasons, tacitly expect them simply to coexist in this
way. "Avant-garde" is not necessarily tied to any historical
period; it refers in general terms, as any good dictionary will
tell us, to experimental or unconventional activities and movements, especially in the arts. Indeed, in the 1960s, "modernism" was frequently used to refer to a paradigm of the past,
whereas "avant-garde" signified current experimental activity.

Even when both terms are used specifically to refer to the
nontraditional literature of the early twentieth century, one
encounters serious problems in the ways they interrelate. For

---

1. The former, of course, had been a key term for experimental art in Continental criticism, while the latter was rarely used with its determinate -ism ending
before the sixties. As I have pointed out, "modern," although a vaguer term, was
and still is frequently used (in English as well as in the other European languages) in
contexts where it bears the meaning generally attributed to "modernism."

one thing, the significance of the avant-garde is frequently downgraded to that of a preparatory stage for the more significant achievements or "masterpieces" of modernism. Others would grant the avant-garde the chief role of aesthetic revolt in the face of convention, emphasizing modernism's greater indebtedness to tradition. They may even go so far as to completely distinguish between modernism and the avant-garde as contemporaneous practices. Either way, the concepts of modernism and of the avant-garde are heavily interdependent.

Movements, Concepts, and Masterpieces

The following part of M. H. Abrams's definition of "modernism" in his *Glossary of Literary Terms* is representative of the assumed affiliation of the two concepts: "A prominent feature of modernism is the phenomenon of an *avant-garde* . . . , that is, a small, self-conscious group of artists and authors who undertake, in Ezra Pound's phrase, to 'make it new.' By violating accepted conventions and decorums, they undertake to create ever-new artistic forms and styles and to introduce hitherto neglected, and often forbidden, subject matters."[2] The concept of avant-garde is strongly shaped by the awareness of such groups, their manifestos and their collective activity. It is perhaps primarily this awareness that often tends to restrict the concept to the European avant-gardes of the early century—the plural form of the term, as used just now, is indeed almost always reserved for these historically demarcated groups of artists and writers. This feature of the avant-garde has even been used as a means of separating it from modernism. Ihab Hassan takes the avant-garde to comprise the movements, now all but vanished, that agitated the early part of the century, whereas modernism is enacted by "individual talents" and has proven more stable.[3] Hassan apparently sees no contradiction in stating that "individual talents" proved more stable than "movements," and this is actually a widespread view of the

---

2. M. H. Abrams, *A Glossary of Literary Terms*, 4th ed. (New York: Holt, Rinehart and Winston, 1981), p. 110.
3. Hassan, *The Dismemberment of Orpheus*, p. 267.

twentieth-century literary scene. Most modernist canons, as I pointed out in chapter 2, are selective groupings of individual talents, generally with heavy emphasis on isolated achievements rather than on literary production as a historical practice. This is not least so in the case of Hugh Kenner, even though he portrays his individuals as a fairly close-knit group, connected through locale and friendship.

Other critics see the avant-garde movements as integral elements of the total "movement" of modernism. This is how the avant-gardes are dealt with in Bradbury and McFarlane's important symposium, for instance. In one of the essays the editors note how "the movement principle was an essential constituent of Modernism, a basic part of its cohesion and its evolution."[4] Thus far I very much agree with them, and they point out the important fact that some of the works we now know as the masterpieces of modernism, such as *Ulysses*, originally found their way into publication in the same way as the products of the avant-garde groups, especially through the little magazines (203). Their conclusion, however, is as vexing as it is typical. They state that by the twenties, "a good deal of the original movement excitement had passed. . . . Now the great, achieved works of the entire endeavour began to stand out in their significance; and newer ones began to appear, their creation made possible by the already large stockpile of *avant-garde* debate and achievement. Here you could see the Modernist impulse transcending, often, the tendencies which had pushed and forced forward new modes, new presumptions. And works like *Ulysses*, *The Waste Land* or the *Duino Elegies* are acts of modernized imagination for which no movement explanation can ever properly fit" (204–5).

One notes how this conclusion resembles Quinones's approach, discussed above. A select group of "high" modernists, preestablished through the "litanies" of critical tradition, is dissociated from the radical avant-gardes, since "in the final achieved masterpieces of the twenties and thirties, the major Modernists went beyond their earlier associations with the

---

4. Bradbury and McFarlane, "Movements, Magazines and Manifestos: The Succession from Naturalism," in Bradbury and McFarlane, ed., *Modernism 1890–1930*, p. 192.

avant-garde and brought to their works a sense of personal appropriation that resulted in fuller aesthetic experience."[5] We see here the outlines of a strategy according to which nothing but *value judgment* would be applied to distinguish between the avant-garde and a consecrated group of modernist master-pieces. There is no doubt that the terms "high modernism" and "classic modernism," which one sees with increasing frequency, are based largely (and with little critical scruple) on such judgmental groupings in modern criticism. Now I will not argue, like Northrop Frye,[6] that taste and value judgments can be excluded from classificatory criticism and literary typologies (I have already underscored the inevitability of canonization), but I want to stress that value judgments are certainly less appropriate in distinguishing one movement or literary "type" from another than in appraising individual works.

According to this historical reconstruction of twentieth-century nontraditional literature, the avant-gardes are primarily to be judged as the soil out of which sprouts the richer growth of modernism and its masterpieces. It is surprising to observe a similar perspective in one of the best-known books on the avant-garde, Renato Poggioli's *Theory of the Avant-Garde*, although there it is not used to distinguish between modernism and the avant-garde. Poggioli argues that in order to transcend the pitfalls of fashion, the avant-garde must win for itself "the sanction of its own classics" (84). He even goes so far as to say that "it is absolutely indispensable to distinguish the spurious from the genuine avant-gardism which results in art, or at least contains the seeds of some future classicism" (164), even though the avant-garde generally puts a great deal of energy into problematizing precisely such concepts as "art" and "classicism."

The masterpiece argument for such canonization, whether it takes place in the name of modernism or not, seems geared toward a highly traditional notion of the sovereign and organic "work," rather than the "text" of modern textuality discussed in the preceding chapter. It is therefore arguably based on an

5. Quinones, *Mapping Literary Modernism*, p. 19.
6. See Northrop Frye, "Polemical Introduction" to *Anatomy of Criticism: Four Essays* (Princeton, N.J.: Princeton University Press, 1957), pp. 3–29.

aesthetics that modernism has itself called into question. But as we shall see, some theorists of the avant-garde wish to plant modernism squarely in the tradition of the organic work, while reserving the dismantling of organicism for the avant-garde as a different literary "movement" altogether.

There are other problems resulting from the dichotomy of avant-garde movements and modernist canons. The weakness of the "split" between them becomes apparent when we wish to bring them, as theoretical constructs, to bear upon the products of writers who do not easily fit into either one. Where do we place the poetry of Cummings, who despite his early canonization as a modernist by Riding and Graves has rarely been included as a major figure of modernist poetry? Or the writings of Gertrude Stein, who deserves the recognition she now seems to be getting as a major literary innovator of the twentieth century? Must we simply seek to make room for these figures in some arbitrary modernist canons of the Joyce-Proust-Mann type (since the procedures of canon formations are so vague anyway), and are they excluded from the avant-garde simply because they did not participate in the collective effort of some avant-garde group? The case of Stein is illuminating. She is rarely dealt with as a modernist; critics have seen her writing in the context of cubist painting (since she was involved with the cubists and interested in their work) rather than looking at it as a part of, if not an exemplary expression of, contemporary avant-garde literary activity. As a result she has come to seem a unique phenomenon, so that at least one critic, Neil Schmitz, has sought to appropriate her for "postmodernism" without inquiring how this interpretation reflects on her historical significance as someone writing at what most consider the height of modernism.[7]

In countering the use of two mutually exclusive categories that center on specific individuals, groups, or movements, I want to ask how these two concepts, modernism and avant-garde, can justifiably "work together" in outlining a nontraditional textual practice. This is in itself not an original task, for in practice many critics already orchestrate the two terms ad-

7. Neil Schmitz, "Gertrude Stein as Post-Modernist: The Rhetoric of *Tender Buttons*," *Journal of Modern Literature* 3 (1974): 1203–18.

mirably in approaching the same work or category of works. They do so in order to allow for different modes of perspective and emphasis, without overtly speculating about the nature of interdependence of the two concepts.

Here I am bound to run up against the objection that applying the concepts in this manner often results from a lack of awareness of the difference between the use of "modernism" in Anglo-American and "avant-garde" in Continental European criticism. To some extent this is a valid objection, although it need not undermine the kind of criticism I am referring to, and the case can also be overstated. Calinescu claims, for example, that it is "difficult, from a European point of view, to conceive of authors like Proust, Joyce, Kafka, Thomas Mann, T. S. Eliot, or Ezra Pound as representatives of the avant-garde."[8] When the study of the avant-garde has gone beyond the various individual movements, however, the gates of the concept have frequently been open to the modernists Calinescu lists (perhaps with the exception of Mann). When Lukács was writing about expressionism in the 1930s, he very much wanted to forestall the misconception that its "poetics" were restricted to Germany; for lack of a better term he stated that "Expressionism" was an "international movement."[9] Later, probably to underscore its nonrestriction to a single national literature, he adopted the term "Avantgardeismus" for the movement, and in *Wider den mißverstandenen Realismus* its representative is Franz Kafka. Lukács has of course been among the most influential literary critics and theorists of Europe, and it is not surprising to note the same broad use of the concept in the writings of his followers, for instance Leo Kofler in Germany and Peter Egri in Hungary, the latter using Joyce as a representative of avant-gardism.[10] Poggioli, whose *Theory of the Avant-Garde* was first published in Italy in 1962, similarly uses "avant-garde" in the broad sense we are familiar with in the case of "modernism,"

8. Calinescu, *Faces of Modernity*, p. 140.
9. Lukács, "Größe und Verfall des Expressionismus," *Essays über Realismus* (Neuwied and Berlin: Luchterhand, 1971), p. 111.
10. See Leo Kofler, *Zur Theorie der modernen Literatur: Der Avantgardismus in soziologischer Sicht* (Neuwied and Berlin: Luchterhand, 1962); Peter Egri, *Avantgardism and Modernity: A Comparison of James Joyce's* Ulysses *with Thomas Mann's* Der Zauberberg *and* Lotte in Weimar, trans. Paul Aston (Tulsa, Okla. and Budapest: University of Tulsa, Akademiai Kiado, 1972).

taking it to include not only Joyce and Kafka, but even Proust.[11] Whatever we may object to in the works of these critics, it must be acknowledged that they seek to understand the avant-garde as a historical practice rather than just a series of localized group efforts.

Futurism and Experimentation

Its very name proclaims the characteristics most frequently associated with the avant-garde: the effort to move beyond the present and create forms for the future, and the vigorous, even violent, experiments carried out in disowning prevalent modes of aesthetic production. "Futurism" was of course the name of two prominent avant-garde groups, in Italy and Russia, but as Poggioli points out, futurism is arguably, in combination with the notion of *transition*, the one "myth" that unites the different avant-gardes. But Poggioli's concept of the avant-garde, as we have seen, is an extensive one; he states broadly that "for the moderns the present is valid only by virtue of the potentialities of the future, as the matrix of the future, insofar as it is the forge of history in continual metamorphosis, seen as a permanent spiritual revolution" (73).

Critics who want to distinguish between modernism and the avant-garde, however, tend to see the extreme future-orientation of the avant-garde as something that separates it from modernism. Charles Russell argues that while modernism is largely an elaboration upon the "existing culture," the avant-gardists attempt "to imagine and possibly provoke a radical change in society by their work."[12] Such distinctions frequently occur in the context of modernism's alleged historical despair, in other words its pessimism or "wastelandism." In his monograph *Dada and Surrealism*, C. W. E. Bigsby maintains that the surrealists "did not, as did the modernists, counterpose the ordered structure of art to the imminent chaos of the world;

11. Poggioli, *The Theory of the Avant-Garde*, p. 229.
12. Charles Russell, *Poets, Prophets, and Revolutionaries: The Literary Avant-Garde from Rimbaud through Postmodernism* (New York: Oxford University Press, 1985), p. 5.

they pursued a vision of life which employed the iconography of apocalypse . . . to convey a sense of expanded reality rather than to express a sense of desperation."[13]

The problem here is that a distinction drawn along such lines risks a reduction to the question of either "purpose" or "content." One can imagine how Kafka would fare if put through such a trial: he would hardly be found to possess much potential for a future of expanded reality. This problem comes clearly to the fore in Bigsby's book, for instance when he tries to dissociate surrealism from any complicity in the nightmare reality of Nathanael West and William Burroughs, admonishing us not "to confuse style with purpose" (79). Such a "confusion" is bound to occur, however, unless we are adamant intentionalists tracking down whatever material, biographical or otherwise, that might serve to clarify the writer's "purpose." The text's mode of representation carries certain "messages" that link up with our intertextual codes and function in relation with the reader formations prevalent at each historical juncture. Some of the surrealists were among the first admirers of Kafka. I do not think his "purpose" had anything to do with that reception (according to Bigsby, Kafka's apparent "sense of desperation" should actually have worked against their attraction to him). What matters is the fact that Kafka rendered (or "textualized") "reality" in a way that the surrealists found significant and even revolutionary.

It may seem important in this context that some influential modernists, despite breaking with prevalent literary traditions, were deeply involved in "salvaging" fragments of the past. Does this necessarily set them apart from the radical futurism that we find in the avant-garde groups? This is another question that touches on the mode of representation. George Steiner has argued that modernism was "at critical points, a strategy of conservation, of custodianship." It was characterized, in a sense, by a grand "translation" effort, and

the elements of *reprise* have been obsessive, and they have organized precisely those texts which at first seemed most revolutionary. "The Waste Land", *Ulysses*, Pound's *Cantos* are deliber-

13. C. W. E. Bigsby, *Dada and Surrealism* (London: Methuen, 1972), p. 75.

ate assemblages, in-gatherings of a cultural past felt to be in danger of dissolution. . . . The apparent iconoclasts have turned out to be more or less anguished custodians racing through the museum of civilization, seeking order and sanctuary for its treasures, before closing time. In modernism *collage* has been the representative device.[14]

In discussing modernism in literature, Steiner, although an avowed internationalist, draws on a narrow canon of masterpieces in English (something that I too, despite my criticism of such canons, have been forced to do a number of times in this book: in analyzing the concept of modernism, we are constrained to deal with works that have been at the center of modernist studies, if only in order to combat the notion that the concept is restricted to a "natural" reading and interpretation of these works). Steiner may be right in stating that Eliot, Pound, and Joyce were seeking to create sanctuaries for the treasures of the past, and this would indeed mark a difference between them and avant-gardists like Marinetti, who wanted "no part of it, the past, we the young and strong *Futurists!*"[15]

But it is noteworthy that Steiner sees no problem in asserting that the modernist effort constitutes a frantic search for "order" and pointing out that this happens through the device of "collage." For it is precisely the collage technique of these works that has made them, for many readers, so *disorderly* and chaotic, so far removed from any normative textual processing of the past. Rather than being orderly "works," they seem, like so many other modernist pieces, to be "meeting places" of various texts. Even Kafka's fiction, despite its (ironic) echoing of the realist story line, has this collage effect. It is no coincidence that there has been a considerable disagreement concerning the chapter sequence of *Der Prozeß* (which was posthumously published).[16] The text plays a strong sense of a static world up against the sequential "process" of the novel's hero.

---

14. George Steiner, *After Babel: Aspects of Language and Translation* (Oxford: Oxford University Press, 1975), pp. 465–66.

15. Marinetti, "The Founding and Manifesto of Futurism 1909," p. 23.

16. See Hartmut Binder's discussion in *Kafka-Kommentar zu den Romanen, Rezensionen, Aphorismen und zum Brief an den Vater* (Munich: Winkler, 1976), pp. 160–84.

As a mode of representation, collage (together with the sometimes differently used *montage*) is also a predominant characteristic of the products of the avant-garde groups. It may in fact be hard to tell whether the device should be labeled modernist or avant-garde, an issue that would be irrelevant were it not for the critics eager to separate the two terms. Cubist painting is perhaps the artistic field most decisively marked by this device, but since there has been less tendency to separate "modernism" from the "avant-garde" in the visual arts, an inquiry into cubism is hardly going to help us draw the line—in fact, it would more likely serve to bring the concepts closer together. In the case of literary works, it seems to me a determining factor that even elements clearly stemming from practices of the past, such as the various literary styles piled up in the "Oxen of the Sun" chapter in *Ulysses*, inevitably undergo a metamorphosis when they appear in the context of a modern collage. From this perspective, Pound's "making it new" is a highly appropriate phrase and not just a shallow call for novelty, as it is sometimes taken to be. Indeed, "stealing" fragments from the past may result in as fragmentary and disjunctive a style as that associated with avant-gardists who may wish to discard the past altogether (which is of course impossible). The self-conscious creation of fragments is typical for both modernism and the avant-garde. I do not think it would be hard to convince various readers that the following "Poem,"[17] of which I quote only the first eleven lines, was a minor modernist "masterpiece," if they were not already aware that it is a collage by Breton, made by cutting scraps of headlines out of newspapers:

> A burst of laughter
> of sapphire in the island of Ceylon
>
> The most beautiful straws
> Have a faded color
> under the locks

17. André Breton, *Manifestoes of Surrealism*, trans. Richard Seaver and Helen R. Lane (Ann Arbor: University of Michigan Press, 1972), pp. 41–42. The "original" has some typographical variations that I am not able to reproduce.

on an isolated farm
from day to day
the pleasant
grows worse

A carriage road
takes you to the edge of the unknown

Modernist poets like Ezra Pound have been instrumental in creating space for such disjointed poetic discourse, a mode of representation that works through the juxtaposition of verbal fragments rather than linear renderings or holistic imagery. But this practice was already breaking through in the post-Flaubertian novel and in symbolist poetry, especially in Rimbaud, Lautréamont, and the late work of Mallarmé. I therefore differ from Roger Shattuck, who sees avant-gardists like Alfred Jarry and Apollinaire originating a modernist writing based on discontinuity and juxtaposition that breaks with the holistic practices of symbolism. He maintains that "Mallarmé's work comes close to violating our normal powers of thinking; it does not, however, advance beyond the last frontier of reason. Juxtaposition in modern literature began where Mallarmé stopped." Hence, he finds that "*Un coup de dés* is the ultimate instance of classic style," although he admits that "misread, Mallarmé seems a 'modernist' who gathered impressions in random sequence on the page. It is highly possible that the cubists and even Apollinaire deliberately misread him in this fashion, for his obscurity then became suggestive of their methods."[18] Shattuck makes the issue of reception far too dependent on his awareness of what was perhaps a dominant holistic poetics within symbolism. But works like *Un coup de dés* obviously defy such poetics through their disjunctive mode of representation. Even if Shattuck is right about Mallarmé's consistent symbolist methods, one could argue that when it has become easier to "misread" a work in a certain way than to read it according to a definitive poetics, this particular poetics is no longer a valid criterion for the work.

18. Roger Shattuck, *The Banquet Years: The Origins of the Avant-Garde in France, 1885 to World War I*, rev. ed. (New York: Vintage Books, 1968), pp. 335–36.

In view of the fact that fragmentary discourse is generally related to experimental literature, it is surprising how rarely works like *Un coup de dés* and *The Cantos* are associated with experimentation. As soon as writers become prominent members of the canon, in fact, there is clearly much less tendency to emphasize the experimental character of their works. In retrospect, at least, experimentation is not assumed to accord with respectability. Experiments with language or other aesthetic media relate to a certain paranoia concerning "authenticity." Poggioli notes, for instance, that "if in the best cases the experiment does become an authentic experience (in the most profound sense of the word), all too often, in the more literal-minded and narrow avant-gardes, it remains merely an experiment."[19] Here, as frequently in his book, Poggioli is working with precisely the traditional criteria that avant-garde practices are problematizing: the received boundaries of "authentic" art and the aesthetic experience.

I am emphasizing this since, as I have already pointed out, the issue of experimentation is sometimes indirectly used as a means to distinguish between modernism and the avant-garde. As we saw in the above quote from Bradbury and McFarlane, there is a tendency to see avant-garde experimentation as largely a preliminary task of formal exploration, while the real "advance" is made by those who transcend the less firm ground of experiment and destructive aesthetics associated with the avant-garde. This then calls for different critical reactions, the most general of which is probably the downgrading of avant-garde vis-à-vis the "achieved" works of modernism. But it can also lead to a blindness with regard to the experimental features of the latter, while celebrating the more radical and adventurous spirit of the former.

Of course, some of the experiments carried out in the avant-garde groups exceeded most acknowledged modernist "masterpieces" in their norm-breaking endeavor. This is particularly true for the Dadaists, who went to extremes, not only in exploring the boundaries of art, but in playing with the significant borders of difficulty and nonsense.

19. Poggioli, *The Theory of the Avant-Garde*, p. 135.

Beckoefkei 7 eckne Büe 7 P F f
ds Me F 7 aede 5 ucer n racun O 2 chase
A   hea Oletché F Mistrei Edeie Vhj 6
s   ihe H O chchra H -   VDchf
s   5 bxegz F ucea   de S W
       d Pa Odw Ner   R V
       adiiiedtd

It is hard to imagine this first "stanza" of Raoul Hausmann's "Sound-Rel"[20] as a product of any of the celebrated modernists. There is no reason, however, to let that blind us to the experimental character of, for instance, Joyce's fiction, Pound's poetry, or Strindberg's late dramas. The continuum between the norm-breaking practices of Hausmann and these other modernists is perhaps nowhere more visible than in the work of Gertrude Stein. While she did not go to Dadaist extremes, her texts radically exercise the breakdown of conventional language signaled to a slightly lesser extent by such fellow modernists as Joyce, Williams, and Pound. In her development from *Three Lives* (especially the story "Melanctha") through *The Making of Americans* and *Tender Buttons* to *Four Saints in Three Acts*, Stein gradually dismantled the received, self-explanatory correlations between the form of fiction and the characters as well as the objects inscribed within that form. *The Making of Americans* is one of the most powerful illustrations of the crisis of the bourgeois subject so prominent in most modernist texts. In this novel Stein takes repetition, that basic vehicle of ideology and social assimilation, and apparent normative antithesis of modernist defamiliarization, and turns it against itself. Recognizing that repetition is very much the basis of our life patterns, "repeating then is always coming out of every one, always in the repeating of every one and coming out of them there is little changing,"[21] Stein also is aware that in our lives we constantly seek to cloak the tedium of repetition: "Listening to repeating is often irritating, listening to

20. Raoul Hausmann, "Sound-Rel," in Lucy R. Lippard, ed., *Dadas on Art* (Englewood Cliffs, N.J.: Prentice-Hall, 1971), p. 67.
21. Gertrude Stein, *The Making of Americans* (New York: Something Else Press, 1966), p. 191. See Jayne L. Walker, *The Making of a Modernist* (chap. 3, "History as Repetition: *The Making of Americans*"), pp. 43–74.

repeating can be dulling, always repeating is all of living" (279). Stein proceeds to turn repetition into a joyous mode of "de-familiarization," into a "conscious feeling of loving repeating" (271), since "more and more listening to repeating gives to me completed understanding. Each one comes to be a whole one to me. Each comes to be a whole one in me" (279). But Stein also seems aware that these "wholes" hardly correspond to the "fullness of life" desired by the bourgeois subject in accordance with prevalent ideology, and through a kind of counterpoint, Stein's repetitions point in the reverse direction. They enact the understanding that repetition is never an expression of the "same"; repetition is always differentiation and fragmentation. "It does certainly make me a little unhappy that every one sometime is a queer one to me" (482). The whole dialectics caused by this interplay of repetition and estrangement is poignantly uttered in her statement "I am writing for myself and strangers" (289). The self, knit together through repetition, is constantly being dispersed, turning strange by means of that very repetition. But the reverse of that principle enables the self to embrace its other and thus to write *for* strangers, which means that at that moment they are no longer strangers. De-familiarization is driven by the urge of "familiarization."

Do these (partly digressive) reflections bring us any closer to categorizing Stein? Does she belong with "the great moderns," as they are sometimes called? Not everyone wants to grant her that status, typically because she is felt to be too much of an experimenter. "Rather than a novelist, she was an experimenter," says James Mellard, and approvingly quotes David Lodge's claim that the "interest and value" of her work is "largely theoretical, rather than particular and concrete, and can best be appreciated in the context of her own theoretical glosses upon it, in essays and lectures."[22] Does this (in my view exceedingly narrow) understanding of her work indicate that she rather belongs in the avant-garde camp?

Placing Negativity

Analysis and placing of individual writers do not solve the problem of categorization based upon large-scale theoretical

22. Mellard, *The Exploded Form*, p. 45.

constructs (although these can be of tremendous significance in approaching individual writers). We therefore need to inquire again into the critical elaboration of such constructs, especially as concerns the relationship of the two terms in question.

Matei Calinescu is among the critics who wish to draw a firm line between the two concepts, and he chides American critics for not doing so. "In France, Italy, Spain, and other European countries the avant-garde . . . tends to be regarded as the most extreme form of artistic negativism—art itself being the first victim. As for modernism . . . it never conveys that sense of universal and hysterical negation so characteristic of the avant-garde. The antitraditionalism of modernism is often subtly traditional."[23] Calinescu's differential observation, quite in tune with an approach discussed earlier, is based on a selective canon of individual modernists on one side of the fence, and the names of the avant-garde groups futurism, Dada, and surrealism on the other. The contrast he fashions—typical of many similar assertions in recent commentary—is not based on any comparative (or contrasting) textual analysis. The universal negation he mentions is certainly not typical for all the avant-gardes. In a sense, it is arguably true in the case of Dada practices, but Dada took negation considerably further than other avant-garde groups. On the other hand, Calinescu is also talking about how the avant-garde "tends to be *regarded*" (my emphasis). This indicates that his observation might be prompted by avant-garde manifestos, since they are usually the avant-garde works that have gone farthest in penetrating "public" awareness of avant-garde activity—something that to a degree is quite ironic, because some of these manifestos are written in conventional language that is being denounced on behalf of the avant-garde practice in question. Obviously the "destructive" poetics promulgated by these manifestos[24] stands in glaring contrast to the aesthetics prominent in the critical writings of such celebrated modernists as Pound and Eliot, not to mention the aesthetics Stephen Dedalus valorizes

23. Calinescu, *Faces of Modernity*, p. 140.
24. For instance, "*We are a furious wind, tearing the dirty linen of clouds and prayers, preparing the great spectacle of disaster, fire, decomposition*," as Tzara says in his radical "Dada Manifesto" of 1918, in my view one of the few avant-garde manifestos that live up to the poetics they are advocating. In Lippard, ed., *Dadas on Art*, p. 17 (emphasis in original).

in *A Portrait of the Artist as a Young Man*, which so many critics have taken on faith as the "bible of modernism in English."[25] We have seen how modernism can be and has been reduced to a practice of such aesthetics, which immediately eliminates any affiliation with the avant-garde. But as I have already argued, nothing compels us to view modernism in that way.

There is no way we can contend that the various avant-garde groups produced texts that are categorically more deconstructive, more "negative," or formally more radical than the texts of the individuals usually cited in the name of modernism. (I leave aside the additional complication that some of these acknowledged modernists did establish avant-garde groups on a small scale, such as Imagism and Vorticism.) If we consider for instance German expressionism, certainly one of the most significant of the avant-gardes, we are hard put to distinguish its works from modernist practices. Even by giving prominence to the most structurally radical or disruptive poems in Pinthus's seminal anthology of expressionist poetry, *Menschheitsdämmerung*, such as the various poems by Gottfried Benn, August Stramm, Else Lasker-Schüler, and Albert Ehrenstein, we cannot argue that expressionist poetry is more radical, or more negative and subversive with regard to tradition, than the poetry of Eliot, Pound, or Williams.

The same is true for much poetry that came out of the surrealist and futurist movements, although they certainly also produced poetry that in terms of structural radicalism went beyond that of these Anglo-American innovators. To take a different example, if we observe the breakdown of generic and referential codes as an experimental and "negative" feature of nontraditional or postrealist literature, then there is no doubt that Breton's *Nadja*—usually taken to be a representative prose work of the surrealist movement, "with its deliberate incoherence, its cleverly disjointed chapters," as reported in Breton's *Second Manifesto*[26]—is a good deal more conventional, less avant-garde, than *Ulysses* or *The Sound and the Fury*, not to

25. Robert Langbaum, "The Theory of the Avant-Garde: A Review," *Boundary 2* 1 (Fall 1972): 240.
26. Breton, *Manifestoes of Surrealism*, p. 120.

mention *Tender Buttons*. I would even argue that it is clearly more "recuperable" on the level of narrative realism than Kafka's novels.

We may not be able to distinguish between modernism and the avant-garde along the lines of structural disruption or "negation," but some critics have sought to establish this distinction elsewhere. Toward the end of *Poets, Prophets, and Revolutionaries*, which traces an avant-garde tradition from Rimbaud to the present, Charles Russell claims to have "discussed the avant-garde as a subsidiary movement of writers and artists within the culture of modernism" (238). This is not the first time that a critic claims to have done something he has not. Russell is more accurate when he states at the beginning of the book: "Throughout this book, I refer to the separate, if historically parallel, traditions of the avant-garde and modernism." Russell's criteria for this separation run as follows:

> What primarily distinguishes them are their aesthetic responses to alienation from the dominant values of modern culture. Most immediately, we shall note that how a writer sustains the sense of the trans-personal and transcendent dimensions in his or her work may be seen as the basis for classifying the writer as modernist or avant-garde. Briefly stated, modernist writers, who represent the main tradition of modern writing, despair of finding in secular, social history a significant ethical, spiritual, or aesthetic dimension. The works of such exemplary modernists as Proust, Pound, Joyce, Woolf, Gide, and Hemingway all deny the possibility of discerning within the flow of modern history anything but the record of meaningless chaos or evident cultural decline. The avant-garde—represented by Rimbaud, Apollinaire, the dadaists, surrealists, and futurists, as well as Brecht and many of the postmodernists—attempts to sustain a belief in the progressive union of writer and society acting within history, but although this implies an allegiance to a Romantic vision, they are little more able than the modernists, their contemporaries, to find in modern, bourgeois society hope for either art or humanity. (7)

The end result is that "what differentiates modernists from the avant-garde are their social and aesthetic assumptions about their cultural placement" (7). It is not easy to be sure *where*

Russell wants to pinpoint his distinction. He repeatedly mentions the assumptions and purposes of the avant-garde, and according to the above quote we might gather that he is referring to "assumptions" as they appear in the "aesthetic responses" to modern society, that is, as a quality of the texts and not as extratextual intentions. But what about the moment of disillusion plaguing avant-gardists as well as modernists, the inability to find hope for art and humanity? Is that not also transparent in the "aesthetic response," and does that not then eradicate whatever difference may have been implied in the original assumptions? Or is it perhaps a sociological observation based on historical and biographical research outside the avant-garde products?

It seems safer, after all, to assume that Russell does not find this disillusion expressed in avant-garde texts, for it is hard to see how it could coexist with the social "engagement" that Russell sees as one of their prime features. The urge for social "engagement" is indeed Russell's chief means of dissociating an avant-garde, of which he has created a sociological theory, from a modernism, the picture of which is uncritically accepted from a critical tradition that judges modernism a formalist enterprise. It is typical that Russell notes, for instance, that "in the United States especially, post-war literary criticism has been dominated by the New Critics, whose formalist values are clearly tied to the premises of literary modernism" (242). Accordingly, Russell can state that "in essence, modernists prize order—both aesthetic and political" (10), that they cherish the privileged domain of the hermetic, self-bounded artwork, and that "at every turn, modernist writers foster strategies of inwardness and aesthetic privilege which purportedly give strength and validity to private experience and perception in opposition to—but in the ultimate interest of—their society, while in fact they are direct expressions of that society" (14).

Russell fails to relate this view of modernism to any visible reading strategies of his own. What method of reading would show works like *Madame Bovary*, *Un coup de dés*, *Das Schloß*, *Ulysses*, or *Absalom, Absalom!* (the writers of these works being modernists, according to Russell) to be the closed-off, privatized aesthetic spheres Russell takes them to be? One can only assume that he is acknowledging the authenticity of a modernism reconstructed according to a New Critical approach, and using this modernism as "a tradition against which the avant-garde is defined" (9). Hence, he refuses, or at least neglects, to read these modernist works as sociocultural texts, while his own approach to texts he labels "avant-garde" is markedly sociological. In discussing the avant-garde, Russell frequently moves beyond the actual texts in arguing how "at the heart of the avant-garde is a desire to transcend alienation, to rediscover a union with society through identification of the forces which will change culture" (94). Russell also points out the disappointing experience of the avant-gardists who allied themselves with political movements. But all this hardly suffices to pursue his distinction, for one can certainly find the same pattern in the careers of such prominent modernists as Pound and Gottfried Benn.[27]

A distinction based on "purpose" or sociological assumptions can only be a lame one. If we wish to foreground the social intentions of the avant-garde groups, the fact that both Dadaists and Italian futurists wanted to see their work in the context of a cultural reorientation appears less significant than their totally different ideological aims, as we see when we contrast the futurists' blind adherence to modern technology and their war frenzy to the skeptical and pacifist (the other side of their often-denounced "nihilist") activity of the Dadaists. But the activity of both groups was directed against prevalent cultural patterns and the symbolic order, and so was the activity of the modernists Russell dumps on the other side of the fence. And it is in the context of this opposition that we need to deliberate the disruptive qualities of nontraditional texts, avoiding any literal-mindedness about a "sense of desperation" perceived in such texts. Who is to say that the historical pessimism and cultural despair some find foregrounded in modernism is not going to arouse the "futuristic" spirit of calling for cultural and social reorientation? And if Russell is right in stating that "the primary expression of the positive impulse within avant-garde aesthetic activity is the creation of a new poetic language" for expressing and discovering new states of consciousness "for

27. Since Russell places Trakl in the modernist category, I am assuming that he would do the same with Benn and most other German expressionists.

which ordinary language and literary conventions are inadequate" (35), one can certainly also make these claims of future-oriented exploration for the modernists Russell wants to exclude from the avant-garde.

To broach the larger critical and historical implications of Russell's argument, one must conclude that he is seeking to deny modernism a negative cultural role in capitalist-bourgeois society, reserving this status for the avant-garde. Like some of the adamant spokesmen of postmodernism, he is seeking to close modernism off as a functional and challenging paradigm of norm-breaking texts, reducing it to a tame aesthetics sealed off from society. This perspective ultimately makes modernism appear as simply a reflection of existing society. What leads Russell to accept this well-worn picture of modernism? In his eagerness to clear a space for his own theory of the avant-garde, it is obviously more convenient to accept the view of modernism as "the main tradition of modern writing" (7) in order to set up his own category of against-the-mainstream avant-garde than it would be to resist the equation of modernism as an aesthetic practice and the academic institutionalization of modernism.

The main result of this radical splitting of nontraditional art and literature into two opposing halves is a very different perception of the sociocultural meaning of the revolt against tradition. Ultimately it implies a reconstruction of literary history that would eradicate even the basic consensus that I have been assuming concerning the status of modernism. The emergence of a postrealist or generally modernist paradigm that we have earlier seen portrayed as a major cultural rupture is now made much less of an "event." As I shall argue in more detail below, this fragmentation is altogether detrimental to our critical understanding of modern literature, reducing our ability to perceive of the explosive potential and the "negativity" of the modernist paradigm. But before I can move on to discuss how one may preserve the force of aesthetic negativity, we must face the argument that the only way to affirm that negativity is to negate the aesthetic, an argument most forcefully presented by Peter Bürger in his theory of the avant-garde and the "institution of art."

Peter Bürger: Avant-Garde and the Institution of Art

Bürger's *Theorie der Avantgarde* aroused considerable debate when it was published in Germany in 1974.[28] A recent English translation (1984) appears to be confirming its status as a source of considerable influence on present and future avant-garde studies, and hence on our reconsiderations of modern literary history. It is a highly problematic book, which however constitutes a significant challenge to those wishing to (re)constitute modernism as a "negative" paradigm, and thus merits a detailed observation in our context.

Bürger makes his theory of the avant-garde immediately dependent upon his theory of the "institution of art/literature" in bourgeois society. The work of art only functions the way it does because of, and in the context of, the institution of art. This institution is characterized by its relative autonomy from the praxis of life (*Lebenspraxis*). Using Marx's critique of religion and Marcuse's essay "The Affirmative Character of Culture," Bürger argues that art contains an element of social criticism, since it holds up a picture of a better world in which "the atrophied bourgeois individual can experience the self as personality." This moment of immanent criticism, however, is inevitably submerged by the socially affirmative role of art: "Because art is detached from daily life, this experience remains without tangible effect, i.e., it cannot be integrated into that life. The lack of tangible effects . . . characterizes a specific function of art in bourgeois society: the neutralization of critique. This neutralization of impulses to change society is thus closely related to the role art plays in the development of bourgeois subjectivity."[29]

28. See the collection of responses published two years later: W. Martin Ludke, ed., *Theorie der Avantgarde: Antworten auf Peter Bürgers Bestimmung von Kunst und bürgerlicher Gesellschaft* (Frankfurt: Suhrkamp, 1976).

29. Peter Bürger, *Theory of the Avant-Garde*, trans. Michael Shaw (Minneapolis: University of Minnesota Press, 1984), p. 13. Although I will often be critical of Bürger in what follows, I should like to stress that he deserves credit for having been instrumental in emancipating German literary studies from the dominance of intrinsic ("werkimmanente") criticism that was practically unbroken for about two decades after the publication of Wolfgang Kayser's *Das sprachliche Kunstwerk* (1948). More than any other literary scholar, Bürger has sought to make the critical heritage of the Frankfurt School fruitful for literary theory and criticism.

In their aesthetic writings, Bürger notes, Kant and Schiller had already outlined "the completed evolution of art as a sphere that is detached from the praxis of life." At the end of the eighteenth century, however, the actual implications of this autonomy were not very much pronounced, for "within this institution, there still function contents (*Gehalte*) that are of a thoroughly political character and thus militate against the autonomy principle of the institution" (26). But in the course of the nineteenth century, these contents too lose their political character, until "art wants to be nothing other than art. This stage is reached at the end of the nineteenth century, in Aestheticism" (26–27).

In aestheticism, of which French symbolism seems to be representative for Bürger, "the apartness from the praxis of life that had always constituted the institutional status of art in bourgeois society now becomes the content of works" (27). But as art thus reaches its ultimate purification, it also reaches the stage of its self-criticism. Bürger ascribes this task to the avant-garde, the emergence of which constitutes a paradigmatic shift the like of which art has not seen since its emergence as an autonomous realm at the dawn of the bourgeois era. For now, "the other side of autonomy, art's lack of social impact, also becomes recognizable. The avant-gardiste protest, whose aim it is to reintegrate art into the praxis of life, reveals the nexus between autonomy and the absence of any consequences" (22). Bürger sees this sublation of art back into the life-praxis as the chief goal and intention of the avant-garde.

In what remains of this chapter, I will pay special attention to four problematic aspects of Bürger's theory: first, the very concept of the "institution of art"; second, his concept of "avant-garde"; third, the notion of art's autonomy and its subsequent sublation in the praxis of life; and finally, the implied reconstitution of literary history.

Bürger faces the same problems with the concept of the "institution of art" that we found in the case of Jonathan Culler's "institution of literature" and "literary competence." Are we really talking of a unified sphere of social activity, and where do we draw its limits? Are there not several "institutions" just as there are several "literary competences"? We can be certain, for one thing, that Bürger's institution is not limited to some notion of "high" art or literature, such as might be substantiated through interpretation of individual works. In the introduction to *Vermittlung-Rezeption-Funktion* (published as an introduction to the English translation of *Theory of the Avant-Garde*), Bürger criticizes Adorno and Lukács for arguing from within the institution of art, taking the distinction between "high" and "low" literature for granted. "For once the institution of art/literature has been thematized," Bürger points out, "the question about the mechanisms that make it possible to exclude certain works as pulp literature necessarily arises" (p. liii). Since Bürger wants to avoid constructing the institution according to some prejudiced notion of what deserves the label of "art," he would seem to have to include in this category various modes and genres of entertainment often classified as "popular culture." Strangely enough, in *Theory of the Avant-Garde* he remains silent about the relative significance of popular culture in the institution of art (a point I shall return to).

Which aspects of modern literature does the concept of the avant-garde cover? Bürger's only attempt at drawing its boundaries occurs in a note to chapter 2:

> The concept of the historical avant-garde movements used here applies primarily to Dadaism and early Surrealism but also and equally to the Russian avant-garde after the October revolution. Partly significant differences between them notwithstanding, a common feature of all these movements is that they do not reject individual artistic techniques and procedures of earlier art but reject that art in its entirety, thus bringing about a radical break with tradition. In their most extreme manifestations, their primary target is art as an institution such as it has developed in bourgeois society. With certain limitations that would have to be determined through concrete analyses, this is also true of Italian Futurism and German Expressionism. (n. 4, p. 109)

In his foreword to the English translation, Jochen Schulte-Sasse takes it for granted that Bürger's concept of the avant-garde is to be understood in contradistinction to that of modernism, while modernism is understood as a projection of aestheticism. Indeed, from the way Bürger pits his theory against Adorno's aesthetics (based to a great extent on a modernist trajectory from Baudelaire on through Beckett), it might seem safe to assume that the modernist practice of writers such as Kafka, Joyce, Musil, Pound, and Pirandello is excluded from Bürger's avant-garde and that it even belongs to the very culmination of the bourgeois aesthetic tradition against which the avant-garde is protesting (although Bürger himself never specifies his concept with regard to such exemplary modernist writers). As a matter of fact I do *not* think that we can legitimately draw this inference, but that need not concern us for the time being.

Bürger repeatedly risks reducing the avant-garde, on the one hand, to the avant-garde *movements* as historical groups rather than formations of historical praxis, and on the other to the *intentions* of the avant-garde movements (although he never really attempts to reconstruct their purposes from manifestos or by other means). Ultimately, however, he cannot skirt an analysis of the avant-garde (anti)aesthetic *practice* leveled against the bourgeois institution of art. In this analysis he is, ironically, heavily indebted to Adorno, with results I shall discuss in my finaly chapter.

On Art in Bourgeois Society

Turning to art's autonomy and its subsequent avant-garde sublation into the life-praxis, the first question is whether there is any clear link between art's relative autonomy and its role as a neutralizer of social critique. Asserting such an inherent "conspiracy" appears highly dogmatic; after all, Bürger himself stresses the liberating and critical potential released by art's disengagement from its subservient role under feudal government and religious doctrine. Even if art, according to the models of Marx and Marcuse, is a potential source of false satisfaction of certain social needs, there is no reason to believe that all art and literature will fulfill that function.

It is interesting that Bürger partially draws on Habermas's theories in this context, although Habermas's views are in this respect much closer to those of Adorno. Bürger quotes Habermas's statement that "art is a sanctuary for the—perhaps merely cerebral—satisfaction of those needs which become quasi illegal in the material life process of bourgeois society," needs such as "mimetic commerce with nature," "solidary living with others," and the "happiness of a communicative experience which is not subject to the imperatives of means-ends rationality and allows as much scope to the imagination as to the spontaneity of behavior" (25). Habermas speaks of these as the "contents" of art in bourgois society, but clearly we need to take their formal mediation into account. The mediation must be such that it does not obstruct the process of the neutralizing *identification* that clearly takes place when we seek an outlet for these needs in art. But Bürger has a different, somewhat awkward, complaint. He finds Habermas's perspective "problematic in our context because it does not permit us to grasp the historical development of the contents expressed in works. I believe it is necessary to distinguish between the institutional status of art in bourgeois society (apartness of the work of art from the praxis of life) and the contents realized in works of art" (25).

Paradoxically, then, Bürger wants to grasp the historical development of contents, but also to distinguish between art's institutional status and such historical contents. To make his argument, however, he ends up intertwining the two. While the aesthetic function of the contents outlined by both Marcuse[30] and Habermas serves to determine the role of art's autonomy as a neutralizer of critique, Bürger appears to find this neutralizing effect an inevitable and essential feature of art in bourgeois society. Taking this effect as a kind of "constant," he reads the historical development of contents as a process of erosion toward the ultimate goal reached in aestheticism, which "had made the distance from the praxis of life the content of works" (49). It is as if the historical development of contents was unilaterally determined by the rigid institutional status of art.

Bürger never stops to deliberate the significance of formal, or generally structural, developments that can be observed in the art and literature of the period in question. He does point out that since the mid-nineteenth century "the form-content di-

30. Cf. Bürger's quote (ibid., p. 12) from Marcuse: "The cultural ideal assimilated men's longing for a happier life: for humanity, goodness, joy, truth, and solidarity. Only, in this ideal, they are all furnished with the affirmative accent of belonging to a higher, purer, nonprosaic world."

alectic of artistic structures has increasingly shifted in favor of form" (19), but he never relates this assertion to his theory that by the time of aestheticism the *content* of art was its own distance from the life-praxis, nor does he ask whether these formal changes could have had any effect on the neutralizing function of art.

Bürger thus ignores the implications of the radicalized dialectic of form and content, a dialectic that Adorno and Habermas see as initiating profound changes in art and literature, resulting in the emergence of the modernist paradigm. As Habermas notes in his *Legitimation Crisis*:

> This development produces, for the first time, a counterculture, arising from the center of bourgeois society itself and hostile to the possessive-individualistic, achievement- and advantage-oriented lifestyle of the bourgeoisie. . . . In the artistically beautiful, the bourgeoisie once could experience primarily its own ideals and redemption, however fictive, of a promise of happiness that was merely suspended in everyday life. But in radicalized art, it soon had to recognize the negation rather than the complement of its social practice.[31]

In his foreword to Bürger's book Schulte-Sasse sees this historical shift quite differently, even though he quotes the same passage from Habermas as if it supported his own view. He claims (on behalf of Bürger, as it were) that "art dissociated itself from its communicative function in society and radically set itself against society. This change appeared on the level of artistic content; its function remained unchanged and led to refutation of the idea that literature was capable of mediating norms and values" (xxxv).

The common charge that the raging negativity of radicalized art, from the mid-nineteenth century on, entails a rejection of norms and values is easily met by pointing out that negating social practice necessarily involves invoking some "other" of that practice. The negation has an anarchic moment, but it also

---

31. Jürgen Habermas, *Legitimation Crisis*, trans. Thomas McCarthy (Boston: Beacon Press, 1975), p. 85.

involves a moment of calling forth some viable social agent in contrast to the reified structures of bourgeois reality. This is where the weakest aspect of Adorno's theory becomes apparent, that is, his reliance on the monadic subject of aesthetic reception—a point that his critics have made much of, together with his cultural pessimism. Habermas has sought to overcome both shortcomings, but he has relied on another aspect of the bourgeois heritage, namely the Enlightenment's rational critique. Indeed, according to Habermas, the "other" called forth by modernist negativity is actually the ongoing project of the Enlightenment, which has been submerged by capitalist-bourgeois culture.

Hence, it seems to me that the postrealist aesthetics portrayed by these two theorists by no means denies literature the ability to mediate norms and values. If this part of Schulte-Sasse's observation misfires, the rest of his comment is strangely muddled: art dissociated itself from its communicative function, something usually attributed to changes in form, and yet the change that occurred appeared on the level of artistic *content*, whose function, however, remained unchanged. The value that Adorno and Habermas find in the counterculture and negativity established through the radicalized relationship between form and content, however, is the potential reactivation of the *distance* implied in the relative autonomy of art, a distance allowing for a critical endeavor vis-à-vis the capitalist-bourgeois life-praxis.

But what has happened to the function Habermas ascribes to bourgeois art, namely that of a sanctuary for the residual needs not fulfilled by materialistic bourgeois society? We saw how Bürger found this perspective problematic in the light of his own theory, but he later presents his version of the same argument: "The citizen who, in everyday life has been reduced to a partial function (means-ends activity) can be discovered in art as 'human being.' Here, one can unfold the abundance of one's talents, though with the proviso that this sphere remain strictly separate from the praxis of life" (48–49). I have already noted how Bürger reifies this function as the central feature of the institution of art, whose nondialectical relationship with the development of contents can only be asserted by ignoring the radicalized form-content dialectic emerging in the late nineteenth century.[32]

If art is to be viewed as a medium of gratuitous self-fulfillment of the bourgeois subject, however, then the whole modernist project would seem to be directed *against* this function (whether this function is attributable to more narrowly defined "symbolist" works is a question I will broach later). Modernist discourse confronts the bourgeois self with its fragmented, decentered, and altogether damaged image. Even if we follow Bürger in skirting discursive qualities and emphasizing "content," then he seems mistaken in conflating bourgeois self-understanding and art's apartness from the life-praxis.[33] For if we are *made aware* that the art or literature we are consuming does not in any way bear on our everyday reality (compare Bürger's statement that distance from life-praxis gradually becomes the content of art), then this awareness is hardly going to result in the unfolding of the abundance of the self, for this abundance requires the illusion that the realm of enjoyment is a part of one's own life, and not just one more broken piece of an already fragmented reality.

This problem brings us back to the part of the "institution" ignored by Bürger in his discussion of nineteenth- and early-twentieth-century art and literature, the part on whose behalf we can lay more of a claim to the neutralizing function Bürger confers on the development toward aestheticism: popular culture. Bürger argues: "During the time of the historical avant-garde movements, the attempt to do away with the distance between art and life still had all the pathos of historical progressiveness on its side. But in the meantime, the culture industry has brought about the false elimination of the distance between art and life" (50). It is hard to see why the culture industry should only serve this role in the post-avant-garde era. Modern-

---

32. Bürger's neglect of the issue of linguistic and formal mediation is well represented in this programmatic statement: "Art in bourgeois society lives off the tension between the institutional framework (releasing art from the demand that it fulfill a social function) and the possible political content (*Gehalt*) of individual works" (*Theory of the Avant-Garde*, 25).

33. "When it is genuinely bourgeois, this art is the objectification of the self-understanding of the bourgeois class. Production and reception of the self-understanding as articulated in art are no longer tied to the praxis of life" (ibid., 47).

ism developed from the start alongside, and often in hostile relationship with, popular culture. *Madame Bovary*, which is often seen as the pioneer modernist novel, is not least a macabre parody of the popular romances that serve falsely to eliminate "the distance between art and life" for Emma Bovary and help her "unfold the abundance of [her] talents."

The Sublation of Art

What happens to art should it manage to transcend the institution of art? According to Bürger, as Schulte-Sasse notes, "we should come to see that avant-garde artists were actively attacking the institution of art. Their effort was not to isolate themselves, but to reintegrate themselves and their art into life" (xxxvi). But why should we wish to see art simply as part and parcel of the reified and materialist life-praxis of capitalist society? Would that make it any different from popular culture? The disastrous dissolution of art into social life is what Eagleton sees happening in the postmodern era, in which "the very autonomy and brute self-identity of the postmodernist artefact is the effect of its thorough *integration* into an economic system where such autonomy, in the form of the commodity fetish, is the order of the day."[34] After remarking that the "praxis of life to which Aestheticism refers and which it negates is the means-ends rationality of the bourgeois everyday," Bürger adds: "Now, it is not the aim of the avant-gardistes to integrate art into *this* praxis. On the contrary, they assent to the aestheticists' rejection of the world and its means-ends rationality. What distinguishes them from the latter is the attempt to organize a new life praxis from a basis in art" (49). While this would seem to be a key issue for Bürger's total argument, he never elaborates on it, perhaps because this new life-praxis is the unknowable "other," for "when art and the praxis of life are one, when the praxis is aesthetic and art is practical, art's purpose can no longer be discovered, because the existence of two distinct spheres (art and the praxis of life) that

34. Eagleton, "Capitalism, Modernism and Postmodernism," *Against the Grain*, pp. 133–34.

is constitutive of the concept of purpose or intended use has come to an end" (51).

It must not be overlooked, however, that Bürger's image of this utopic state derives not least *from art*. Hence, while the institution of art is to be dissolved, the life-praxis is to become "aesthetic" and to have "a basis in art." Perhaps this goes to show that our notion of "the good life" is very often in some way tied up with art, and while we may not like art's social function in present society, we have our opinions about how it should serve to create a better one. While we may loathe the notion of "art" as a separate realm, we do not wish it to be erased without a trace. This double bind between the revolt against art and the preoccupation with it is prevalent in the work of several avant-gardists, and probably no one has worked more self-consciously with the concept of art than they. When Marcel Duchamp mounted a bicycle wheel on a kitchen stool and then exhibited the piece as a work of art, he was not sublating art into the praxis of life. He was powerfully demonstrating that the prevalent *context* (and hence the "institution") of art was not a "safe" container with predictable ingredients. Duchamp's greatest innovation, as Lucy Lippard says, "was the simple [sic] declaration that *anything is art if the artist says it is*."[35] This also makes it clear that our registration of something as "art" hinges on our knowledge of the status of the "artist," and more broadly speaking on our awareness of art as a distinctive sphere of social praxis. Any gesture, however violent, toward destroying art while working in its context will only carry its meaning because of our preclassification of aesthetic activity.

At the same time, it would be a narrow understanding of the avant-garde if we took its radical practice to be only directed against "art" as a concept or institution. This reduction of its practice is constantly implicit in Bürger's book, in particular when he seeks to argue that the avant-garde was responding to the aestheticists' ultimate purification of art. Since Bürger constantly refers to the "intention" of the avant-garde, it must be stressed that in their manifestos, avant-gardists like Tzara, Marinetti, and Breton certainly do not exert themselves attack-

35. Lippard, ed., *Dadas on Art*, p. 139.

ing symbolist writing. Their main target, besides the general burden of tradition, is bourgeois life-praxis and conventional language and discourse, which is both laden with the deadening values of the past and susceptible to the ideological manipulations of the present (although the Italian futurists were not on the alert for the latter). In the case of Zürich Dada, for instance, Rudolf Kuenzli has shown how avant-gardists aimed their radical semiotic warfare against the sign system of conventional, communicative language, which was being debased through relentless war propaganda.[36]

Hence, while many avant-gardists probably shared the "belief that art is not half so interesting or so important a business as daily life," as Calvin Tomkins puts it,[37] they used the context of art to observe the interesting business of daily life. And ultimately, as Bürger admits, the "attempt to reintegrate art into the life process is itself a profoundly contradictory endeavor. For the (relative) freedom of art vis-à-vis the praxis of life is at the same time the condition that must be fulfilled if there is to be a critical cognition of reality" (50). Bürger concludes, I think correctly, that the reintegration of art into life "has not occurred, and presumably cannot occur, in bourgeois society unless it be as a false sublation of autonomous art" (54). If such reintegration is to have any laudable effects, it would have to take place in a radically different society.

On the other hand, the concept of the "autonomy of art" is easily misunderstood and misapplied. As Bürger remarks, the "category 'autonomy' does not permit the understanding of its referent as one that developed historically. The relative dissociation of the work of art from the praxis of life in bourgeois society thus becomes transformed into the (erroneous) idea that the work of art is totally independent of society" (46). Here Bürger cogently outlines the dilemma of art in bourgeois society, for the relative autonomy that art needs to establish a critical distance from society can be transformed, as Eagleton points out, into the illusory independence from society, which

36. Rudolf E. Kuenzli, "Dada gegen den Ersten Weltkrieg: Die Dadaisten in Zürich," in Wolfgang Paulsen and Helmut G. Hermann, ed., Sinn aus Unsinn: Dada International (Bern and Munich: Francke, 1982), pp. 87–100.

37. Calvin Tomkins, The Bride and the Bachelors: Five Masters of the Avant-Garde (New York: Penguin Books, 1976), p. 2.

is simply a feature of the general fetishization taking place in that very society.

Channeling Literary History

In my final chapter I shall discuss Bürger's theory of the nonorganic avant-garde work; but first I want to touch briefly on the restructuring of literary history that is often implied in Bürger's theory and sometimes carried out. According to one of Bürger's central criteria, it is "from the standpoint of the avant-garde that the preceding phases in the development of art as a phenomenon in bourgeois society can be understood" (19). The avant-garde is attacking the institution of art, whose neutralizing implications were made visible by aestheticism. Accordingly, the development of bourgeois art is seen as a logical unfolding toward aestheticism. This is a full-scale teleology; one must face "the fact that in Aestheticism, art in bourgeois society comes into its own."[38]

This view of the development of nineteenth-century bourgeois literature might seem simply to exclude the profuse realist and naturalist tendencies of that period, in particular the prominence of the novel, the bourgeois genre par excellence. In *Theory of the Avant-Garde* it appears that Bürger sees realism as simply a phase in this evolution toward aestheticism. He states that the self-criticism of art that sets in with the avant-garde "makes possible the 'objective understanding' of past phases of development. Whereas during the period of realism, for example, the development of art was felt to lie in a growing closeness of representation to reality, the one-sidedness of this construction could now be recognized. Realism no longer appears as *the* principle of artistic creation but becomes understandable as the sum of certain period procedures" (22).

38. Peter Bürger, *Theorie der Avantgarde* (Frankfurt: Suhrkamp, 1974), n. 16, p. 46: "die Tatsache, daß im Ästhetizismus die Kunst in der bürgerlichen Gesellschaft zu sich selbst kommt." The English translation, "becomes conscious of itself" (111), does not do full justice to the Hegelian teleology implicit in the German phrase "zu sich selbst kommen." "Comes into its own" seems to me more accurate.

In a later work Bürger outlines the problem very differently. Here the development, in the name of the autonomy doctrine, toward aestheticism is countered by a bourgeois-Enlightenment institutionalization of literature, a tradition that sees itself as a "medium of the moral-political self-understanding of the citizens."[39] Bürger's example of this tradition is naturalism. It might seem logical to place realism as a whole within this trajectory, except that Bürger sees this tradition as a historical formation in *opposition* to the *dominant* (aestheticist) institution of bourgeois art. One can only begin to wonder what defines "dominance" in literary history, if realism is not to be considered a dominant literary category of, especially, nineteenth-century fiction. The issue becomes even more complicated when we take into account that Bürger's view of the social function of the organic work, which as we shall see includes realism, does not really allow for the organic work to be judged as an oppositional aesthetic category.

Avant-Garde as Modernism

Bürger's theory of the institution of art and his concept of aestheticism are to a considerable extent pitted against Adorno's aesthetic theories. In the latter half of his book, however, when he comes to analyze the fundamental characteristics of the avant-garde work of art, Bürger draws heavily on Adorno. In fact, as soon as he no longer limits his discussion to the avant-garde movements and their intentions and begins to outline avant-garde textual practices under the concept of "the nonorganic work," Bürger's book turns into a theory of modernism that is much indebted to Adorno's (implicit as well as explicit) theory of modernism. While Bürger criticizes Adorno's belief that "the avant-gardiste work is the only possibly authentic expression of the contemporary state of the world" (85), the concept "avant-gardiste" is here not confined to the avant-garde

39. Peter Bürger, "Einleitung: Naturalismus und Ästhetizismus als rivalisierende Institutionalisierungen der Literatur," in Christa Bürger, Peter Bürger, and Jochen Schulte-Sasse, ed., *Naturalismus/Ästhetizismus* (Frankfurt: Suhrkamp, 1979), p. 13.

movements, but includes Adorno's broader conception of non-traditional literature and art.[40]

Unlike Schulte-Sasse, therefore, I do not see modernism as a form of projection of Bürger's concept of aestheticism. It may well be that Bürger can classify a great deal of aestheticist or symbolist literature under his concept of the "organic" or "classicist" work, but he gives us no good reasons to place the works of Joyce, Kafka, Pound, or other representative modernists within an aestheticist trajectory. On the contrary; since the emergence of these works is more or less contemporary with the activities of the avant-garde movements, it does indeed make more sense to see them as being involved in the same historical "project." Thus, except for the fact that he limits himself to the avant-garde *movements*, I find myself in agreement with Bürger when he states that through the avant-garde, "the historical succession of techniques and styles has been transformed into a simultaneity of the radically disparate. The consequence is that no movement in the arts today can legitimately claim to be historically more advanced *as art* than any other" (63). In chapter 3 I discussed how I saw this eclecticism emerging through the modernist subversion of the very authority of tradition, which ultimately leads to the (at least apparent) simultaneous availability of all traditions.

Does all this mean that I simply want to *equate* the terms "modernism" and "avant-garde"? No, for while the terms are often used in a manner indicating them to be synonymous, there are important functional differences between them. For one thing, as I pointed out at the beginning of this chapter, "avant-garde" carries a general sense of exploration and experimentation that, unlike "modernism," is nonspecific in histor-

---

40. It is striking to note that while Schulte-Sasse, in his foreword, claims that "the equation of the two terms stems from an inability to see that the theoretical emphases of modernist and avant-garde writers are radically different" (ibid., xv), he no fewer than four times uses the concepts interchangeably (first "modernism" and then "avant-garde," or vice versa) in referring to the same phenomena: "Major Theories of Modernism" and "understanding the avant-garde" (xv); "avant-garde writers" and "Derrida's attitude toward modernism" (xix); "the modernist theater" and "the avant-garde theater" (xx); and "artistic praxis of the avant-garde," "the writing practice of artistic modernism," and "the positivity of the avant-garde art program" (xxii). His introduction thus bears ample witness to the fact that the two concepts are far from being mutually exclusive.

ical terms. However, our awareness and understanding of the concept of the avant-garde and its experimental aura is very much shaped by the nontraditional literature and art of the early twentieth century, which some refer to as the "modernist era." In that case, "modernism" is necessarily the broader term, while the concept of the "avant-garde" has proven to enjoy a good deal of "free-play" *within* the overall reach of modernism. At the same time, nothing that is modernist can escape the touch of the avant-garde.

"Avant-garde" frequently has some explicit references of its own, in particular with regard to the avant-garde *movements*. But it can only lead to a reductive understanding of both "modernism" and "avant-garde" if we see the activities of these movements as something categorically different from the radical textual practices that can be observed both inside and outside the movements as such. In fact, one way to radicalize the concept of modernism fruitfully is to read "modernist" works from the perspective of the avant-garde. This is what Richard Sieburth has done in "Dada Pound," in which he studies Pound's leanings toward the Paris avant-garde during a crucial period of his career. He points out, for instance, that Pound's strategies of quotation in *The Cantos* may to a considerable extent be derived from Francis Picabia's emphatic foregrounding in his work of "such intertextual devices as citation, plagiarism, transcription, translation, parody, and pastiche."[41] He also touches on the significant fact that Pound's "celebrated midwifery of *The Waste Land*," which resulted in a more disjointed, formally more radical poem than Eliot would have delivered, "is an event very much contemporary with his Dada phase" (66). Such critical endeavors help us, in Sieburth's words, to resist "academic institutionalization" that serves to "domesticate an open, plural text into a massively monadic aesthetic object whose readability and respectability are no longer in question" (68).

When used in conjunction with modernism, "avant-garde" tends to signify the more radical, norm-breaking aspects of modernism. This is one of the relevant designated uses of the

41. Richard Sieburth, "Dada Pound," *South Atlantic Quarterly* 83 (Winter 1984): 52.

term. Frederick Karl has outlined this function of the avant-garde: "As the cutting edge of Modern, the avant-garde establishes the point at which Modern must enter its new phase in order to keep up with itself. The avant-garde points toward the future and as soon as it is absorbed into the present, it ceases to be itself and becomes part of Modernism."[42] While I agree that "avant-garde" constitutes the cutting edge of modernism, formulating its relationship with modernism in this manner runs the risk of having the two concepts slide apart, with all the ensuing value judgments and fruitless distinctions discussed earlier: seeing the avant-garde as simply a preparatory stage for the masterpieces of modernism or judging the avant-garde as the only significant revolt, while modernism is merely a classicism in disguise. The avant-garde should be seen as more than turning outward (or forward) with respect to modernism; it is no less important that it turn *inward*, teasing out the radical elements of modernism whenever it appears to be losing its edge.

Some critics may only be satisfied if they can pronounce a clear-cut division between the two terms. Certain workable points of distinction are certainly an advantage. But rather than enforce a rigid separation, I find it a good deal more critically stimulating and historically challenging to work on the assumption that while texts such as *Ulysses*, *Der Prozeß*, *Nightwood*, and *The Cantos* are modernist works, they are also avant-garde in their nontraditional structure and their radicalized correlations of form and content, and that while the avant-garde movements are historical phenomena in their own right, they are also salient motors of modernism.

42. Frederick R. Karl, *Modern and Modernism: The Sovereignty of the Artist, 1885–1925* (New York: Atheneum, 1985), p. 13.

5

Realism, Modernism, and the Aesthetics of Interruption

"REALISM" IS the only concept that appears to compete with "modernism" on the same scale in the overall landscape of twentieth-century literature. However, as I have pointed out, some critics have problems locating "realism" in their models of modern literature. One can safely say that while realism, however strictly defined, has been the predominant literary doctrine in Eastern Europe (since the mid-forties in the Soviet Union, the stronghold of socialist realism), the concept of realism has frequently been somewhat of an embarrassment to the literary establishment of the West. Several critical authorities have declared realism outmoded or dead, and even those antagonistic to modernist practices sometimes appear to have found little "realistic" relief. Gerald Graff writes: "Weary though we have become of modernist experimental modes, and wryly cynical about the quasi-theological claims that used to be made in their name, we do not know how to break out of them."[1] The view that modernism wields a hegemonic power over our literary sensibilities is not uncommon, as may be gathered from the preceding discussion. It has, for instance, been endorsed by Fredric Jameson, who states that in literature today, "amidst a weariness with plotless or poetic fiction, a return to intrigue is achieved, not by the latter's rediscovery, but rather by pastiche

1. Graff, *Literature against Itself*, p. 224.

of older narratives and depersonalized imitation of traditional voices, similar to Stravinsky's pastiche of the classics criticized by Adorno's *Philosophy of Music*." Consequently, this brand of "postmodernism" appears to be simply another extremity of the modernist monster. Jameson adds:

> In these circumstances, indeed, there is some question whether the ultimate renewal of modernism, the final dialectical subversion of the now automatized convention of an aesthetic of perceptual revolution, might not simply be . . . realism itself! For when modernism and its accompanying techniques of "estrangement" have become the dominant style whereby the consumer is reconciled with capitalism, the habit of fragmentation itself needs to be "estranged" and corrected by a more totalizing way of viewing phenomena.[2]

As is frequently the case with Jameson's observations, this passage is packed with thought-provoking and provocative ideas. First, why should realism bring about the "final" subversion of automatized convention? Does it foreshadow some final and ultimate turn into a totalized culture, one characterized by a "transparent" realism that under new social conditions would no longer risk serving as an ideological cloak hiding actual social constraints out of view; a realism that would therefore no longer need the devices of deautomatization? Leaving aside the question of whether such a culture is desirable, one wonders if this kind of realism is conceivable before the actual emergence of such a society. Second, are the modernist techniques of estrangement to be equated with the habitualized fragmentation of capitalist society? This is a question of the utmost importance, one I shall arrive at later in this chapter. But finally, is this an accurate depiction of the literary situation today?

In asking this question, we are again confronted with the issue of the institutional "politics" and the social distribution of literary culture. In what cultural context have critics suffered such alarming overexposure to modernism? Where has it become the "dominant style"? For whom have modernist prac-

2. Jameson, "Reflections in Conclusion," p. 211 (ellipses in original).

tices become automatized, and in what way? While it may seem easy to answer these questions by referring to the institutionalization of modernism in the modern literary academy, we are still left with the question of the fate of realism. Even by portraying the literary academy as a most isolated ivory tower, it is hard to imagine it as having "forgotten" realist discourse to such an extent that realism might serve to "shock" it out of its automatized modernism. I believe this would hold true even if we were able to restrict ourselves to an observation of what is generally conceived of as "literary" or "aesthetic" discourse. In 1959 Raymond Williams wrote:

> The major tradition of European fiction, in the nineteenth century, is commonly described as a tradition of "realism," and it is equally assumed that, in the West at any rate, this particular tradition has ended. The realistic novel, it was said recently, went out with the hansom cab. Yet it is not at all easy, at first sight, to see what in practice this means. For clearly, in the overwhelming majority of modern novels, including those novels we continue to regard as literature, the ordinary criteria of realism still hold.[3]

More than three decades later, this is still the case. We must, of course, allow for relative modification and development in the category of realism—Iris Murdoch is a realist writer, but surely Harold Bloom is mistaken in seeing her fiction as an embodiment of "the incongruous form of the 19th-century realistic novel."[4] Fredric Jameson, while desiring a new wave of realism, does not appear to see any authentic realist projection into the twentieth century taking place. He says that no one would seriously want "to return to the narrative mode of nineteenth century realism: the latter's rightful inheritors are the writers of bestsellers, who—unlike Kafka or Robbe-Grillet, really do concern themselves about the basic secular problems of our existence, namely, money, power, position, sex, and all those humdrum daily preoccupations which continue to form the

---

3. Raymond Williams, "Realism and the Contemporary Novel," *Partisan Review* 26 (Spring 1959): 202.
4. Harold Bloom, "A Comedy of Worldly Salvation," *New York Times Book Review*, January 12, 1986.

substance of our daily lives all the while that art literature considers them unworthy of its notice."[5]

It would be interesting to speculate, in view of Jameson's interest in the "revival" of realism, how a neorealism should go about deautomatizing this best-seller mode of realism while also breaking with the habitualized disruptions of modernism, since both practices have, it seems, become thoroughly integrated into capitalist culture. But this picture of modern literary culture betrays a lack of awareness of the development of "serious" realist fiction throughout this century, the significance of which is reflected by the prominence of such contemporary realist writers as Saul Bellow and John Updike in the United States, Graham Greene and Iris Murdoch in Britain, Heinrich Böll and Siegfried Lenz in Germany. Even the American universities, whose professors and writers' workshops are often held responsible for the experimental postmodernist vogue on the west side of the Atlantic, have recently been the breeding ground for a good deal of neorealist writing.[6]

It is my contention that the dialectical relationship of modernism and realism is of utmost significance for an understanding of our present literary culture. This position is not without its risks, since once the concepts are used for the purpose of grouping modern literature into two opposing categories they can obviously become severely restrictive. I shall begin, therefore, by examining some cases of such dualistic construction of modern literary history.

Realism vs. Modernism: The Ultimate Binary System?

It sometimes seems that the concept of realism is no longer an issue in literary studies. As the disputes surrounding "differences" within modernism grow ever more refined and specific, realism can even appear outmoded as a target of theoretical and critical scrutiny. But unless modernism is recast as a thoroughly conservative literary mode (a form of realism, in a sense)

5. Fredric Jameson, "Beyond the Cave: Demystifying the Ideology of Modernism," *Bulletin of the Midwest Modern Language Association* 8 (Spring 1975): 18.
6. The spectrum of American neorealism is well represented in two special issues of *Granta*: no. 8, 1983 ("Dirty Realism") and no. 19, 1986 ("More Dirt").

that supplies the dialectical opponent of postmodernism, realism has generally been indispensable as a background against which to understand and study modernism. In many cases, as Jameson notes, realism has served as the "straw man" designating whatever modernism *is not*:

> Thus, we may observe that the division of literature into these two starkly antithetical tendencies (form-oriented vs. content-oriented, artistic play vs. imitation of the real, etc.) is dictated by the attempt to deal adequately with modernism, rather than the other way round. . . . The concept of realism which thereby emerges is always that with which modernism has had to break, that norm from which modernism is the deviation, and so forth.[7]

It is by no means fair to say that the dualistic categorization has always been carried out only to deal adequately with modernism; critics have frequently striven to deal with the two concepts on an equal basis (I am also thinking of some of Jameson's own writings). When Stephen Spender's *Struggle of the Modern* appeared in 1963, it was felt that with his polarization of "modern" and "contemporary" he had clarified the antithetical developments of the two major trends in the twentieth century, without prejudicing either. But such polarization of course always involves the risk of essentializing the distinction, as when Daniel Fuchs, in buttressing Saul Bellow's opposition to modernism, maintains that "one must choose between Spender's categories, and Bellow is in the camp of the prose contemporaries, not the poetic moderns; the realists, not the visionaries."[8]

Most of Spender's dualistic observations had actually been prefigured by Edmund Wilson. While *Axel's Castle* is of course more about "symbolism" than about its "naturalist" antithesis, Wilson cannot be said to favor the former over the latter. Intrigued by modernist writing, he also has great reservations about it; much like Auerbach in the final chapter of *Mimesis*, he faces modernism with admiration and terror. It is interesting to note how his value judgments oscillate throughout the

---

7. Jameson, "The Ideology of the Text," p. 233.
8. Daniel Fuchs, "Saul Bellow and the Modern Tradition," p. 76.

book, depending on whether he is observing structural elements of modernist works or their social and cultural implications. He sees in these works a literary genius that nevertheless bodes cultural decadence and a crisis of humanism, for "when we turn back to consider even the masterpieces of that literature . . . we are oppressed by a sullenness, a lethargy, a sense of energies ingrown and sometimes festering" (283). Wilson sets up his oppositional categories partly by pairing antithetical writers, such as Bernard Shaw versus Yeats (59) and Anatole France versus Valéry (86), and he demonstrates how one is immersed in the affairs of the social world, highlighting its objective reality as his *content*, while the other, directing his creativity into aesthetized *form*, ultimately opts for a subjective and solipsistic retreat from the world into "Axel's castle."

A common response to such a portrayal of the modernist enterprise is that, far from rejecting the "real world," modernism is seeking reality at a different level of human existence, reality as it is processed by the human consciousness. This perspective is central to Auerbach's analysis of *To the Lighthouse* to the extent that he is willing to accede to its constituting a modern "realism." In Woolf herself we find, of course, a vehement advocate of the "realism" of consciousness, who places it in radical opposition to traditional realism. She attacks writers like Arnold Bennett and H. G. Wells for pouring all their energy into descriptions of the human environment and the creation of convincing characters. Responding to Bennett's demand that characters must be real if the novel is to be successful, she states: "But, I ask myself, what is reality? And who are the judges of reality?"[9] The one word she feels best characterizes the traditional realists, or the "Edwardians," is *materialists*. She even claims that they "write of unimportant things," whereas "Georgians" like herself find more important "material" by looking inside even "an ordinary mind on an ordinary day. The mind receives a myriad impressions—trivial, fantastic, evanescent, or engraved with a sharpness of steel. From all sides they come, an incessant shower of innumerable atoms."[10]

9. Woolf, "Mr. Bennett and Mrs. Brown," *Collected Essays* 1, p. 325.
10. Virginia Woolf, "Modern Fiction," *Collected Essays* 2 (London: Hogarth Press, 1972), pp. 104, 105, 106.

This question of the *perspective* involved in rendering reality has been at the center of many similarly polarized debates about modern literature. One of the most important of these is the controversy in *Das Wort* in the late 1930s, in which there was a fierce debate over expressionism and realism as diverging aesthetic and cultural tendencies.[11] It is telling that Ernst Bloch, the chief authority on the expressionist side, worked with the concept of "experienced reality" ("Erlebniswirklichkeit"), while Lukács, the self-evident leader of the advocates of realism, constantly demanded that literature reflect "objective reality." But a great deal more was at stake than epistemological disagreements, for the debate was felt to be decisive not only for the nature and function of realism but for socialist aesthetic and cultural policies, for the roles and relationships of experimentation and tradition, and generally for the reception of the bourgeois cultural heritage and the stance that antibourgeois cultural forces should adopt with regard to this heritage.

One of the participants, Béla Balázs, pointed out that a major decision concerning cultural policy in the Soviet Union had been made when experimental theater director Wsewolod Meyerhold, who had much in common with Brecht, was ousted from his position, while Konstantin Stanislavsky, the naturalist champion of the "illusionist" theater, was elevated and honored. "The names of these two great directors signify two different styles of dramatic art. More than that: two opposing principles of art in general."[12] Stanislavsky is taken to be representative for the realist urge to present both the outside world and the human character as unified and in their totality, whereas Meyerhold is typical of the formalist and expressionist tendency to present both as fragmented and estranged from normative perception.

The broader cultural implications of this distinction become apparent when Balázs states that Stanislavsky is "the *greatest realist of the stage*; he is appreciated and loved because he

11. A total of fifteen people took part in the controversy, which is sometimes mistakenly referred to as the Brecht-Lukács debate (the essays and notes that Brecht wrote in the midst of the debate were not published until a decade after his death). All the essays, together with those of Brecht and other relevant material, have been collected by Schmitt in *Die Expressionismusdebatte*.

12. Béla Balázs, "Meyerhold und Stanislawsky," in Schmitt, ed., *Die Expressionismusdebatte*, p. 121 (my translation).

brought one of the purest values of bourgeois culture uncorrupted across into the socialist culture—where such heritage is appreciated" (129). This equation of realism with the salvageable elements of bourgeois culture further leads to a concept of tradition that is filtered through the prevalent concept of realism—causing realism to serve a somewhat contradictory dual role. It constitutes an accessible storehouse of all recognized tradition, which actually covers both bourgeois and prebourgeois culture; it is not uncommon for spokesmen of such "realism" to lay claim to the Greek tragedians, Cervantes, and Shakespeare in the name of their concept. On the other hand, the concept designates a mimetic, verisimilar mode of representation modeled primarily on nineteenth-century realism. It was of course this latter realism that Lukács and others drew upon in their battle against modernism. Nineteenth-century realism was to some extent a natural horizon of tradition when it came to linking tradition with contemporary aesthetic praxis, since it so obviously had served to "democratize" the language of literature. Through its emphasis and dependence on contemporary social affairs, realism brought literature in close contact with the prevalent communicative and pragmatic function of language. This was also the reason for the modernists' revolt against realism and for their frequent equation of realism with tradition, an equation they have in common with the modern advocates of realism.

The sanction of nineteenth-century realism as an effective alternative to the chaos of avant-garde writing is staunchly upheld by Lukács. With untiring references to the achievements of Goethe, Balzac, and Tolstoy, he argues how their method of presenting a totalized reflection of society in all its contradictory richness is still viable in modern writing. The one modern writer who most fully lives up to this realist heritage is Thomas Mann, and in his *Wider den mißverstandenen Realismus* Lukács sets Mann up as a representative of one of the poles of modern bourgeois literature, "critical realism." The other pole, "decadent avant-garde," is represented by Kafka. This polarization is dramatically foregrounded by Lukács's chapter heading "Franz Kafka oder Thomas Mann?" (49).

In reading Lukács, the ultimate implication of the modernist/realist binary system comes clearly to view; it entails

nothing less than the division of all twentieth-century literature into two categories. It is no doubt this very implication
that has made many critics shy away from the two concepts.
Due to their lack of precision and tendency to elude manageable bounds, they seem to lack the well-defined, "technical"
use that is often demanded of critical tools (although this has
by no means prevented countless critics from using them without care or consistency). This dichotomy seems particularly
problematic in the case of poetry, since the traditions questioned by modernist poets are rarely subsumed under the rubric
of "realism."

In narrative literature, however, the polarization has frequently been taken for granted. Michel Zeraffa, for instance,
holds that "there cannot be a reasonable sociology of the novel
unless it is recognized from the start that there are two kinds of
approaches, the one appearing to carry on the realist tradition
and the other seemingly bearing the stamp of artistic creation."[13] (The striking opposition of "realist tradition" and "artistic creation" is a variant of the binary system, a variant that
expresses the aesthetic prejudices frequently involved in such
dichotomies.) I believe, in fact, that the entire issue of modernism is especially momentous and foregrounded in the case of
narrative, for the aesthetic proclivities of modernism seem
bound to go against the very notion of narrativity, narrative
progression, or storytelling in any traditional sense. One way to
define modernism would be to say that it resists reality-fabrica-
tions that are recuperable as "stories" or as situations that can
readily be reformulated in sociopragmatic terms.

Before exploring the nature of that resistance, I want to problematize further the dichotomy between modernism and realism. Dividing the entire literary field into two halves will inevitably prove to be restrictive in many respects. First, where and
how do we place popular culture? Labeling the whole so-called
culture industry "realistic" hardly seems productive. Those
who endorse this dichotomy often do not address the question
of popular culture at all. Second, the frequently encountered
grouping of individual writers into opposing "camps" can be

13. Michel Zeraffa, *Fictions: The Novel and Social Reality*, trans. Catherine
Burns and Tom Burns (Harmondsworth, Eng.: Penguin Books, 1976), p. 23.

treacherously arbitrary, even when the principles behind the division may be fully valid as theoretical constructs.

The same holds true for the use of individual writers as representatives of the contrasting modes of writing. Lukács's valorization of Thomas Mann as a representative of the modern projection of the realist novel is a case in point, since Mann is taken by several critics to belong to "high modernism." It seems evident that Mann relies on realist discourse and referential sociocodes to a much greater degree than for instance Joyce, the early Faulkner, or Gertrude Stein. The question is how much Mann (like Kafka, for instance) makes use of that discourse to ultimately undermine it by estranging us from the social reality to which it traditionally relates. It is tempting to agree with Irving Howe that in Mann's work "formal experiment is virtually absent, yet the spirit of modernism is extremely powerful,"[14] but this does not go far toward clarifying Mann's status. If we "ask in what way Thomas Mann contributes to the 'modernity' of the novel," notes J. P. Stern, "our first answer will be: by an increase in the consciousness portrayed and a corresponding increase in the consciousness of the portrayal." Stern concludes: "The chief mode of literature in the new century (and not of literature only) is a weakening of the nexus between the private and social spheres," that is, a "burgeoning of consciousness beyond the world of common indication, and thus the undermining of the realistic convention."[15]

Lukács deplores this drifting apart of social and personal experience. It bears witness to a lack of social awareness in handling the decisive role of the representational *perspective*, which governs the equilibrium between "objective reality" and its "aesthetic reflection." For the ideal of literary representation is an artistic effigy of this reality, one that is appropriate in content, formally homogeneous and closed.[16] This reflection of the objective world, moreover, has to incorporate, through its balance of the typical and the particular, the totality of social life in all its contradictions.

---

14. Howe, "The Culture of Modernism," *Decline of the New*, p. 13.
15. J. P. Stern, "The Theme of Consciousness: Thomas Mann," in Bradbury and McFarlane, ed., *Modernism, 1890–1930*, pp. 425, 428.
16. See Lukács, *Wider den mißverstandenen Realismus*, p. 59.

In order for Mann's *Zauberberg* to qualify for this kind of realism, we have to see the world of the sanatorium as a microcosm reproducing the social reality of the outside world through a reliable narrative perspective. There are numerous indications, however, that the narrative is not presenting us with a "reflection" of "objective reality." Frequently the irony shimmering through the text seems to call the reliability of the narrative voice into question, and although not as mischievous as in Joyce's *Ulysses*, the narration, instead of being that of realist storytelling, continuously creates the impression of parodying realist traditions. Mann thought of himself as one of the writers who had taken radical leave of the realist tradition, primarily through the stringent use of parody, an aesthetic quality he later attributed to his modernist hero, Adrian Leverkühn. "In the affairs of style I only know my way in parody. In this I am close to Joyce," says Mann in his "Entstehung des Doktor Faustus."[17]

There are other features of *Der Zauberberg* that seem to relate it to modernism, such as the manifold, often flagrantly self-conscious, manipulations of time and its relation to narrativity, and the rich but elusive allegorical implications of sickness, which has some affinity with Walter Benjamin's concept of allegory as the presentation of history as a process of decay. While *Der Zauberberg* is not a *Künstlerroman*, like some of Mann's other novels, its hero is in a sense an unshaped artist, "Hans Castorp, the unwritten sheet,"[18] who is torn between the representatives of two clashing historical philosophies: Settembrini, the champion of European Enlightenment, humanism, rationality, and progress (and ironically also of war), and Naphta, who stands for apocalyptic schism and deep scepticism with regard to reason and rationality and who unhesitatingly forecasts the end of the Western bourgeois era. As an aesthetic category, modernism arguably takes place where these two philosophies converge upon one another, and it is significant that the sanatorium, or the magic mountain in gen-

17. Thomas Mann, quoted in Viktor Žmegač, "Konvention, Modernismus und Parodie: Bemerkungen zum Erzählstil Thomas Manns," in Peter Pütz, ed., *Thomas Mann und die Tradition* (Frankfurt: Athenäum, 1971), p. 2 (my translation).

18. Thomas Mann, *Der Zauberberg* (Frankfurt: Fischer Taschenbuch, 1967), p. 40.

eral, comprises a kind of aesthetic realm. There, life is depragmatized to an extreme degree, and the bustling "real life" on the "Flachland" is contemplated from an estranging distance that makes time, daily activities, and human relations take on radically different proportions. In a sense the whole novel could be considered an exercise in perceptual "defamiliarization." Close to its end, Castorp's stay on the magic mountain is referred to as the "adventurous years of estrangement" ("abenteuerliche Jährchen der Entfremdung" [p. 749]). But an examination of these dimensions of the novel would have to be balanced with the question of how many of these features, which serve to break the codes of realism, are easily "naturalized"[19] due to the realistic overtones of the novel's narrative progression, which after all does not contain any radical syntactic disjunctions. And ultimately the magic mountain seems to be closer to our normative world than, for instance, the castle hill of one of Kafka's novels.

As this brief discussion may suggest, however, Mann's work can be effectively used to dismantle the dualistic opposition of realism and modernism, a dualism that may in fact prove to be the most deconstructable of all binary systems (although I want to stress that this in itself does not undo the usefulness of the concepts in question). It is of course frequently maintained that a central task of postmodernism is precisely the deconstruction of these boundaries. As David Lodge notes in a recent version of the modernist/realist binary system, postmodernism therefore offers an interesting challenge to the explanatory power of the dualistic typology,[20] frequently by pursuing a "both-and" rather than an "either-or" policy with regard to this dualism.

But this pursuit, as I have already pointed out, is far from being restricted to the postmodern era. *Madame Bovary*, which is so often referred to as the pioneer modernist novel, may in fact be the best example of this both-and aesthetics, as is reflected in the fact that it has also frequently served as one of the outstanding *realist* novels of the nineteenth century. Jonathan Culler, author of perhaps the most radical reading of Flaubert as

---

19. For the concepts of "naturalization" and "recuperation," see Culler, *Structuralist Poetics*, pp. 113–60.

20. Lodge, *The Modes of Modern Writing*, pp. 220–21.

a modernist,[21] admits that "we can read Flaubert as realist or modernist, though the power and interest of those two readings differ greatly."[22] This coincides with Gerald Bruns's observation in *Modern Poetry and the Idea of Language*, a book in which he fruitfully explores the dialectics of "hermetic" and "orphic" forms of poetic language, that there are "two *Madame Bovary*s, one a representation of life, a tour de force in the realistic mode, the other an adumbration of an impossible book—a book which, given the nature of language as a semiotic system, cannot exist in a pure state but only in a relationship of competition with the reality which language seeks conveniently to articulate"; the latter book is written in a style that seeks to radically "distance the work from the world represented in the work" (148–49).

Realism as Literature and Language

Before rushing to the conclusion that the modernist/realist dichotomy is thus ultimately based on two oppositional uses of language, we need to take a closer look at the general coverage of the concept of realism, although I will offer nothing like a survey of the vast literature relating to the definition of realism. As a concept, "realism" evinces many of the behavioral features we find in the case of "modernism." Both have considerably broader reference than most other typological concepts of literary history, such as "expressionism," "romanticism," or "classicism," and both have an obvious tendency to break loose from their moorings as period terms. Partly as a result, both concepts have assumed central positions in theoretical and critical debates in literary studies. In dealing with both concepts, the critic is best off deciding, as Peter Demetz says, "to play a floating game with the concept."[23]

One can discern three major aspects of the concept of real-

21. Jonathan Culler, *Flaubert: The Uses of Uncertainty* (Ithaca, N.Y.: Cornell University Press, 1974).

22. Jonathan Culler, *"The Uses of Uncertainty* Re-viewed," in Paul Hernadi, ed., *The Horizon of Literature* (Lincoln: University of Nebraska Press, 1982), p. 306.

23. Peter Demetz, "Zur Definition des Realismus," *Literatur und Kritik* 16/17 (August 1967): 333.

ism, although they are usually found in composite forms. "Realism" is, first, a period term for the dominant trend of nineteenth-century literature, especially narrative fiction; second, a certain type of mimetic (and usually narrative) processing of objective reality, and third, a fictional or literary embodiment of the communicative language acknowledged by the "public sphere."

In René Wellek's scheme of period concepts, realism signifies the dominant literary trend from "the end of romanticism" until such time when "realism and naturalism had run their course and would be replaced by a new art, symbolic, neoromantic or whatever else it might call itself."[24] As in the case of "symbolism," Wellek's emphasis on the historical demarcation of the *period* sits uneasily alongside his general definition, according to which realism is "the objective representation of contemporary social reality." As a theory of exclusion, this "rejects the fantastic, the fairy-tale-like, the allegorical and the symbolic, the highly stylized, the purely abstract and decorative" (240–41), while "type" and "objectivity" remain the main "watchwords" of realism (246).

While I agree that realism has strong and important historical ties with nineteenth-century social developments, it is hard to see why it should be restricted to that period. In *On Realism*, however, J. P. Stern goes too far in dissolving realism as a period term. While it is true that "the moment we accept the statement 'Shakespeare is more realistic than Ben Jonson' as meaningful, the case for realism as a strict period term is lost," it is decisive, as Stern in fact notes, that our judgment "of what is and what is not realistic is closer to the judgment of the nineteenth century than to that of earlier ages."[25] Our criteria for judging realism are predominantly shaped by the realist tradition consolidated by nineteenth-century literary practice.

An analysis of the historical backbone of realism, however, arguably takes the concept beyond the nineteenth century, unveiling its entanglement with philosophical realism and the Enlightenment. This is what Ian Watt does when he appraises

---

24. Wellek, "The Concept of Realism in Literary Scholarship," *Concepts of Criticism*, p. 240.
25. J. P. Stern, *On Realism* (London: Routledge and Kegan Paul, 1973), p. 41.

the "rise of the novel" in eighteenth-century Britain in terms of the emergence of realism. This approach has the benefit of eschewing the overemphasis on the nineteenth-century "realistic" reaction to the thematic or scenic idealism of either classicism or romanticism. "If the novel were realistic merely because it saw life from the seamy side, it would only be an inverted romance," Watt says. "The novel's realism does not reside in the kind of life it presents, but in the way it presents it."[26] Realistic representation is characterized by close attention to the "correspondence between the literary work and the reality which it imitates" (11)—by a pursuit of verisimilitude that places the individual firmly in a physical and social setting, whereby the rendering of particularity (and the rejection of universals) is closely aligned with holistic characterization and presentation of background (19). Realism mediates between the representational "closeness to the texture of daily existence" (24) and the portrayal of "individual life in its larger perspective as a historical process" (26).

I shall later address the question why it is that this type of literary presentation comes into full flowering in the nineteenth century. For the moment I want to examine the second aspect of realism, that is, the type of reality processing involved. In asking which mimetic details are relevant for a realistic presentation, Stern responds: "Clearly, all those that contribute, and no more than contribute, to the achieved whole ('the total form') of the realistic fiction: a 'total form' which fulfils and enriches our expectations by way of a continuity."[27] But in order to meet our expectations and establish what might be called the "realist contract" with the reader, a certain amount of redundancy has to be built into the message. It is this redundancy that Barthes points to as the crucial "reality effect;"[28] that which by its sheer presentness emits the signal: "this is reality." Such details must not become too weighty, for then they may rupture the wholeness of the "total form." It was for this reason that Lukács denied naturalism (from Flaubert

26. Ian Watt, *The Rise of the Novel: Studies in Defoe, Richardson and Fielding* (Harmondsworth, Eng.: Penguin Books, 1963), p. 11.
27. Stern, *On Realism*, p. 73.
28. Roland Barthes, "The Reality Effect," in *The Rustle of Language*, pp. 141–48.

through Zola into the twentieth century) a place in the realist tradition; he saw the naturalist emphasis on the various details of social life initiating the modernist tearing of details out of the unified fabric of the realist text.

Realism, then, portrays social reality as a "whole" and ultimately as a "common ground," and as Lukács demonstrates so persuasively in his *Theorie des Romans*, this holds true even when the relationship between individuals and society is predominantly characterized by conflict. Stern is not far off the mark, therefore, when he notes that the area in which realism is most fully at home is "where human relationships are formalized and protected against the caprice of solipsism, in the social institutions of a given age" (91). The emphasis on the workings of social institutions, perhaps predominantly the family but also the political arena, official administrations, schools, churches, newspapers, and judicial system, is still clearly visible in prominent contemporary realists—the whole career of Heinrich Böll, for instance, can be seen as an extended attempt at a dialogue with such institutions. Realism is preoccupied with a "world of shared reality," as Stern puts it (150), and it depends upon the reader's willingness to "share" that reality. As a kind of summary, and as a lead into a discussion of the further implications of realistic "form," let me quote Peter Demetz's fourfold definition of the realist "syndrome" (whereby not all qualities have to be present for the work to be legitimately realistic):

> 1. the possibility of a inclusive narrative; 2. the question of the typical, which replaces the heroic; 3. the development ("Bildung") of man, of the image of man, in the determining network of material forces and 4. the problem of a mode of representation in which the "I" serves a world which preserves its validity independent of creative sensibility.[29]

The first feature designates the creation and "encircling" of a sphere of reality that is thus under unified "control." The third relates to the historical determinants of realism: realism is an expression of a secularized and systematized bourgeois society.

29. Demetz, "Zur Definition des Realismus," p. 336 (my translation).

The second feature, the foregrounding of the typical, runs parallel to the important fourth one, a mode of representation brought to bear on a world that preserves its substantiality independent of the "creative sensibility." This brings me to the third aspect of realism, according to my previous tripartite approximation: its reliance on normative, communicative language. Its depiction of a shared reality demands that it be mediated through a shared language. David Lodge has set forth a "working definition of realism in literature" as *the representation of experience in a manner which approximates closely to descriptions of similar experience in nonliterary texts of the same culture.*[30]

In actuality, the term "literary" can be misleading here. If the avant-garde threatens to explode the domain of art by showing that it is as much a place of non-sense as of meaning, realism constantly threatens art, and thus also helps recharge it, from the other side. Realism tends to minimize or erase the relative boundaries between literature and "ordinary" social discourse. We might therefore reformulate Lodge's definition to say that realist discourse in literature is constantly nourished and motivated by the dominant modes of cultural representation in the respective society.

Through its language, therefore, in its very form, realism implicitly presents culture as a unified sphere and, to exaggerate slightly, reflects a fully "democratic" and egalitarian society—a society in which meaning is evenly "shared" (no matter what the actual political situation in the respective society may be). Realism is a mode of writing in which the subject "comes to terms with" the object, where the individual "makes sense" of a society in which there is a basis of common understanding. One could perhaps say that nineteenth-century realism consolidates as a re-creation of the "public sphere," at a time when some see that sphere as entering a process of fragmentation.[31] Realist discourse is in some ways an ideal(istic) form of what Habermas calls *communicative rationality.*

Hence, it should be clear how realism could come to serve as

30. Lodge, *The Modes of Modern Writing*, p. 25 (emphasis in original).
31. See Terry Eagleton's discussion of criticism and the public sphere in *The Function of Criticism: From* The Spectator *to Post-Structuralism* (London: Verso, 1984).

a locus of literary traditions in the course of the nineteenth century: through its systematized and rationalized mimeticism on the one hand, and holistic cultural implications on the other, its discourse could be taken to subsume other traditions, in particular those which also depended heavily on epic and mimetic representation. This explains why Roland Barthes sees modernism revolting not just against realism but against the totality of "classical language," which is transparent, which is "always reducible to a persuasive continuum. . . . It establishes a universe in which men are not alone, where words never have the terrible weight of things, where speech is always a meeting with the others,"[32] and why he states that "readerly texts" make up "the enormous mass of our literature."[33]

Before attending to the revolt against realist discourse, I want to mention briefly a problem that lies beyond the scope of this study but is nevertheless significant for modernist studies. It seems to me that in postrealist times (that is since realism became fully established as a literary mode and the revolt against it began), largely because of this collaboration of fictional realism and communicative language, "realism" has become less dependent on the second aspect of the concept, that is, the typological restraints on its mimetic facilities. A novel or other piece of narrative no longer has to incorporate an inclusive or "encircling" depiction of nonidealized contemporary reality to register as "realistic." The very use of a received mimetic-realist discourse and an unobstructedly unfolded narrative is intertextually preregistered as a sign of a world-within-reach. This development has served to bridge the gap between the kind of fiction at the center of nineteenth-century realism and various other narrative modes. We live in a "strange world," Charles Newman says, where "confessional autobiography is considered 'realistic' rather than self-indulgent."[34] Realism, it is safe to say, has reincorporated much of the "fantastic," and it is realism, rather than any narrowly defined postmodernism, that has bridged the gap between "art literature" and popular fiction (ambivalent as such a move is in the present kind of

32. Barthes, *Writing Degree Zero*, p. 49.
33. Roland Barthes, *S/Z*, trans. Richard Miller (London: Jonathan Cape, 1974), p. 5.
34. Newman, *The Post-Modern Aura*, p. 43.

society). Of special challenge to a contemporary theory of realism would be the "verisimilitude" of science fiction,[35] much (but by no means all) of which is written in "realistic" language, besides relying on the realist tradition in characterization and narrative structure. It seems we are dealing with a cultural situation in which the "futuristic" (if that is the right word), high-tech-ridden environment of a science fiction novel, because of the way its verisimilitude is exercised, is more of a "shared reality" for us than is the world of Kafka's novels. This indicates the power a realist discourse has to invoke our cooperation. Interrupting this power is therefore a major undertaking, and perhaps a hopeless one.

Realist Discourse—Modernist Interruption

In an essay on Gertrude Stein, William Gass writes: "In every art two contradictory impulses are in a state of Manichean war: the impulse to communicate and so to treat the medium of communication as a means, and the impulse to make an artifact out of the materials of the medium and so to treat the medium as an end."[36] This utterance is exemplary of one of the most frequently used arguments in the defense of modernist writing. "Consult your own experience," Paul Valéry writes, "and you will find that we understand each other, and ourselves, only thanks to our *rapid passage over words*."[37] As a contrast to this experience, he speaks of noticing "in myself certain states which I may well call *poetic*, since some of them were finally realized in poems," and in these states "I found myself for a time jolted out of my habitual state of mind" (141). We note the parallel to the formalist theory of defamiliariza-

35. Each subgenre operates its own kind of verisimilitude, a reader-contract through which the work "tries to convince us it conforms to reality and not to its own laws," as Tzvetan Todorov notes in his "Introduction to Verisimilitude," *The Poetics of Prose*, trans. Richard Howard (Ithaca, N.Y.: Cornell University Press, 1977), p. 83.
36. William Gass, "Gertrude Stein: Her Escape from Protective Language," *Fiction and the Figures of Life* (Boston: Nonpareil Books, 1971), p. 94.
37. Paul Valéry, "Poetry and Abstract Thought," *An Anthology*, ed. James R. Lawler, trans. Denise Folliot (London: Routledge and Kegan Paul, 1977), p. 140 (emphasis in original).

tion, and Valéry, needless to say, saw it as poetry's business to prevent the rapid passage over words, to lend words back their weight and stop them from receding into the background of communication, and thus dying.

This may remind us of another aesthetician of death, Maurice Blanchot, who sees the linguistic "naming" of things as being a sacrifice of reality: "Death alone allows me to grasp what I want to attain; it exists in words as the only way they can have meaning."[38] Any summary discussion can only do injustice to Blanchot's complex theory-performance, much of which is geared toward the distinction between "literary language" and "common language" (44). This distinction is then redoubled within the domain of literature:

> If one looks at it in a certain way, literature has two slopes. One side of literature is turned toward the movement of negation by which things are separated from themselves and destroyed in order to be known, subjugated, communicated. . . .
>
> But there is another side to literature. Literature is a concern for the reality of things, for their unknown, free and silent existence. . . . In this way, it sympathizes with darkness, with aimless passion, with lawless violence, with everything in the world that seems to perpetuate the refusal to come into the world. (48–49)

Blanchot obviously sees the chief function of literature as residing on this second slope, in the fact that its language is also an *obstacle to communication*. His argument, dating from 1949, to some extent prefigures that of Roland Barthes in *Writing Degree Zero* (1953). There, Barthes counters the transparency and reassuring effect of classical language with the opacity of modern writing (écriture), which "manifests an essence and holds the threat of a secret, it is anti-communication, it is intimidating" (20). The classical novel, contrariwise, "escapes the terror of an expression without laws: reality becomes slighter and more familiar, it fits within a style, it does not outrun language" (32).

Now even if we grant such aesthetics the argument that

---

38. Maurice Blanchot, "Literature and the Right to Death," in *The Gaze of Orpheus and Other Literary Essays*, trans. Lydia Davis (New York: Station Hill Press, 1981), p. 43.

modernist writing is resisting an escape into the security of the normative language of communication, how can we be sure that modernist language, in turn, is not an escape from human and social interaction? Gass's essay on Stein is (ironically?) subtitled "Her Escape from Protective Language." Does this also constitute an "escape" into the isolation of a "poetic effect"? As soon as we wish to define modernism through its defiance of realist discourse, and ultimately of communicative language, we run the risk of simply reiterating the formalist theory of "poetic language." The poetic language fallacy, as Mary Louise Pratt calls it,[39] operates on two levels. It serves to distinguish "poetic" from "ordinary" or "communicative" language by locating linguistic and structural deviation against the dominant background of language use. It then redoubles this distinction by bringing it to bear on the already differentiated sphere of literature, with obvious prejudice for texts that break the norms of literary production. I have already discussed the ambivalence of the theory of defamiliarization, which is a central device in this context. It involves, on the one hand, a purification and specification of the verbal act *as art*; it holds forth, on the other, the potential to challenge ideological and social norms.

In order for the social aspect of defamiliarization to be at all functional—and this is decisive for my view of modernism—the first level of the poetic language theory has to be dismantled: we must not be able to distinguish categorically between literature and nonliterature on the basis of linguistic difference. And I think my discussion of realism has made clear that such a distinction is in fact not feasible. Realism therefore proves to be an inevitable intertextual basis for an understanding of modernist writing as *social text*. It helps us to understand that there is no *intrinsic* linguistic quality that makes works "literary." To look at a representative, in fact a seminal, attempt at specifying "literary language," let us recall Roman Jakobson's model of the six factors involved in verbal communication and their respective functions:[40]

---

39. See Pratt's critique in the first chapter of *Toward a Speech Act Theory of Literary Discourse*, pp. 3–37.
40. Roman Jakobson, "Closing Statement: Linguistics and Poetics," in Thomas E. Sebeok, ed., *Style in Language* (Cambridge: MIT Press, 1960), pp. 353, 357.

Context (referential)

Addresser   Message (poetic)   Addressee

(emotive)   Contact (phatic)   (conative)

Code (metalingual)

In poetic language, Jakobson argues, the poetic function, "the set (Einstellung) toward the MESSAGE as such, focus on the message for its own sake" (356), dominates the other functions, whereas the referential function is generally at the forefront of most communicative messages. Jakobson lucidly argues that the poetic function is operative, though not dominant, in non-poetic utterances, for instance in the phrase "I like Ike" (357). He tells us that this is a political slogan, and that the poetic function is secondary (presumably to the referential one). But only the fact that he *already knows* it is a political slogan helps him to determine the relative weight of the functions. If it had been a line from a poem by William Carlos Williams, the poetic function would undoubtedly have been deemed the dominant one. Hence, the factor that helps us to determine whether an utterance is poetic or not is, ironically, the sphere of the referential function, namely the *context* of the utterance. We always need to be aware of this context to know whether a text is "literary." Often we immediately and unconsciously supply the necessary context, and whatever expectations go with it, through our preregistered knowledge of genres. As a relatively autonomous sphere of text-production, literature exists only as a social convention, not as a safeguard of a specific literary function or essence.

But if a text requires the referential function to signal its cultural position, then it should also be obvious that a significant and inextricable part of the context is language itself—and from this perspective the medium is not to be separated from the context. Even if we understand the message to be focusing on itself, it is *referring* to its language as social reality.[41] Once we have adopted this perspective, the aesthetics of the "other slope" of language acquires social significance and helps us

41. For a critique of poetic "essentialism" and a forceful argument for a "restoration" of the referential function in literary studies, see Constanzo Di Girolamo, *A Critical Theory of Literature* (Madison: University of Wisconsin Press, 1981).

approach the modernist enterprise. For this "slope" is not "poetic language"; it is the "other" of language in a more violent sense, since it resists the communicative-semiotic function of language.

A significant element of the often bewildering "referential function" of modernist works is the very crisis of language, referentiality, and communication that they enact through their structural properties. This explains why the theories of so ideologically radical a scholar as Adorno come in some respects very close to the aesthetics promulgated by such aesthetes as Valéry and Gass. Through its disposition to the dialectics of the "double nature of language as a discursive, significatory medium—primarily of communication—and as expression," modernist literature resists the false availability of meaning: "The so-called unintelligibility of precisely the legitimate contemporary art is a consequence of an inherent essence of art. At the same time this provocation passes historical judgment on intelligibility which has degenerated into misunderstanding" ("über die zum Mißverständnis degenerierte Verständlichkeit").[42]

The problem with Adorno's approach is that he reproduces the poetic language fallacy by restricting this resistance to normative communication to *art* as an *isolated realm*. Such resistance to hegemonic social formations can theoretically occur in any sphere of cultural activity. In *Subculture: The Meaning of Style*, Dick Hebdige shows how such subcultures as punk "represent symbolic challenges to a symbolic order."[43] Modernism arguably constitutes a form of "subculture," and Hebdige in fact unveils a number of parallels between certain youth subcultures and avant-garde practices. One might object that if modernism is a subculture, it is thoroughly assimilated to modern bourgeois society—but by now so is punk. Any attempt to interrupt the seemingly cohesive symbolic order of a capitalist bourgeois-democratic society is inevitably threatened by assimilation into that order.

42. Adorno, "Voraussetzungen," *Versuch, das Endspiel zu verstehen*, p. 110 (my translation).

43. Dick Hebdige, *Subculture: The Meaning of Style* (London: Methuen, 1979), p. 92.

I think it would be misleading, therefore, to insist that interruption of prevalent social discourse is initiated by modernism
or limited to modernist practices. We might even want to argue,
as Benjamin does in discussing interruption as a cardinal element in Brecht's epic theater, "that interruption is one of the
fundamental devices of all structuring. It goes far beyond the
sphere of art."[44] We might even note, since Adorno sees modernist interruption and anticommunication as directed against
intrumental rationality and the dialectics of Enlightenment,
that one of the champions of the Enlightenment, Denis Diderot, was a man who cherished interruption. In Diderot's
Jacques le fataliste, the action is halted by a narrator who
asserts his right to continue the story in whatever way he
pleases (prefiguring many narrators of the "postmodern" era).
At one point Jacques exclaims, "I've been interrupted so often
that I should do as well to start all over again."[45] An even more
radical book of interruptions is Sterne's *Tristram Shandy*,
whose ceaselessly interrupted and deferred story begins with
an interrupted act of coitus, setting the scene for the coexistence of creativity and interruption that characterizes the
whole novel.[46] Victor Shklovsky's famous comment that "*Tristram Shandy* is the most typical novel in world literature"[47]
springs from the idea that the slightest trace of plot construction in a novel is already an interruption of a "straight" story,
and that Sterne was therefore using the creativity of "plotting"
to the hilt.

Modernist interruption, however, occurs in a cultural context that is quite different from that of eighteenth-century
France or England, and unlike the above cases, it has to be seen
as an instrumental element of an emerging cultural paradigm.
Despite my criticism of Adorno's programmatic aesthetics, I
wish to stress that he sees the provocative unintelligibility of

44. Walter Benjamin, "What Is Epic Theater?" *Illuminations*, ed. Hanna
Arendt, trans. Harry Zohn (New York: Schocken Books, 1969), p. 151.
45. Denis Diderot, *Jacques the Fatalist and His Master*, trans. J. Robert Loy
(New York: Norton, 1978), p. 14.
46. "*Did ever woman, since the creation of the world, interrupt a man with
such a silly question?*" Laurence Sterne, *Tristram Shandy*, ed. Howard Anderson
(New York: Norton, 1980), p. 2 (emphasis in original).
47. Victor Shklovsky, "Sterne's *Tristram Shandy*: Stylistic Commentary," in
Lemon and Reis, *Russian Formalist Criticism*, p. 57.

art passing a *"historical* judgment on intelligibility which has degenerated into misunderstanding."[48] The striking and often-quoted interruption of traditional poetic diction effected by Eliot's third line of "Love Song of J. Alfred Prufrock" can be read to signal the historical-cultural disenchantment that spurs the modernist self-conscious and incongruous production of fragments:

> Let us go then, you and I,
> When the evening is spread out against the sky
> Like a patient etherised upon a table[49]

Interruption, then, much like defamiliarization—when read against the purist grain of formalist aesthetics—can be understood as a revolt against perceptual and ideological anesthesia. In the expressionist controversy, Ernst Bloch, the paramount theoretician of the expressionist camp, objected to the unbroken, totalized world that Lukács had inherited from idealist philosophical systems and now wished to set up as a model for modern literary production. Bloch points out that "perhaps real reality is also an interruption."[50] Similarly, in a letter to Lukács following the controversy, Anna Seghers wonders if "realism" should not mean "tendency towards becoming aware of reality."[51]

The twin notions that reality is also interruption and that realism should primarily involve the process of *becoming aware* of reality show an obvious affinity with Brecht's theory of the "Verfremdungseffekt," which he was in fact developing at the time of the controversy, partly under the influence of the Russian formalist theory of defamiliarization. Behind the theories of Bloch and Brecht lies the assumption that ideology, in Althusser's words, "represents the imaginary relationship of

---

48. Adorno, "Voraussetzungen," *Versuch, das Endspiel zu verstehen*, p. 110 (my emphasis).

49. T. S. Eliot, *The Complete Poems and Plays of T. S. Eliot* (London: Faber and Faber, 1969), p. 13.

50. Ernst Bloch, "Diskussionen über Expressionismus," in Schmitt, ed., *Die Expressionismusdebatte*, p. 186.

51. "Ein Briefwechsel zwischen Anna Seghers und Georg Lukács," in Schmitt, ed., *Die Expressionismusdebatte*, p. 271.

individuals to their real conditions of existence,"[52] and that it takes on the form of a bounded, holistic world view. In order to get closer to these real conditions, the world as we see it must not simply be reproduced in another holistic mold. Rather, it has to be estranged, our imaginary relationship with it has to be interrupted.

This explains the aversion of certain Marxists to realist writing. Peter Bürger critiques Lukács's theory of "organic" realism by stating that the organic work "intends the impression of wholeness," and that it "seeks to make unrecognizable the fact that it has been made."[53] The organic "wholeness" of the literary text may reinforce the latent detachment of literature from other social practices, a detachment that is inevitably inherent in the relative autonomy of literature. The work will therefore not contribute to our understanding of how meaning, and hence ideology, is *produced*. Adorno is even more critical of realism, since he sees it as a fake image of a reconciliation between reality and the perceiving subject. In contrast to this illusory rapprochement, Adorno notes, we can observe how the formalism involved for instance in Joyce's disentangling of the empirical time continuum manages to show what has happened to time in modern reality.

> Such convergences prove formalism to be the true realism, while procedures regulated to reflect the real feign a nonexistent reconciliation of reality with the subject. Realism in art has become an ideology, just as the mentality of so-called realistic people, who act according to prevalent institutions and whatever these desire or offer; they do so not, as they imagine, to become free from illusions, but only to take part in weaving the veil with which repression cloaks the circumstances involved, lending them the semblance of natural conditions.[54]

Adorno here polemically foregrounds the latent connection between the meanings of the word "realistic" as it is used for

---

52. Louis Althusser, "Ideology and Ideological State Apparatus (Notes towards an Investigation)," *Lenin and Philosophy and Other Essays*, trans. Ben Brewster (New York: Monthly Review Press, 1971), p. 162.

53. Bürger, *Theory of the Avant-Garde*, p. 72.

54. Adorno, "Voraussetzungen," *Versuch, das Endspiel zu verstehen*, pp. 115–16 (my translation).

literature and for "real life." To be "realistic," as a philosophy of
life, is generally to settle for what one can have in some given
circumstances—while the circumstances themselves are not
necessarily questioned.

We could argue, analogously, that one of the communicative
traps for realistic discourse is the degeneration of its referential
function into a phatic function, for which Jakobson gives us an
extreme and funny example from Dorothy Parker: " 'Well!' the
young man said. 'Well!' she said. 'Well, here we are,' he said.
'Here we are,' she said, 'Aren't we?' 'I should say we were,' he
said, 'Eeyop! Here we are.' 'Well!' she said. 'Well!' he said,
'well.' "[55] In other words, we are making sure the communicative channel is open, irrespective of whether actual communication is taking place. We may even seek to confirm that we
share a discourse and a reality, even if this is only so in a very
limited sense; we have an urge to test if the world as we know it
(and not some "other" reality) is still "out there." This primarily affirmative function of language is one of Adorno's main
targets.

To be sure, the campaign against realism is at times over-
heated. Judging realist discourse as the inevitable vehicle and
symbolic reflection of a positivist, technocratic-instrumental-
ized and repressive social system ultimately leads to a wholesale condemnation of the very language we continually use in
most of our everyday interaction. Such a radical modernist
perspective has obvious affinities with the antirational project
of some modern thinkers, who tend to emphasize the negative,
self-destructive elements of reason as furthered by the Enlightenment. The shortcomings of this general approach are frequently reflected in the implicit assumptions that, first, such a
cultural signifying system is not able, in different ways, to
critique itself, and second, that modernist and antirational revolts against the episteme embodied in the Enlightenment tradition actually suggest that this tradition, with all its weight of
logic and rationality, could be discarded. I find it more fruitful
to look at modernism as a practice that works in opposition to
rational and realist discourse but that, in its "negativity," only
preserves its significance and its signifying power against the

55. Jakobson, "Closing Statement," pp. 355–56.

background of the tradition that produces and legitimatizes that discourse.

Toward the Nonorganic Text

In "Beyond the Cave," Fredric Jameson argues that modernism functions very much like a "cancelled realism"—an argument with which I concur, although the inferences I draw from this act of negation diverge from Jameson's. He suggests "that realism—but also that desacralized, post-magical, commonsense, everyday, secular reality which is its object—is inseparable from the development of capitalism, the quantification by the market system of the older hierarchical or feudal or magical environment, and thus that both are intimately linked to the bourgeoisie as its product and its commodity."[56]

Jameson argues that the conflicting aesthetic positions of realism and modernism "correspond in the long run to two quite different cultures: there was a culture of realism, that of the nineteenth century . . . and there is today a different culture altogether, that of modernism" (8). As Jameson's subsequent arguments make clear, however, modernist culture, were it to exist, would look radically different from dominant twentieth-century bourgeois culture. Drawing on Deleuze and Guattari, Jameson points out that the "most revealing and authentic" of modernist strategies "is surely the emergence of schizophrenic literature, or the attempt to come to terms with the pure primordial flux itself" (13). Surely, for better or worse, Western culture still has not entered such a state. From any normative perspective, therefore, "modernist culture" (still) does not exist. This calls for a closer look at Jameson's depiction of the cohabitation of classical capitalism and realist discourse (like Jameson, I choose to skirt the question of why and how this discourse also developed in the different economic system of Russia).

What happens under capitalism is the decoding of "earlier types of realities or code-constructions" (12), or, as Jameson puts it in another essay, "the secularization of the older sacred

56. Jameson, "Beyond the Cave," pp. 8–9.

codes, the systematic dissolution of the remaining traces of the hierarchical structures which very unequally and over many centuries characterized the organization of life and practices under the *ancien régime* and even more distantly under feudalism itself. The process is evidently at one with the whole philosophical programme of secularization and modernization projected by the Enlightenment *philosophes*."[57] While Jameson comes dangerously close to equating the project of the Enlightenment with the foundations of capitalism, it is obvious that realist discourse is heavily dependent on both. In decoding and desanctifying earlier "versions" of reality, it "takes command," in language, of secularized reality, "mapping" it with an unprecedented mimetic closeness.

As for the emergence of modernism, Jameson's explanation is profoundly unsatisfactory: "At length, as the nineteenth century itself wears on, we begin to detect signs of a kind of fatigue with the whole process of decoding. . . . There appear perhaps to be fewer and fewer codes in the older sacred sense to serve as the object of such semiotic purification." Modernism then emerges as an attempt to "recode the henceforth decoded flux of the realistic, middle-class, secular era."[58] Astoundingly, Jameson speaks as if realism were an "innocent" medium, and as if the reality of which it is a product had not recodified society and culture in its own terms. In its heavy emphasis on narrative construction, realism is a prime code maker. At various points in "Beyond the Cave," Jameson in fact points out the identity between realism and both historical thinking and ideology (both of which necessarily exist as systems of codes). It is perhaps this dual relation that leads Jameson to assert that "realism is the most complex epistemological instrument yet devised for recording the truth of social reality, and also, at one and the same time, that it is a lie in the very form itself, the prototype of aesthetic false consciousness, the appearance which bourgeois ideology takes on in the realm of narrative literature" (9–10).

Working through Jameson's theory of modernism leads me to

---

57. Fredric Jameson, "The Realist Floor-Plan," in Marshall Blonsky, ed., *On Signs* (Baltimore: Johns Hopkins University Press, 1985), p. 373.

58. Jameson, "Beyond the Cave," p. 16.

a conclusion implicit in his analysis, even though he decidedly steers away from such implications. If Jameson is right in detecting a joint effort in the secularizing practices of both classical capitalism and realist discourse, then we can judge the emergence of modernism in terms that are quite different from his. Modernism can be seen to emerge because realism, as a form of historical thinking, is felt to deal inadequately with secularized reality *in its own terms*, so to speak. Even though realism may be highly critical of capitalist reality (as many nineteenth-century realists were), it evinces a tendency to reproduce the narrative structures and the symbolic order that form the basis of this society and its ideology.[59] As a mode of cultural resistance (and in this sense even the insistence on "l'art pour l'art" can be seen as a form of resistance), modernism seeks to distance itself from this symbolic order, but it does so without providing a new "culture"; rather, it functions at a second remove from the capitalist-bourgeois symbolic order. Saying that it functions at a second remove may sound too idealistic, however, since modernism cannot escape being "polluted" by prevalent depictions and conceptions of lived reality. But modernism seeks to resist or subvert the immediate contact with reality that the codes of realism appear to supply. Thus, I agree with Jameson that "modernist works are essentially simply," or not so simply,

> cancelled realistic ones; that they are in other words not apprehended directly, in terms of their own symbolic meanings, in terms of their own mythic or sacred immediacy, the way an older primitive or overcoded work would be, but rather indirectly only, by way of the relay of an imaginary realistic narrative of which the symbolic and modernistic one is then seen as a kind of stylization. . . . Let me suggest, in other words, to put it very crudely, that when you make sense of something like Kafka's *Castle*, your process of doing so involves the substitution for that recoded flux of a realistic narrative of your own devising. (16–17)

59. I want to stress, however, that I do not think that reproducing the symbolic order is necessarily an act of uncritical assent. This would ultimately mean that we are unable to practice any cultural criticism in normative communicative language. I believe that there is more than a single form of cultural resistance, and as I shall argue toward the end of this book, modernist resistance by itself by no means ensures critical posture.

Suggestive as these remarks are, Jameson's conclusion is disappointing. While I agree that the reading of such works is "a two-stage affair"—we are led through a hermeneutic process of seeking to understand the work in terms of our previously established sociocultural code system—I find it hard to accept that after our own recreation of a "realistic" subtext, this text is simply interpreted "according to the procedures we reserved for the older realistic novel in general" (17). What Jameson ends up seeing here is enhanced alienation, as we are driven "deeper into the contradictions of our own scientific and causal thought-modes," and he reveals that Lukács—and this is not the only time Lukács shows up at a crucial moment in Jameson's work—

> turns out in the long run to have been right after all about the nature of modernism: very far from a break with that older over-stuffed Victorian bourgeois reality, it simply reinforces all of the latter's basic presuppositions, only in a world so thoroughly sub-jectivized that they have been driven underground, beneath the surface of the work, forcing us to reconfirm the concept of a secular reality at the very moment in which we imagine ourselves to be demolishing it. (17–18)

Jameson fails to acknowledge the potential dialectical productivity of the interplay between the "two texts." It is enough to think of works in which the realist text is not so much suppressed—I am thinking for instance of what Bruns calls the two *Madame Bovarys*—to see that it is far from being unaffected by the modernist subversion. In modernist works that evince a more radical "forgetting," to use Nietzsche's term, of their realist past, this negated past is still called upon in forming a basis of communication with the text. But to say that we fully reconstruct an understanding of the text in terms of realist discourse implies that no matter how we seek to interrupt tradition, it has, "always already," reclaimed us into its sovereign wholeness.

It is precisely to elude incorporation into a holistic continuum, reflected in the organic wholeness of individual works, that modernism manifests itself in nonorganic texts. At this point I should like to incorporate Bürger's theory of the avant-garde work into my approach to modernism. A connection between the two is to be found in the concept of modernism that can be extracted from Adorno's aesthetic theory. While Bürger is critical of Adorno's theory when discussing the institution of art in bourgeois society, he draws heavily on Adorno's theory of modernism in his description of the avant-garde work of art (he even refers to Adorno's portrayal of modernist art as a theory of the avant-garde).

A basic feature of the avant-garde work, according to Bürger, is that it is made up of fragments without the aim of making them cohere with one another in a traditional sense. I have already discussed how the modernist work frequently has a collage texture, giving the impression that it is a meeting place of various textual scraps rather than a unified work. As Bürger quotes from Adorno: "The semblance (*Schein*) of art being reconciled with a heterogeneous reality because it portrays it is to disintegrate as the work admits actual fragments (*scheinlose Trümmer*) of empirical reality"—and, as Bürger notes, "the insertation of reality fragments into the work of art fundamentally transforms that work. The artist not only renounces shaping a whole, but gives the painting a different status, since parts of it no longer have the relationship to reality characteristic of the organic work of art."[60] Like Bürger, I disagree with Adorno's view that "the avant-gardiste work is the only possible authentic expression of the contemporary state of the world" (85). As Bürger acknowledges, however, Adorno's stance on this particular issue does not prevent him from giving an accurate account of the avant-garde—Adorno's aesthetic theory, as I have already argued, should perhaps primarily be understood as a *theory of modernism*.

A salient feature of that theory, Bürger says, again quoting Adorno, is the observation that in the modernist work "the negation of synthesis becomes a compositional principle" (79), a principle also at the heart of Benjamin's theory of baroque allegory, which Bürger does not fail to read "as a theory of the avant-gardiste (nonorganic) work of art" (68). In presenting his theory of baroque allegory, in *Ursprung des deutschen Trauerspiels* (1928), Benjamin himself points out its "remarkable analogies to present-day German literature" (by which he

60. Bürger, *Theory of the Avant-Garde*, p. 78.

means primarily German expressionism), analogies "most apparent in the use of language."[61] I do not think we can say, as Lukács did when attacking (and acknowledging the importance of) Benjamin's book, that it is really a thinly disguised treatise on contemporary modernist literature.[62] Parts of it, however, especially the chapter on "Allegory and Trauerspiel," can stand basically unaltered as a theory of modernism. One of the most striking aspects of Benjamin's whole argument is the way he separates allegory from the "theological symbol," which so drastically shaped romanticist aesthetics. In its insistence on "the indivisible unity of form and content," the symbol can have "an immeasurably comforting effect on the practice of investigation into the arts."

> The unity of the material and the transcendental object, which constitutes the paradox of the theological symbol, is distorted into a relationship between appearance and essence. The introduction of this distorted conception of the symbol into aesthetics was a romantic and destructive extravagance which preceded the desolation of modern art criticism. As a symbolic construct, the beautiful is supposed to merge with the divine in an unbroken whole. (160)

It is almost as if Benjamin had foreseen the fate of modernism at the hands of aesthetic criticism; the way modernist disjunctions and fragmentary structures have consistently been gathered in by critical authorities and embraced as "an unbroken whole," and, indeed, as a "theological symbol."

In baroque allegory the "false appearance of totality is extinguished" (176), as fragments are piled up, joined together without much regard for conventional textual synthesis, with the result that "it is as something incomplete and imperfect that objects stare out from the allegorical structure" (186). This structure of fragments resembles nothing so much as ruins: "In the ruin, history has physically merged into the setting. And in this guise history does not assume the form of the process of an

---

61. Walter Benjamin, *The Origin of German Tragic Drama*, trans. John Osborne (London: Verso, 1977), p. 54.
62. Lukács, *Wider den mißverstandenen Realismus*, pp. 42–43; *The Meaning of Contemporary Realism*, pp. 41–43.

eternal life so much as that of irresistible decay. Allegory thereby declares itself to be beyond beauty. Allegories are, in the realm of thoughts, what ruins are in the realm of things" (177–78).

It is not least language itself which lies in ruin, which has been fragmented to the degree that it is made useless for "practical," communicative purposes. Even works that appear to invite us into a holistic textual world turn out to be "ruinous" amalgamations of contorted language. We may discover that the fragmentary beginning of *Finnegans Wake* ("riverrun, past Eve and Adam's, from swerve of shore to bend of bay") is apparently recuperated at the end of the novel ("A way a lone a last a loved a long the"[63]), but the expectation that an awareness of a cyclical form is somehow going to create an unbroken whole through which to understand the work is bound to be frustrated to no end in reading the text supposedly "contained" within this cycle. *Finnegans Wake* is an extreme example of modernist writing in that "the rhetorical and instrumental subordination of narrative language to narrative representation can no longer be taken for granted," to quote another of Jameson's acute observations without accepting his interpretive perspective.[64]

In such writing, words, syntactic features, and generic qualities strive to break free from their conventional referential functions. Modernist practice is, not least, characterized by a radical realization that language has lost its innocence (if it ever had one), and that there may be something false about using it strictly as a communicative medium. One of the most famous and most discussed expressions of this loss of innocence is to be found in *A Farewell to Arms*:

> I was always embarrassed by the words sacred, glorious and sacrifice and the expression in vain. We had . . . read them, on proclamations that were slapped up by billposters over other proclamations, now for a long time, and I had seen nothing sacred and the things that were glorious had no glory. . . . There were many words that you could not stand to hear and finally only the names of places had dignity. Certain numbers were the same way and cer-

---

63. James Joyce, *Finnegans Wake* (New York: Viking Press, 1959), pp. 3, 628.
64. Jameson, *Fables of Aggression*, p. 7.

tain dates and these with the names of places were all you could say and have them mean anything.[65]

Less discussed, however, is the limited extent to which Hemingway, even at his most "hard boiled," displays this skepticism, this view of the futility of received language, *in practice* (and the same could be said of some other writers who have explicated this crisis of language, such as Hugo von Hofmannsthal, the author of *The Lord Chandos Letter*). It is noteworthy, though, that Hemingway's novel is set in World War I, and the above passage thus addresses the very crisis to which the Dadaists were responding in their semiotic attacks on the social sign-system,[66] attacks that constitute the most radical of modernist antireferential practices. There, the objects or words that stare out from the allegorical structure are frequently not even recognizable as words.

But what is the referential status of words or even letters that have been so radically displaced from their contextually codified functions? In discussing the fate of the object once it has been shorn of its initial significance (although I do not believe such intertextual ties can be fully severed), Benjamin claims that "it is now quite incapable of emanating any meaning or significance of its own; such significance as it has, it acquires from the allegorist. . . . In his hands the object becomes something different."[67] This seems to me one of the most baffling, but also one of the most challenging, aspects of Benjamin's theory of allegory. Who is the allegorist? It could be the writer, who rearranges the disjointed fragments and thus establishes a difference, an otherness (inherent in the very term *"allegoria"*), by making them refer to something else. At the same time, this reference is hardly just in the power of the writer. For the reader does not, because of the metamorphic difference that has been wrought upon the objects or words, have a sound basis to estab-

65. Ernest Hemingway, *A Farewell to Arms* (London: Jonathan Cape, 1957), pp. 161–62.

66. See Ruedolf E. Kuenzli, "The Semiotics of Dada Poetry," in Stephen C. Foster and Rudolf E. Kuenzli, ed., *Dada Spectrum: The Dialectics of Revolt* (Madison, Wisc.: Coda Press; Iowa City: University of Iowa, 1979), pp. 52–70, and his "Dada gegen den Ersten Weltkrieg."

67. Benjamin, *The Origin of German Tragic Drama*, p. 184.

lish any unequivocal frame of reference for the allegory; indeed, it would seem that the reader has to negotiate an otherness in his or her own terms. Does that not make the reader an allegorist?

Negativity and the Reader

Such thorough questioning as we find in Benjamin and Adorno's theories of modernism of what might be called the identity of texts clearly assumes that the reader is ready to accept an attitude of radical negativity with regard to received modes of communication. These aesthetics of negativity have recently come under fire from one of the most prominent aestheticians of reader response. Hans Robert Jauss seeks to argue that "if a new Enlightenment through aesthetic expression is to counter the anti-Enlightenment of the culture industry, the aesthetics of negativity must stop denying the communicative character of art. It must rid itself of the abstract "either-or" of negativity and affirmation and attempt to turn the norm-breaking forms of avant-gardist art into norm-creating achievements of the aesthetic experience."[68]

Perhaps the greatest problem with Jauss's critique is his ahistorical use of the concept of "aesthetic experience," which leads him to base it on "communication as catharsis" (xxxiii), and, centrally, on "identification." There is little doubt that identification is a core element of language use and communication, but to make it central to aesthetic experience is to surmise that aesthetic experience, like language, has its "natural" place or function as a medium of communication. While Adorno may be criticized for holding too tightly onto the sovereignty of the aesthetic experience, he at least seeks to define its role historically in modern society, a society that makes it necessary to be skeptical of identification, because of its easily manipulable aspects, intertwined with all the subtleties of power that modern democracy has to suffer. Jauss does not even grant Adorno's strategies of distancing and aesthetic-critical

68. Hans Robert Jauss, *Aesthetic Experience and Literary Hermeneutics*, trans. Michael Shaw (Minneapolis: University of Minnesota Press, 1982), p. xxxviii.

reflection the full status of "aesthetic experience," as becomes obvious when he says that his criticism of Adorno is "meant to introduce the attempt to justify aesthetic experience vis-à-vis a theoretical claim that neglects or suppresses the *primary* modes of this experience, especially *its communicative efficacy*, in favor of the higher level of aesthetic reflection" (21, my emphasis).

The claim that Adorno's aesthetics of negativity is "inappropriately one-sided in its emphasis on what is social in art, for it leaves out communicative functions" (16) indicates that Jauss has misunderstood Adorno's notion of anticommunication to be a wholesale rejection of communication. Adorno's theory of negative mimesis depends of course on traditional referentiality and communicative channels, even while it aims at subverting them (the same could be said of how Derrida's concepts of "différance" and deconstruction depend on our awareness of identity and mimetologism). Identification and referential efficacy are indisputable bases of social communication, but what is to be resisted is their congealment into a seductive power through which we come to equate enjoyment with identification and assent, as we see happening in this passage from Wayne Booth's *Rhetoric of Fiction*:

> The implied author of each novel is someone with whose beliefs on all subjects I must largely agree if I am to enjoy his work. . . . It is only as I read that I become the self whose beliefs must coincide with the author's. Regardless of my real beliefs and practices, I must subordinate my mind and heart to the book if I am to enjoy it to the full. The author creates, in short, an image of himself and another image of his reader; he makes his reader, as he makes his second self, and the most successful reading is one in which the created selves, author and reader, can find complete agreement.[69]

To pursue the implications of this view in a broader social context,[70] we might want to ask what kind of "readers" of

69. Wayne Booth, *The Rhetoric of Fiction* (Chicago and London: The University of Chicago Press, 1961), pp. 137–38.

70. Booth in fact elaborates on this context in his *Modern Dogma and the Rhetoric of Assent* (Notre Dame: University of Notre Dame Press, 1974). In this book, Booth voices a vehement disapproval of the skepticism inherent in modern-

culture are being "educated" through such handling of texts. Booth is likely to argue that such enjoyment through assent will enhance pluralistic tolerance for various cultural attitudes, but the ideological result might also prove to be subordination to existing cultural norms. This would concur with Franco Moretti's view that in Western capitalist society, "the substantial function of literature is to *secure consent*. To make individuals feel 'at ease' in the world they happen to live in, to reconcile them in a pleasant and imperceptible way to its prevailing cultural norms."[71]

Such social consumption presupposes a largely passive reception of cultural products, but it seems to me that one of the things modernist writing does *not* perpetrate, categorically speaking, is passive reception. In fact, while modernist works may be the vehicles of various ideological messages, they share an aggressively negative stance toward passive consumption. In a manner reminiscent of Barthes's theory of the "writerly text," Richard Poirier argues that "modernism manifests itself whenever a text chooses to demonstrate that one of its primary purposes is to expose the factitiousness of its own local procedures. In order to do this, it must make the experience of reading in some way almost directly analogous to the experience of writing."[72] From one angle this may seem to go completely against the grain of the act of reading, but if reading is an *act*, the question is whether creative intervention is any less a "natural" response to texts (including traditional or realist texts) than is identification. It is noteworthy that Jauss's colleague in the Konstanz school of reader-response aesthetics, Wolfgang Iser, places as much emphasis on intervention as Jauss does on identification.

According to Iser, the reading of a text, the appropriation of

---

ist practices (which he sees as being a significant factor in the student riots of the late sixties, for instance). The book contains some memorable utterances springing from this disapproval: "What do we know about the *arena of change*, the mind or self, if we know what no one in this hall seriously doubts? Remember: we must not cheat and fall back into modernism" (111). There are even some almost desperate remarks: "Sometimes we *understand* each other" (113; emphasis in original).

71. Moretti, *Signs Taken for Wonders*, p. 27 (emphasis in original).

72. Poirier, "The Difficulties of Modernism and the Modernism of Difficulty," p. 138.

an unfamiliar horizon of ideas and attitudes, is almost always a challenging experience. He notes that "the incorporation of the unfamiliar into our own range of experience has been to a certain extent obscured by an idea very common in literary discussion: namely, that the process of absorbing the unfamiliar is labeled as the *identification* of the reader with what he reads."[73] The extent to which Iser has gone in downgrading the role of identification is reflected in his assertion, in *The Act of Reading*, that "one only communicates that which is *not* already shared by sender and receiver."[74] But identification in terms of the reality shared by sender and receiver forms the basis of reference necessary for reading to even occur. Furthermore, we are all familiar with passive modes of reception that do not take us outside the received communicative "contract." Literature, like any other use of signs, frequently does little more than to confirm precisely that which is already shared. For Iser, however, "the reader's enjoyment begins when he himself becomes productive, i.e., when the text allows him to bring his own faculties into play" (108). Iser even comes close to ascribing an inherent adversarial function to literature, as we see when he discusses the structure underlying the reigning cultural model of reality: "The literary text, however, interferes with this structure, for generally it takes the prevalent thought system or social system as its context, but does not reproduce the frame of reference which stabilizes these systems" (71).

While Iser's theory is thus at least slightly idealistic, he nevertheless presents us with a valuable analysis of what happens when familiar consistency-building is intercepted in texts. He describes how, "whenever the flow is interrupted and we are led off in unexpected directions, the opportunity is given us to bring into play our own faculty for establishing connections—for filling in the gaps left by the text itself." He adds: "With 'traditional' texts this process was more or less unconscious, but modern texts frequently exploit it quite differently.

73. Wolfgang Iser, *The Implied Reader: Patterns of Communication in Prose Fiction from Bunyan to Beckett* (Baltimore: Johns Hopkins University Press, 1974), p. 291.
74. Wolfgang Iser, *The Act of Reading: A Theory of Aesthetic Response* (Baltimore: Johns Hopkins University Press, 1978), p. 29 (emphasis in original).

They are often so fragmentary that one's attention is almost exclusively occupied with the search for the connections between the fragments."[75] While Iser's theory is certainly applicable to traditional and realistic texts (as his own analyses demonstrate), its explanatory power only becomes fully apparent in the case of modernist writing, for it is here that the dialectics between what he calls "consistency-building" and the gaps or "blanks" that challenge it become highly prominent.

Consistency-building relates to the forming of a gestalt for the text, which involves the "process of grouping together all the different aspects of the text to form the consistency that the reader will always be in seach of. While expectations may be continually modified, and images continually expanded, the reader will still strive, even if unconsciously, to fit everything together in a consistent pattern" (283). In the case of modernism, as I have argued, consistency-building occurs through the constitution of a "realist" subtext that however is challenged, since the text interrupts the cultural matrix from which this subtext is drawn. In search of a code to explain a sign-function, we rummage through the various cultural patterns underlying our modes of communication, for, as Umberto Eco explains in his *Theory of Semiotics*, the act of communication, the use of a sign, *"presupposes a signification system as its necessary condition."*[76] What happens, then, in the case of a modernist disruption of conventional signification systems? Eco provides us with the following answer: "Faced with uncoded circumstances and complex contexts, the interpreter is obliged to recognize that the message does not rely on previous codes and yet that it must be understandable; if it is so, non-explicit conventions must exist; if not yet in existence, they have to exist (or be posited). Their apparent absence postulates their necessity" (129).

If we observe modernist writing in terms of communication, it seems apt to place it at the boundaries of received conventions and those "not yet in existence"; modernism both carries on and retards communication through its play with the ab-

75. Iser, *The Implied Reader*, p. 280.
76. Umberto Eco, *A Theory of Semiotics* (Bloomington: Indiana University Press, 1976), p. 9 (emphasis in original).

sence that postulates the necessity of the presence of codes. Modernist practice can therefore be analyzed as "rule-changing creativity" characterized by *"ratio difficilis"* (183–88), and in certain cases in terms of "a radical code-making, a violent proposal of new conventions" (254). But how far does modernism go in establishing new codes? What Eco has to say of the "aesthetic idiolect" may help us answer that question:

> Insofar as it is accepted by an artistic community and produces imitations, mannerisms, stylistic habits, etc., it becomes a *movement-idiolect*, or a *period-idiolect*, studied by criticism or the history of ideas as the main artistic feature of a given historical group or period. Insofar as it produces new norms accepted by an entire society, the artistic idiolect may act as *a meta-semiotic judgment changing common codes.* (272, emphasis in original)

As should be fully apparent by now, I do not think modernist practices have decisively changed prevalent signification systems of the cultural order. Modernism has largely remained a branch of "idiolects." This may be taken as a failure of modernism to enter fully what may be called social consciousness. But this also means that modernism has remained in a position of potential challenge to the cultural order. I think this prolonged estrangement of modernism from the "common codes" of society goes far toward explaining why modernism has been such a hotly contested field of research and why there are such radically divergent opinions of its meaning and function as a cultural practice. Precisely through its position of negativity, modernism not only challenges the prevalent communicative discourse of the sociosymbolic order, but also helps us to focus on and debate the nature and function of that very discourse. Even scholars like Foucault, who see the "return" of language in the modernist literature of the late nineteenth century, signifying the emergence of a new episteme, admit that the preceding Western episteme "still serves as the positive ground of our knowledge."[77]

Timothy Reiss, generalizing under the influence of Foucault, has argued how modern Western discourse, the "analytico-

77. Foucault, *The Order of Things*, p. 385.

referential," riding the wave of the European "desire for conquest, dominion, and possession,"[78] grew to be "the single *dominant* structure and the necessary form taken by thought, by knowledge, by cultural and social practices of all kinds. This dominance still exists today" (23). Reiss acknowledges, however, that this discourse is going through a period of crisis that is leading to a "significant and complete conceptual change" (9). This is certainly one reason for the significance of modernism: not only do we feel that it acts out the crisis of the symbolic order, of the system of codes that are still, however, essential for us as producers and receivers of signs and meaning, we also seek in it the *other* of the order that is still our world, an other which can at least hint to us what it is like *not* to be caught in the prevalent sociosymbolic network of meaning.

It may be objected that in speaking of modernism in terms of social codes and the symbolic order, I am forgetting what may seem a nonexplicit convention that plays a role in our attitude toward modernism, namely, the convention that partly regulates our traffic in the field of practice called "art." One of the major principles of this convention in bourgeois society is the act of bracketing off the individual work in order to contemplate it in relative isolation. It is a principle well represented by Mukařovský's dictum that "only as an integral work does the work of art fulfill its function as an aesthetic sign."[79] By making this convention cohere with the modernist rupture of conventional referentiality, several critics have, as I have shown, sought to portray the modernist work as the very perfection of such integral wholeness.

By adopting another perspective, however, we may see that precisely this convention also lends modernism a significant background for its subversive practices. As Eco points out in *A Theory of Semiotics*, in most communicative situations codes are complicated in order to introduce redundancy and elimi-

78. Timothy J. Reiss, *The Discourse of Modernism* (Ithaca, N.Y., and London: Cornell University Press, 1982), p. 21. The title of Reiss's book is misleading, to say the least. The modern Western discourse whose development Reiss is tracing is certainly not that of "modernism"; in fact, it is precisely the discourse of the social modernity that modernism can be seen as revolting *against*.

79. Jan Mukařovský, "Intentionality and Unintentionality in Art," *Structure, Sign and Function*, trans. and ed. John Burbank and Peter Steiner (New Haven, Conn., and London: Yale University Press, 1978), p. 89.

nate malfunction through noise (32–47). In aesthetic communication, however, tradition prescribes significance to each and every detail, since it is always taken to contribute to the integral whole of the work. This is why Kermode, in his discussion of modernism, is plainly wrong in asserting that "novelty in the arts is either communication or noise. If it is noise there is no more to say about it."[80] In art, noise occurs in a context that has already prescribed its significance. Modernism frequently makes use of this preestablished value in order to collapse practical hierarchies that we recognize from our enculturation as social beings. Using noise as communication—which in itself is a referential commentary on the "achievements" of instrumental communication that prevails in society—has been a major avant-garde device.

This cultural situation also helps to explain why works that greatly elaborate the processes of signification are often closely associated with those that blatantly reject such processes. As Iser remarks, using Joyce as an example, "overdetermination of a literary text does not, as one might suppose, produce semantic clarity but, on the contrary, splits the text up into a whole semantic spectrum." Further on, Iser says: "The blanks that arise out of the overprecision of representation cause the reader to become more and more disoriented."[81] Radical deployment of blanks and negations leads to a heightened level of "negativity" that is the "structure underlying the invalidation of the manifested reality" (229). Modernist texts carry within them a potentially radical cultural displacement that opens up the spectrum of received signification systems. Eco notes, in the case of "extra-coding," how "the criss-cross of circumstances and abductive presuppositions, along with the interplay of various codes and subcodes, makes the message (or the text) appear as an *empty form to which can be attributed various possible senses*" (139). It is precisely this momentary appearance of an empty form that modernism uses to break open received modes of communication and to question prevalent codes through which signs receive their signifying power. While "codes control the emission of messages," messages can, as Eco stresses,

80. Kermode, *The Sense of an Ending*, p. 102.
81. Iser, *The Act of Reading*, pp. 48, 207.

"restructure the codes" (161). Modernist practices often point toward an (impossibly) revolutionary restructuring of the codes, and thus toward a cultural reorientation the impact of which is hard to imagine because of the very "openness" of the semiotic revolt.[82]

As a Conclusion: Dialectics of Modernism

In this final section I shall not offer a summary conclusion of all my arguments. Such a procedure never does much justice to the process of working through the issues at hand and can only serve to reduce the value of deliberating the problematics of an entire cultural paradigm. There are of course certain obvious patterns in my argumentation, many of them, I hope, underpinning one of my chief aims, which runs alongside and interweaves with my critical examination of the emergence and the "creation" of a modernist paradigm. I am referring to my wish to show how modernism contains the rudiments of an adversary culture; how it tends to negate the cultural experience most readily furthered by bourgeois society; how it problematizes and seeks to interrupt the predominant modes of communication in this society. Instead of trying to put my various arguments in some kind of nutshell, I shall attempt to open up my previous discussion onto a broader horizon of cultural inquiry. There, I hope, after having frequently been compressed into issues regarding "literary" or "aesthetic" function, these

---

82. The challenging implications of Eco's discussion of the "open form" in *Theory of Semiotics* make his discussion of the "open text" in *The Role of the Reader* all the more disappointing. While he is right in noting that the reading of an "open text" does not simply involve "indiscriminate participation," he goes to the other extreme by judging such reading as "an oriented insertation into something which always remains the world intended by the author" (62). Thus, "when reading *Ulysses* one can extrapolate the profile of a 'good *Ulysses* reader' from the text itself. . . . As referred to an unsuitable reader (to a negative Model Reader unable to do the job he has just been postulated to do), *Ulysses qua Ulysses* could not stand up. At most it becomes another text" (9). I do not think that the text ever functions as "the text itself"; in fact, it makes more sense to say that it is *always* "another text," depending on the historical and readerly context into which the text enters. For a good critique of the-text-itself aesthetics, which includes a brief discussion of Eco's *The Role of the Reader*, see Tony Bennett, "Texts, Readers, Reading Formations," *Bulletin of the Midwest Modern Language Association* 16 (Spring 1983): 3–17.

arguments can be reconstituted as a criticism concerned with the function and treatment of *cultural products* in a broad sense.

It is a commonplace, in some circles, to assert that modernism has by now been fully assimilated into its cultural environment. Certain critics even hold that its aesthetics have been appropriated by its longtime enemy the culture industry or, through an even broader implication, by commercialism in general.

Various scholars have called attention to the parallels between the avant-garde, or modernism in general, on the one hand, and commercially engineered *fashion* on the other.[83] Both might, from this perspective, seem to effect a fragmentation and "interruption" of cultural continuities. Both evince a desire for "the new" and for some kind of shock effect, which can, however, only enjoy a short life of "success," since it rapidly gets assimilated by novelty-hunting recipients who will soon need another and "different" kind of newness. It has even been argued, for instance by Bruce Robbins, that "the techniques of the modernist classics have been incorporated into modernist commercials." Robbins quotes Andreas Huyssen's statement that by the 1960s, "the use of visual montage, one of the major inventions of the avant-garde, had already become standard procedure in commercial advertising, and reminders of literary modernism popped up in Volkswagen's beetle ads: 'Und läuft und läuft und läuft.' "[84]

But we should avoid short-circuit explanations on the basis of such parallels. The question to ask is whether "shock" and fragmentation serve the same *function* in both realms. Does an audience fed on modern commercials experience them at all as interruptions of its normative, lived experience in bourgeois society? It seems to me that while commercialism may seem bent on "refreshening" reality, its "shock" is ultimately *affirmative*; it is not out to estrange us from our familiar world. On

83. See Poggioli, *The Theory of the Avant-Garde*, pp. 79–84, although I disagree with Poggioli that the avant-garde transcends fashion only by creating its own classics (p. 84).

84. Bruce Robbins, "Modernism in History, Modernism in Power," in Robert Kiely, ed., *Modernism Reconsidered* (*Harvard English Studies* 11) (Cambridge, Mass., and London: Harvard University Press, 1983), pp. 234–35.

the contrary: it wishes to make us believe that the world we already know has a variety of purchasable excitements in store. Commercial interruption is always ultimately a form of repetition; thus, the commercial "und läuft und läuft und läuft" ("and runs and runs and runs") is typically—and in a way symbolically—a phrase that the audience (possibly prospective customers) is expected to learn and to associate pleasantly with a certain product. The social context in which a text, a message, is produced and communicated plays a determining role in its concretization. The commercial text, while it may require some "defamiliarization" (frequently in some form of "sensation"), is ultimately to bear a clear message; after all, its aim is not primarily to ask us to see reality anew, but to buy something. Such commercials are to be "lived" as a means of gaining access to the material environment, and as such they enter into other structures of bourgeois instrumental rationality.

In other words, commercials do not, however fragmentary they may appear, function as nonorganic texts, and they do not carry with them a sense of crisis in communication and meaning-production. They do not negate our normative social experiences. This is not to say that modernist devices cannot be appropriated for commercial purposes. A commercial may even use Stein's "A rose is a rose is a rose is a rose" (probably the phrase Huyssen sees behind the Volkswagen ad), thereby lending it the definite frame of reference that it strives to stave off. But is there *any* cultural product, however deviant, that is not cooptable for commercial purposes? Dick Hebdige explains that while punk represented "symbolic challenges to the symbolic order," when its stylistic innovations started attracting the media's attention the first step toward its cooptation was already taken. The material objects that the radical practices of punk had sought to empty of meaning are again turned into marketable commodities.[85]

If modernism has been coopted by commercialism, an equivalent form of assimilation has been taking place in the academy, as I discussed in chapter 2. Eagleton has mentioned how critics such as Lyotard refuse "to confront the disturbing fact

85. Hebdige, *Subculture*, pp. 92–93.

that modernism proved prey to institutionalization."[86] It is actually not difficult to imagine the academy, on behalf of the cultural order, as it were, institutionalizing various antibourgeois tendencies. But can the bourgeois order possibly erase every sign of an adversary culture—can there be total hegemony? The pessimism implicit in Adorno's writings seems to indicate that Western society is heading for precisely this totalized "rational" order. Raymond Williams has similarly pondered whether it is possible to have a hegemonic culture that would even produce and limit "its own forms of counterculture," but he rejects this notion, since it means reducing cultural objects to finished products of fixed positions.[87] As Schulte-Sasse points out, "every historical situation contains ideological ruptures and offers alternatives of thought."[88] One could perhaps, like Schulte-Sasse, chide Adorno for neglecting the potential of perhaps every cultural product to function in resistance to a hegemonic ratification, causing a fracture in the cultural order. We can also, however, adopt Adorno's theory of negativity without subscribing to his pessimism or what some undoubtedly call his "Schwarzmalerei." After all, the analyses Adorno has given us of the "negative" function of modernism clearly portray it as going against its dominant, "respectable" function in the modern academy. One might say, then, that if modernism proved prey to institutionalization, the institution has embraced a force that has the potential to rupture its totalized order.

This raises the question of whether modernism has an equivalent relation of negativity to other cultural "institutions." Having established the parallel between modernism and commercialism, Bruce Robbins, in the essay quoted above, concludes that "Leopold Bloom, advertising canvasser, is thus prophetic of what the literary modernism he embodied would become" (235). It seems to me that this assertion can be stood

86. Eagleton, "Capitalism, Modernism and Postmodernism," *Against the Grain*, p. 135.

87. Williams, *Marxism and Literature*, p. 114. Williams notes that *"no mode of production and therefore no dominant social order and therefore no dominant culture ever in reality includes and exhausts all human practice, human energy, and human intention"* (p. 125; emphasis in original).

88. Schulte-Sasse, foreword to Bürger, *Theory of the Avant-Garde*, p. xxix.

on its head, for we can just as well say that Bloom's function in *Ulysses* is indicative of how commercial products can be stripped of their intended function. Such products are context-dependent. Once torn out of the context they were intended for, they can be held up for critical reflection.

Once the various ads that Leopold Bloom encounters on June 16, 1904 have been processed through Joyce's narrative, they have been stripped of what Adorno would call their "positivity." They no longer appear as instrumental elements of an objective reality, but as arbitrary texts: cultural products serving certain purposes. "He eyed the horseshoe poster over the gate of college park: cyclist doubled up like a cod in a pot. Damn bad ad. Now if they had made it round like a wheel. Then the spokes: sports, sports, sports: and the hub big: college. Something to catch the eye."[89] As so often, we find Bloom "reading" his environment, in this case analyzing an ad with a view to its function and its dependence on the interplay of vision and desire. At the same time the ad has been robbed of its function and the reader receives it in a de-reified form as just one more linguistic fragment among many others making up the novel's massive textual flow. The stream imagery is sometimes used by Joyce in this context, as when Bloom sees a more successful ad by the river: "Good idea that. Wonder if he pays rent to the corporation. How can you own water really? It's always flowing in a stream, never the same, which in the stream of life we trace. Because life is a stream. All kind of places are good for ads" (153). Bloom is well aware of the power of commercial reportage, as we see most clearly in the Aeolus chapter: "It's the ads and side features sell a weekly not the stale news in the official gazette" (118). He may not be consciously critical of its power as this notion passes through his mind (although it is preceded by another, perhaps symbolic, thought as he passes by the printing machines: "Machines. Smash a man to atoms if they got him caught. Rule the world today"), but through the representation of his mental processes, commercial messages are torn out of the fabric where they belong, while at the same time their normative contexts are deliberated. At one point Bloom explains that "for an advertisement you must have repetition.

89. Joyce, *Ulysses*, p. 86.

That's the whole secret" (323). But the reader becomes aware that the ads that get repeated in the novel, such as the HELYS men and the Plumstree Potted Meat, occur in situations that manipulate and change their significance.

Joyce treats other elements of popular culture and the consciousness industry in a similar manner, constantly calling attention to them as "texts" occurring in different situations, arbitrary scraps of the semiotic flood of a single day. It seems to me that because of their manipulable and disjointed structures, modernist texts are well equipped to "reprocess" the messages of the culture industry in this way. Franco Moretti argues convincingly that Joyce's text unveils important elements of modern advertising and commodity fetishism by applying a principle of value equivalence that is irreducibly opposed to the hierarchical principles of bourgeois culture. But Moretti concludes by saying that this does not make *Ulysses* critical of any ideologies, since Joyce's experiments lack "any motivation and purpose."[90] This highlights the weighty issue of *reception*. Do we really have to be aware of an author's "motivation and purpose" for a text to be "critical"? Jameson contends, in discussing how *Ulysses* comes to terms with reification and alienation of the modern city, that the "recurrence of events and characters" throughout the novel is a process that continually suspends solidification of the text into a "codified symbolic order," a process, therefore, of "dereification."[91]

If this is the case, then the text has at least opened up a space for critical reception. But this means that the reader is in fact being asked not just to read and receive the text but to consciously *read into* it. In a sense, therefore, as Poirier has pointed out, modernism seeks to make the experience of reading analogous to that of writing;[92] it strives toward Barthes's ultimately unthinkable "writerly" text. Poirier also phrases the same idea differently: "Modernism happened when reading got to be grim" (125). There is no need to see grim reading as being restricted to the reception of isolated literary works. Why

90. Moretti, *Signs Taken for Wonders*, p. 207.
91. Jameson, "Ulysses in History," pp. 132–33.
92. Cf. the quotation above at n. 72 from Poirier, "The Difficulties of Modernism and the Modernism of Difficulty," p. 138.

should this activation of our self-conscious textual processing not reach beyond the work into our other involvements in signifying practices? Is it not possible to think of modernism as a pedagogic project, helping us to resist "innocent" reception and possible subjugation as we confront the rhetorical powers of various channels of communication?

This is what Anthony Libby suggests. He claims that "at least in non-totalitarian societies, one primary instrument of political oppression or manipulation is rhetoric,"[93] and that what modernism does to language is therefore of a primary political importance, since it breaks through habitualized communicative structures and calls signifying practices into question. From this perspective, modernism is seen as a potentially subversive semiotic force: what happens if we bring "modernist" reading practices to bear upon other "readerly" material? Perhaps this could be a version of the practice, mentioned by Eco, of changing the "content" of messages

> by acting on the circumstances in which the message will be received. This is a "revolutionary" aspect of a semiotic endeavor. In an era in which mass communication often appears as the manifestation of the domination which makes sure of social control by planning the sending of messages, it remains possible (as in an ideal semiotic "guerilla warfare") to change the circumstances in the light of which the addressees will choose their own ways of interpretation. In opposition to a *strategy* of coding, which strives to render messages redundant in order to secure interpretation according to pre-established plans, one can trace a *tactic* of decoding where the message as expression form does not change but the addressee rediscovers his *freedom of decoding*.[94]

Eco is clearly driven by the awareness that passive reception is perilous and alienating in a modern society of mass communication. Similarly, Richard Howard has pointed out, in a prefatory note to Barthes's *S/Z*, that "only when we know . . .

---

93. Anthony Libby, "Conceptual Space, The Politics of Modernism," *Chicago Review* 34 (Spring 1984): 21.

94. Eco, *A Theory of Semiotics*, p. 150, n. 27 (emphasis in original). See also Eco's "Towards a Semiological Guerilla Warfare," *Travels in Hyperreality*, trans. William Weaver (New York: Harcourt Brace Jovanovich, 1986), pp. 135–44.

what we are doing when we read, are we free to enjoy what we read. As long as our enjoyment is—or is said to be—instinctive, it is not enjoyment, it is terrorism" (p. ix).

But has modernism tended to foster a critical attitude of any particular kind? Bürger notes that while an avant-garde refusal to provide conventional forms of meaning is experienced as a shock by the recipient, this does not have any unequivocal results: "The problem with shock as the intended reaction of the recipient is that it is generally nonspecific. Even a possible breaking through the aesthetic immanence does not insure that the recipient's change of behavior is given a particular direction."[95]

The important thing is what happens *beyond* the shock effect, and Bürger goes on to discuss how trying to grasp for meaning can lead the recipient on to observing the principles of construction in the work (as we saw *Ulysses* inviting us to do). From this perspective, modernism is a mode of skeptical hermeneutics, critical of habitualized practices handed down to us by tradition. It is no coincidence, therefore, that Jürgen Habermas has recently been a staunch defender of modernism and its legacy, most notably in his already famous essay "Die Moderne: Ein unvollendetes Projekt."[96] Thus, in discussing the avant-garde's "anarchistic intention of blowing up the continuum of history," he notes that "the time consciousness articulated in avant-garde art is not simply ahistorical; it is directed against what might be called a false normativity in history."[97] The avant-garde can help us break the shackles of a bourgeois tradition that has placed ever-increasing value on instrumental rationality, and thus modernist practices can help revitalize the critical project of the Enlightenment and the communicative rationality that Habermas sees as a potential force countering the systematically distorted communication that to a high degree characterizes modern society.

But while resurrecting communicative rationality may be a

95. Bürger, *Theory of the Avant-Garde*, p. 80.
96. Jürgen Habermas, pub. in English as "Modernity versus Postmodernity," *New German Critique*, no. 22 (Winter 1981): 3–14, but later under its original title: "Modernity—An Incomplete Project," in Hal Foster, ed., *The Anti-Aesthetic*, pp. 3–15.
97. Habermas, "Modernity versus Postmodernity," p. 5.

potential role of modernism, the modernist function of interruption, by itself, is not unidimensional. Even if modernist
works are canceled realistic ones, as I have argued in Jameson's
wake, this hardly means that they lead us to construe any
single *specifically* different version of a "realistic" world. In
some ways modernism has certainly given us the "freedom of
decoding" that Eco mentions. This freedom, however, is also
the "other" of social modernity and its normative discourses.
We might do well here to recall Calinescu's arguments that
since the emergence of modernism, we can speak of two mutually conflicting modernities. If modernism is the other *modernity*, we must not overlook its potential role as a vehicle of the
other. In appearing to serve as the antithesis of regulative social
modernity, modernism does not only call for an "enlightened"
response. The "anarchistic" element that Habermas detects in
the avant-garde certainly does not always lead us to a determinate meaning. Its reference is often violently unclear; it often
seems, more than anything, to be a *search for meaning*, a search
caught between an enlightened response to the crisis of language and an anarchic abandonment amid the "ruins" of that
language.

Perhaps no one has realized this dialectic of modernism in a
more illuminating manner than Walter Benjamin, nowhere
more so than in his comments on the gesture ("Gestus") in the
works of two of his favorite writers, Franz Kafka and Bertolt
Brecht. The interruptions Brecht devised for his plays are of
special interest to Benjamin, for they break the work into a
series of gestures, and " 'making gestures quotable' is one of the
substantial achievements of the epic theater."[98] By isolating
and foregrounding various gestures involved in the theater performance, Brecht's (undeniably modernist) experiments aimed
at ripping apart the holistic fabric of both the work and our
received world view. With each of his gestures, however, Brecht
wanted to tear the audience out of its habitualized mode of
perception in order to present it with an "enlightened" vision of
the world. "We do not just want people to see simply 'differently,' we want them to see in quite a specific manner"[99]—

98. Benjamin, "What Is Epic Theater?" *Illuminations*, p. 151.
99. Bertolt Brecht, "Über gegenstandslose Malerei," *Über Politik und Kunst*,
ed. Werner Hecht (Frankfurt: Suhrkamp, 1971), p. 106.

something that Brecht, in refusing to resort to traditional methods, sometimes found hard to do. The process of the theatrical gesture, as Brecht understood it, involved not only pointing and seeing but also identifying, and, in more than one sense, *grasping*.

But Walter Benjamin finds no less significance in the gestures he observes in Kafka's work, and does not seem much troubled by their difference from those aimed for by Brecht. In the case of Kafka, the gesture—which is of course a referential act— takes place in "a code of gestures which surely had no definite symbolic meaning for the author from the outset; rather the author tried to derive such a meaning from them in ever-changing contexts and experimental groupings. . . . Like El Greco, Kafka tears open the sky behind every gesture," he "divests the human gesture of its traditional supports and then has a subject for reflection without end."[100] In Kafka's troubled gestures we see the modernist crisis of both the subject and its/our language. And his gesture lays no less of a claim on the reader than that of Brecht. At the end of *Der Prozeß* a window is opened, and "a person, feeble and thin in the distance and elevation, bent way forward with a jerk and stretched the arms still farther out" (194). Who is this gesture meant *for*? Josef K., or perhaps the baffled reader? And what does it *mean*? Is somebody offering help (interpretation), or is somebody asking for assistance (meaning)? In this way, the gesture may be enacting the very crisis we are experiencing as subjects and users of language. But while it may seem impossible to know what this gesture means, the act of reference is still there.

Kafka's own discourse is functioning at a metalevel in this case, describing as well as enacting a modernist crisis in meaning-production (and as a "story" or novel his narrative is certainly a significant example of that crisis). The communicative crisis we associate with modernism can be described as an urge to carry out the act of reference without the instrumental function of reference. What remains is the *act*—which we can link up variously with Nietzsche's "life and action," Lacan's "Real," or Artaud's "life." Perhaps we can see a relation between Kafka's window gesture and Artaud's notion of an act

100. Benjamin, "Franz Kafka: On the Tenth Anniversary of His Death," *Illuminations*, pp. 120–22.

with which "we are not referring to life as we know it from its surface of fact, but to that fragile, fluctuating center which forms never reach. And if there is still one hellish, truly accursed thing in our time, it is our artistic dallying with forms, instead of being like victims burnt at the stake, signaling through the flames."[101]

Signaling without using forms—this notion is not to be taken literally, since signaling requires the use of forms: the act involves the reference. But Artaud's statement is largely aimed at conventional communicative (including aesthetic) uses of language. We live in an age when language no longer adheres to life; "it is this painful cleavage which is responsible for the revenge of *things*" (8–9). This revenge occurs in the spectacle, in extreme gestures and physical expressions and in a "contagious delirium" (26). The theater is to be the arena of the "terrible and necessary cruelty which things can exercise against us" (79), it is to make language "express what it does not ordinarily express: to make use of it in a new, exceptional, and unaccustomed fashion; to reveal its possibilities for producing physical shock . . . to turn against language and its basely utilitarian, one could say alimentary, sources" (46).

The theater of cruelty is to make use of gestures (motioning, pointing, physical and linguistic expression) without the subsequent identification and grasping of what is being "pointed out" by the gestures. This idea is very much in tune with much poststructuralist theory, and it is hardly surprising that Jacques Derrida is strongly attracted to Artaud's theory of (non)reference. "The theater of cruelty is not a *representation*," Derrida says. "It is life itself, in the extent to which life is unrepresentable. Life is the nonrepresentable origin of representation."[102] This theater pursues the origin of representation (the nonrepresentable), even as it realizes that this origin does not exist. In destroying mimetic representation it seeks to make its own representation the impossible "autopresentation of pure visibility and even pure sensibility" (238). This is "less a question

101. Antonin Artaud, *The Theater and Its Double*, trans. Mary Caroline Richards (New York: Grove, 1958), p. 13.

102. Jacques Derrida, "The Theater of Cruelty and the Closure of Representation," *Writing and Difference*, trans. Alan Bass (Chicago: University of Chicago Press, 1978), p. 234.

of constructing a mute stage than of constructing a stage whose clamor has not yet been pacified into words" (240).

The "not yet" in Derrida's statement is a gesture toward (the nonexistent) origin of social representation, but he is of course referring to the violence done to the received and codified system of representation upon which we rely in any normative act of communication. That such violence is a major characteristic of modernist practice need not be harped on. We must move beyond the plain affirmation and reiteration of the modernist dispersal of meaning. The belief that there is a need for more than affirmation in our dealings with modernism is a major incentive behind the aesthetic theories of both Julia Kristeva and Jürgen Habermas.

In their differences, the writings of Kristeva and Habermas powerfully illustrate the dialectics so crucial for representation in modernist practice. Their differences in some ways correspond to those between the dramatic aesthetics of Artaud and Brecht and their varying notions of "gesture." But both Kristeva and Habermas respond to modernist practice in light of the fact that most of our social communication does *not* take place in such a disruptive manner.

In *Revolution in Poetic Language*, Kristeva explicates two functions of language, "*two modalities* of what is, for us, the same signifying process. We shall call the first 'the semiotic' and the second 'the symbolic.'"[103] The symbolic function is necessary "to express meaning in a communicable sentence between speakers. This function harbors coherence . . . or, in other words, social identity." This "thetic character of the signifying act, which establishes the transcendent object and the transcendent ego of communication (and consequently of sociability),"[104] has to be acknowledged, since it establishes a coherent relation between the subject and social discourse and enables the subject to communicate according to the inherent "contract" of language.

Kristeva's view of the historical development of the thetic language of communication runs in part parallel to that of

103. Julia Kristeva, *Revolution in Poetic Language*, trans. Margaret Waller (New York: Columbia University Press, 1984), pp. 23–24.
104. Kristeva, "From One Identity to an Other," *Desire in Language*, p. 131.

Adorno, except that where he stresses the increasingly ossified instrumentalization of normative communication, she emphasizes the patriarchal nature of the transcendental rationality underpinning such communication: the thetic function is a phallic function, just as the symbolic order is a patriarchy. Like Adorno, however, she sees a "revolution in poetic language" starting to take place in the late nineteenth century. This revolution, according to Kristeva, radically unbinds the "semiotic" energy of language. This energy is largely tapped from the *chora*, the "nonexpressive totality formed by the drives and their stases in a motility that is as full of movement as it is regulated." The *chora*, which is the "medium" of our presymbolic relationship with the mother, "is not yet a position that represents something for someone (i.e., it is not a sign). . . . The theory of the subject proposed by the theory of the unconscious will allow us to read in this rhythmic space, which has no thesis and no position, the process by which signifiance is constituted."[105]

What Kristeva calls "signifiance" involves the subject in the radically *other* of meaning, as language stripped of reference falls "back" on the physical, gestural, "semiotic" properties of language. Signifiance introduces an "aimless wandering within the identity of the speaker and the economy of its very discourse,"[106] and turns the subject into what Kristeva calls "sujet en procès," i.e., a subject that is both "in process" (aimlessly wandering) and "on trial." It is put on trial by thetic language due to its lack of adherence to the contract of social communication.

This latter sense of the concept is pivotal, for Kristeva wishes to forestall any "idealism" regarding the "escape" from the protective/protected language of the symbolic order. As soon as the semiotic properties of language seek to express themselves, they begin to be "grasped" by the policing faculties of the symbolic function. "All enunciation, whether of a word or of a sentence, is thetic. It requires an identification";[107] and Kristeva stresses, in a statement undoubtedly aimed at poststruc-

---

105. Kristeva, *Revolution in Poetic Language*, pp. 25–26.
106. Kristeva, "From One Identity to an Other," *Desire in Language*, p. 137.
107. Kristeva, *Revolution in Poetic Language*, p. 43.

turalist/deconstructive swerves into idealism, that without this acknowledgment "any reflection on significance, by refusing its thetic character, will continually ignore its constraining, legislative, and socializing elements: under the impression that it is breaking down the metaphysics of the signified or the transcendental ego, such a reflection will become lodged in a negative theology that denies their limitations."[108]

The disruptive semiotic function, however—and this is the latent force that Kristeva sees in modernist practices—"shows the constraints of a civilization dominated by transcendental rationality" (140), and thus destroys the "naturalness" of its limitations, showing them to be "subject" to flexibility and change. This radical "poetic function departs from the signified and the transcendental ego and makes of what is known as 'literature' something other than knowledge: the very place where social code is destroyed and renewed" (132).

From this social perspective, therefore, significance is a form of "defamiliarization"; the experience of the subject in process/ on trial makes language (and whatever it mediates) strange for us. Thus, the physical and gestural spontaneity advocated by Kristeva and Artaud can in fact be seen as a form of estrangement. While Derrida may in one sense be right in saying that Artaud's theater is irreconcilable with the "Verfremdungseffekt,"[109] in another sense the theater of cruelty is close to Brecht in blowing open received structures of signification and mediation. The "spontaneity" aimed for by Artaud's "spectacle" and "trance" is clearly a form of alienation from the immediacy that we "live" in normative habitualized communication.

It is precisely with regard to this "explosive" moment of reception that Habermas seems to share some of Kristeva's basic ideas about the "poetic revolution" of modernism. Both theorists see avant-garde strategies as having considerable emancipatory potential as they encounter the layers of the sociosymbolic order built into our structures of reception or into our "horizon of expectations," to use Jauss's term. This

---

108. Kristeva, "From One Identity to an Other," *Desire in Language,* p. 131.
109. Derrida, "The Theater of Cruelty and the Closure of Representation," *Writing and Difference,* p. 244.

encounter, by upsetting the subject's prevalent positioning in language, can serve to create a new space for the subject's understanding and expression. Such emancipation presupposes, however, that the crisis created in the relationship of subject and language is dealt with by our "thetic" or "rational" capacities.

This is where Kristeva and Habermas differ from Adorno, and in different ways also from thinkers like Lacan and Derrida. The latter tend to see rationality, as an instrument of the symbolic order, having always already engulfed the act of emancipation, or they assume that we can at most hope for brief interims of deconstructive "freedom." Habermas and Kristeva, on the other hand, hold that such margins of "otherness" can influence and even significantly change the "order" of our social discourse and interaction.

Habermas's view of communicative rationality is to a large extent based on the general argument that our perception of distorted communication arises from our built-in awareness of the ideal of undistorted social interaction, in which the subject is free from external domination. In this Habermas sees himself as opposed to the post-Enlightenment trend that dominates twentieth-century philosophy. He takes this trend to task in a recent book that bears the somewhat misleading title *Der philosophische Diskurs der Moderne*—misleading, because the thinkers involved, including Adorno, Horkheimer, Heidegger, Bataille, Foucault, and Derrida, have all, according to Habermas, followed Nietzsche's example in giving up the critical project of "the modern" and giving themselves over to "the postmodern," whose chief characteristic is the attempt totally to negate subject-centered reason.[110]

Our ability even to criticize reason and the "rational order," argues Habermas, involves the Enlightenment's legacy of rationality, democracy, and critique. This means, for instance, that any social discourse presupposes the existence of a relatively autonomous subject, the concept of which we can therefore not do without in critical theory. Hence, Habermas op-

110. Habermas, *Der philosophische Diskurs der Moderne: Zwölf Vorlesungen* (Frankfurt: Suhrkamp, 1985), p. 104. The title of the chapter on Nietzsche gives us a better idea of Habermas's main line of argument than the book title: "Eintritt in die Postmoderne: Nietzsche als Drehscheibe."

poses Adorno and Marcuse's proclamation that psychoanalysis is obsolete, and states that the Frankfurt School, like psychoanalysis, has sought to break "the power of the past over the present . . . through future-oriented memory."[111]

Habermas argues that the "postmodern" thinkers falsely equate social modernity with rationality, not realizing that what has happened is precisely the sliding apart of the two.[112] This state actually calls for an enhanced and revitalized rational critique of modernity and the pragmatic, instrumental rationality that serves to underpin its "order." Within the symbolic universe Habermas sees critique and communicative rationality as having space to battle the hegemonic tendencies of instrumental rationality, a space for the development of the capacity "to question the validity of social roles and norms of action."[113]

It is in this development that Habermas sees the importance of aesthetic practices, for like Kristeva, he sees them as part of the model for an unconstrained ego identity. Aesthetic expression, in particular the radicalized aesthetics of modernism, has emancipatory potential in that it can help to break the shackles that normative instrumental rationality forces upon our perception of, and contribution to, social life. What Iser would call the radical *blanks* in such texts can serve to open up the fractures of the symbolic order. Habermas also shares with Kristeva a critique of the "postmodern" thinkers who tear the modernist element of disruption out of its relation with theoretical and practical rationality.

That Habermas goes a step further in this direction than Kristeva can be seen from his employing the concept "Vernunftmoment" ("rational element")[114] for the disruptive potential of the avant-garde. While we can argue, along Habermas's lines, that this element of significatory "displacement" makes the receiver an "external observer," somewhat in the

111. Jürgen Habermas, "Moral Development and Ego Identity," *Communication and the Evolution of Society*, trans. Thomas McCarthy (Boston: Beacon Press, 1979), p. 69.

112. Habermas, *Der philosophische Diskurs der Moderne*, p. 12.

113. Habermas, "Moral Development and Ego Identity," *Communication and the Evolution of Society*, p. 84.

114. Habermas, *Der philosophische Diskurs der Moderne*, p. 117.

spirit of a Brechtian spectator, it seems overhasty to assume that he or she will automatically fill up the "blank" with "metalanguages" of skeptical hermeneutics and rational critique.[115] Rather, in order for it to resist the power of instrumental understanding, this semiotic gap must be experienced as an *interruption*, a dialectical hesitation, as it were, between sense and non-sense, approaching Artaud's "unique language halfway between gesture and thought."[116]

Given such reservations, we can still look to Habermas for a fruitful view of modernism as an adversary culture and as an aesthetic force blowing open the social strata of false normativity. And by working through the parallel traits of the seemingly very different theoretical projects of Habermas and Kristeva, I hope to have elucidated the dialectic at work behind an apparent contradiction of modernist aesthetics. This "contradiction" has in a sense emerged as a reformulation of a related opposition discussed earlier, namely, between modernism as, on the one hand, a culturally subversive force, and an aesthetic-formalist project on the other. But in this dialectic there is no escape from the issue of the social function of modernist practice, since the role of its interruption points both toward the *opening up of critical space* and a *liberation from the repressive forces of rationality*. Clearly the critical element is pivotal in order for modernism to be a breeder of "grim reading." By interrupting the "realistic" processes of habitualized communication, modernism holds forth strategies of creative reading that can be used to unveil the discrepancies of a meaning production tending toward hegemony and to carry on a semiotic warfare against the homogenizing forces of mass communication.

But the need for such critique arises from the desire to be freed from social repression, from the violence and reproductive potential of the "transcendental signified." This revolutionary aspect of modernist interruption runs parallel to the "postmodern" or post-Enlightenment tradition Habermas has

115. For Habermas's notion of metalanguages and the external observer, see "The Hermeneutic Claim to Universality," in Josef Bleicher, ed., *Contemporary Hermeneutics: Hermeneutics as Method, Philosophy and Critique* (London: Routledge and Kegan Paul, 1980), pp. 181–211.

116. Artaud, *The Theater and Its Double*, p. 89.

recently taken to task for, in a sense, bringing "skeptical her-meneutics" to the point of rejecting any "rational" order, in-cluding, therefore, the basis of any critique except "blind" negation. It is precisely in this blindness that Kristeva sees the dangers of the radicalized "semiotic" function of language, in the "lost" subject and in the cult of the signifier: "Psychosis and fetishism represent the two abysses that threaten the un-stable subject of poetic language, as twentieth-century litera-ture has only too clearly demonstrated."[117] Hence, as Haber-mas would insist, we can only "distance" ourselves from the symbolic order by supplementing the "revolution in poetic language" with a critical observation of prevalent principles of construction and mediation.

This goes far toward explaining the importance of Haber-mas's contribution to the debate about modernism and post-modernism. The main problem with Habermas's view of mod-ernism, however, stems from his insistence on the separation of differentiated fields of knowledge, philosophy and literature in particular. This insistence blinds him to the way in which thinkers like Nietzsche, Adorno, and Derrida have elucidated the dialectics of modernism, partly by erasing the boundaries between aesthetic, philosophical, and ideological concerns. From Habermas's perspective the projects of Adorno and Der-rida are undermined by the fact that they prove unable to perform their critique of subject-centered reason without fall-ing back upon the medium of that reason.[118] But the same holds true for any "understanding" of modernist practices, and it is hard to see why the receiver of post-Enlightenment philos-ophy should not also supply this discourse with the "Vernunft-moment" integral to the critique of instrumental rationality. For Habermas, however, the interruptive practices of the avant-garde seem operative only within a differentiated aesthetic/literary field. He therefore risks deflating the potential force of modernist interruption.

We see an analogous procedure at the end of Mary Louise Pratt's study of literary discourse from the perspective of speech-act theory, when she acknowledges that linguistic rule-

---

117. Kristeva, "From One Identity to an Other," *Desire in Language*, p. 139.
118. Habermas, *Der philosophische Diskurs der Moderne*, p. 219.

breaking carries social weight as an expression of "hostility," provoking the breakdown of the "cooperative principle," but adds that in literature such threats are thought to be (in William Labov's words) "insulated from further consequences."[119] From this vantage point, modernist practices could be seen as a kind of "outlet" for deviance, a temporary collapse of communication, "allowing people to express real hostility in a nondestructive way" (222).

The relevance of modernism depends upon our resisting the insulation of literature. The relative autonomy of literature must not be reified into a rigid separation of "literary" expression from social discourse. Modernism must reach beyond a purely aesthetic function if its "destructive" practices are to be a critical and potentially subversive force, if its interruptions are to unearth the ruptures inherent in every historical moment. And since no linguistic expression can avoid being contaminated by the sociosymbolic order, our awareness of such ruptures or interruptions is inevitably a form of historical consciousness.

As a historical paradigm, then, modernism is caught between the crisis or even breakdown of modern rational discourse and the attempts of that very discourse to critique its own social and ideological effects and functions. The various individual devices of modernist disruption or interruption are elements of a paradigmatic effort to interrupt the "progress" of rationality, and perhaps to initiate a "new" discourse, which we can, however, not really know, since it is (still) the negativity of the discourse in which we are immersed. It is the other (of) modernity, or, to put it differently, it is modernity held in abeyance.

Such (in Habermas's words) future-oriented memory, however, is a way to think about the present. Or, even better, it is a means of *speaking* about the present. We can observe modernist interruption as a gesture halting monological speech in its various social and political guises. By interrupting a discourse (or by consciously making "use" of an interruption), we are implicitly claiming the right to participate in and even change that discourse; we are insisting on our right to speak and write. I doubt that anyone has put this more succinctly than Ernst

119. Pratt, *Toward a Speech Act Theory of Literary Discourse*, p. 221.

Bloch in his already quoted statement that "perhaps real reality is also an interruption."[120] But if this is a lesson we can gather from the century-long history of modernist practices, it is obvious that the main thrust of modernism today is hardly aimed at tradition as such, but at an instrumental rationality that is seeking to incorporate even the disruptive forms of its opposition. In the meantime modernism, in its own negative way, may have become a "tradition." But if so, it is a tradition powerfully emitting a message that a dedicated aesthetician of interruption, Walter Benjamin, formulated in a now familiar statement: "In every era the attempt must be made anew to wrest tradition away from a conformism that is about to overpower it."[121]

120. Bloch, "Diskussionen über Expressionismus," in Schmitt, ed., *Die Expressionismusdebatte*, p. 186.
121. Benjamin, "Theses on the Philosophy of History," *Illuminations*, p. 255.

Bibliography

A list of critical and theoretical sources consulted for this study.

Abrams, M. H. *A Glossary of Literary Terms*, 4th ed. New York: Holt, Rinehart and Winston, 1981.

Ackroyd, Peter. *Notes for a New Culture: An Essay on Modernism*. New York: Barnes and Noble, 1976.

Adams, Robert M. *After Joyce: Studies in Fiction after* Ulysses. New York: Oxford University Press, 1977.

———. "What Was Modernism?" *Hudson Review* 31 (Spring 1978): 19–33.

Adorno, Theodor W. *Ästhetische Theorie* (*Gesammelte Schriften*, vol. 7). Ed. Gretel Adorno and Rolf Tiedemann. Frankfurt: Suhrkamp, 1970. Trans. C. Lenhardt: *Aesthetic Theory*. London: Routledge and Kegan Paul, 1984.

———. *Prisms*. Trans. Samuel and Shierry Weber. Cambridge, Mass.: MIT Press, 1981.

———. *Über Walter Benjamin*. Ed. Rolf Tiedemann. Frankfurt: Suhrkamp Taschenbuch, 1970.

———. *Versuch, das Endspiel zu verstehen: Aufsätze zur Literatur des 20. Jahrhunderts I*. Frankfurt: Suhrkamp Taschenbuch, 1973.

———. *Zur Dialektik des Engagements: Aufsätze zur Literatur des 20. Jahrhunderts II*. Frankfurt: Suhrkamp Taschenbuch, 1973.

Alter, Robert. *Partial Magic: The Novel as a Self-Conscious Genre*. Berkeley: University of California Press, 1975.

Althusser, Louis. *Lenin and Philosophy and Other Essays*. Trans. Ben Brewster. New York: Monthly Review Press, 1971.

Altieri, Charles. "An Idea and Ideal of a Literary Canon." In Robert van

Hallberg, ed., *Canons*. Chicago: University of Chicago Press, 1984, pp. 41–64.

Apel, Karl-Otto, et al., ed. *Hermeneutik und Ideologiekritik*. Frankfurt: Suhrkamp, 1971.

Apollonio, Umbro, ed. with an intro. *Futurist Manifestos*. New York: Viking, 1973.

Artaud, Antonin. *The Theater and Its Double*. Trans. Mary Caroline Richards. New York: Grove, 1958.

Auerbach, Erich. *Mimesis: The Representation of Reality in Western Literature*. Trans. Willard R. Trask. Princeton, N.J.: Princeton University Press, 1953.

Bakhtin, Mikhail. *Problems of Dostoevsky's Poetics*. Ed. and trans. Caryl Emerson. Minneapolis: University of Minnesota Press, 1984.

———. *Rabelais and His World*. Trans. Helene Iswolsky. Bloomington: Indiana University Press, 1984.

Ball, Hugo. *Der Künstler und die Zeitkrankheit: Ausgewählte Schriften*. Ed. Hans B. Schlichting. Frankfurt: Suhrkamp, 1984.

Barth, John. "The Literature of Exhaustion." *Atlantic Monthly*, August 1967, pp. 29–34.

———. "The Literature of Replenishment: Postmodernist Fiction." *Atlantic Monthly*, January 1980. pp. 65–71.

Barthes, Roland. *Critical Essays*. Trans. Richard Howard. Evanston, Ill.: Northwestern University Press, 1972.

———. *Image-Music-Text*. Ed. and trans. Stephen Heath. Glasgow: Fontana/Collins, 1977.

———. *The Rustle of Language*. Trans. Richard Howard. New York: Hill and Wang, 1986.

———. *S/Z*. Trans. Richard Miller. London: Jonathan Cape, 1974.

———. *Writing Degree Zero*. Trans. Annette Lavers and Colin Smith. New York: Hill and Wang, 1968.

Baudelaire, Charles. *Baudelaire as a Literary Critic: Selected Essays*. Ed. and trans. Lois Boe Hyslop and Francis E. Hyslop, Jr. University Park, Pa.: Pennsylvania State University Press, 1964.

Baudrillard, Jean: *Selected Writings*. Ed. Mark Poster. Stanford: Stanford University Press, 1988.

———. *Simulations*. Trans. Paul Foss, Paul Patton, and Philip Beitchman. New York: Semiotext(e), 1983.

Baumgart, Reinhard. *Aussichten des Romans oder Hat Literatur Zukunft?* Münich: Deutscher Taschenbuch Verlag, 1970.

Beebe, Maurice. "What Modernism Was." *Journal of Modern Literature* 3 (July 1974): 1065–84.

Bell, Daniel. "Beyond Modernism, Beyond Self." *The Winding Passage: Essays and Sociological Journeys, 1960–1980*. New York: Basic, 1980.

———. *The Cultural Contradictions of Capitalism*. New York: Basic, 1976.

Benjamin, Walter. *Illuminationen: Ausgewählte Schriften*. Ed. Siegfried Unseld. Frankfurt: Suhrkamp Taschenbuch, 1980.

——. *Illuminations*. Ed. Hanna Arendt; trans. Harry Zohn. New York: Schocken Books, 1969.

——. *The Origin of German Tragic Drama*. Trans. John Osborne. London: Verso, 1977.

——. *Reflections: Essays, Aphorisms, Autobiographical Writings*. Ed. Peter Demetz; trans. Edmund Jephcott. New York: Harcourt Brace Jovanovich, 1978.

——. *Versuche über Brecht*. Ed. Rolf Tiedemann. Frankfurt: Suhrkamp, 1978.

Bennett, Tony. "Texts, Readers, Reading Formations." *The Bulletin of the Midwest Modern Language Association* 16 (Spring 1983): 3–17.

Benstock, Shari. *Women of the Left Bank: Paris, 1900–1940*. Austin: University of Texas Press, 1986.

Bergonzi, Bernard. "The Advent of Modernism." In Bernard Bergonzi, ed., *The Twentieth Century* (*History of Literature in the English Language*, vol. 7). London: Barrie & Jenkins, 1970, pp. 17–45.

Berman, Marshall. *All That Is Solid Melts into Air: The Experience of Modernity*. New York: Simon and Schuster, 1982.

Bigsby, C. W. E. *Dada and Surrealism*. London: Methuen, 1972.

Binder, Hartmut. *Kafka-Kommentar zu den Romanen, Rezensionen, Aphorismen und zum Brief an den Vater*. Munich: Winkler, 1976.

Blanchot, Maurice. *The Gaze of Orpheus and Other Literary Essays*. Trans. Lydia Davis. New York: Station Hill Press, 1981.

Bloch, Ernst, et al. *Aesthetics and Politics*. London: New Left Books, 1977.

Bloom, Harold. *The Anxiety of Influence: A Theory of Poetry*. New York: Oxford University Press, 1973.

——. "The Dialectics of Literary Tradition." *Boundary 2* 2 (Spring 1974): 528–38.

Booth, Wayne C. *Modern Dogma and the Rhetoric of Assent*. Notre Dame: University of Notre Dame Press, 1974.

——. *The Rhetoric of Fiction*. Chicago: University of Chicago Press, 1961.

Bradbury, Malcolm. "The Novel in the 1920's." In Bernard Bergonzi, ed., *The Twentieth Century* (*History of Literature in the English Language*, vol. 7). London: Barrie & Jenkins, 1970, pp. 180–221.

——. *The Social Context of Modern English Literature*. New York: Schocken Books, 1971.

——, ed. *The Novel Today: Contemporary Writers on Modern Fiction*. Glasgow: Fontana/Collins, 1977.

——, and James McFarlane, ed. *Modernism 1890–1930*. Harmondsworth, Eng.: Penguin Books, 1976.

Brecht, Bertolt. *Brecht on Theatre*. Ed. and trans. John Willet. London: Methuen, 1978.

————. *Gesammelte Werke*, vols. 15–19. Frankfurt: Suhrkamp, 1967.

————. *Schriften zum Theater: Über eine nicht-aristotelische Dramatik*. Frankfurt: Suhrkamp, 1977.

————. *Über Politik und Kunst*. Ed. Werner Hecht. Frankfurt: Suhrkamp, 1971.

Breton, André. *Manifestoes of Surrealism*. Trans. Richard Seaver and Helen R. Lane. Ann Arbor: University of Michigan Press, 1972.

Broch, Hermann. *Die Schlafwandler: Eine Romantrilogie (Kommentierte Werkausgabe*, vol. 1). Ed. Paul Michael Lützeler. Frankfurt: Suhrkamp Taschenbuch, 1978.

Brooks, Cleanth. *Modern Poetry and the Tradition*. Chapel Hill: University of North Carolina Press, 1939.

————. *The Well Wrought Urn*. New York: Harcourt, Brace & World, 1975.

Bruns, Gerald L. *Modern Poetry and the Idea of Language: A Critical and Historical Study*. New Haven, Conn.: Yale University Press, 1974.

Buchloh, Benjamin H.D., Serge Guilbaut, and David Solkin, ed. *Modernism and Modernity: The Vancouver Conference Papers*. Halifax, Nova Scotia: Press of the Nova Scotia College of Art and Design, 1983.

Bürger, Christa, and Peter Bürger, ed. *Postmoderne: Alltag, Allegorie und Avantgarde*. Frankfurt: Suhrkamp Taschenbuch, 1987.

Bürger, Christa, Peter Bürger, and Jochen Schulte-Sasse, ed. *Naturalismus/Ästhetizismus*. Frankfurt: Suhrkamp Taschenbuch, 1979.

Bürger, Peter. "The Significance of the Avant-Garde for Contemporary Aesthetics: A Reply to Jürgen Habermas." *New German Critique*, no. 22 (Winter 1981): 19–22.

————. *Theorie der Avantgarde*. Frankfurt: Suhrkamp, 1974. Trans. Michael Shaw; foreword Jochen Schulte-Sasse: *Theory of the Avant-Garde*. Minneapolis: University of Minnesota Press, 1984.

————. *Vermittlung—Rezeption—Funktion: Ästhetische Theorie und Methodologie der Literaturwissenschaft*. Frankfurt: Suhrkamp Taschenbuch, 1979.

Calinescu, Matei. "Avant-Garde, Neo-Avant-Garde, Post-Modernism: The Culture of Crisis." *Clio* 4 (1975): 317–40.

————. *Faces of Modernity: Avant-Garde, Decadence, Kitsch*, Bloomington: Indiana University Press, 1977.

Cawelti, John G. *The Six-Gun Mystique*. Bowling Green, Ohio: Bowling Green University Popular Press, n.d.

Chefdor, Monique, Ricardo Quinones, and Albert Wachtel, ed., *Modernism: Challenges and Perspectives*. Urbana: University of Illinois Press, 1986.

Chiari, Joseph. *The Aesthetics of Modernism*. London: Vision, 1970.

Coblentz, Stanton A. *The Literary Revolution*. New York: Frank Maurice, 1927 (rpt. New York: Johnson Reprint Corporation, 1969).

Conradi, Peter. *John Fowles*. London: Methuen, 1982.

Conroy, Mark. *Modernism and Authority: Strategies of Legitimation in Flaubert and Conrad*. Baltimore: Johns Hopkins University Press, 1985.

Craig, David. *The Real Foundations: Literature and Social Change*. London: Chatto and Windus, 1973.

Creighton, Joanne V. "The Reader and Modern and Post-Modern Fiction." *College Literature* 9 (Fall 1982): 216–30.

Cronin, Anthony. *A Question of Modernity*. London: Secker and Warburg, 1966.

Culler, Jonathan. *Flaubert: The Uses of Uncertainty*. Ithaca, N.Y.: Cornell University Press, 1974.

———. *Structuralist Poetics: Structuralism, Linguistics and the Study of Literature*. London and Henley: Routledge & Kegan Paul, 1975.

———. "*The Uses of Uncertainty* Re-viewed." In Paul Hernadi, ed., *The Horizon of Literature*. Lincoln: University of Nebraska Press, 1982, pp. 299–306.

Davies, Alistair. *An Annotated Critical Bibliography of Modernism*. Totowa, N.J.: Barnes and Noble, 1982.

Davison, Ned J. *The Concept of Modernism in Hispanic Criticism*. Boulder, Colo.: Pruett Press, 1966.

DeKoven, Marianne. *A Different Language: Gertrude Stein's Experimental Writing* (Madison: University of Wisconsin Press, 1983).

———. "Gertrude Stein and the Modernist Canon." In Shirley Neuman and Ira B. Nadel, ed., *Gertrude Stein and the Making of Literature*. Boston: Northeastern University Press, 1988, pp. 8–20.

Deleuze, Gilles and Félix Guattari. *Anti-Oedipus: Capitalism and Schizophrenia*. Trans. Robert Hurley, Mark Seem, and Helen R. Lane. Minneapolis: University of Minnesota Press, 1983.

de Man, Paul. "Literary History and Literary Modernity." *Blindness and Insight: Essays in the Rhetoric of Contemporary Criticism*. New York: Oxford University Press, 1971.

Demetz, Peter. "Zur Definition des Realismus." *Literatur und Kritik* 16/17 (August 1967): 333–44.

Derrida, Jacques. *Of Grammatology*. Trans. Gayatri Chakravorty Spivak. Baltimore: Johns Hopkins University Press, 1976.

———. *Writing and Difference*. Trans. Alan Bass. Chicago: University of Chicago Press, 1978.

Di Girolamo, Constanzo. *A Critical Theory of Literature*. Madison: University of Wisconsin Press, 1981.

Donoghue, Denis. "The Holy Language of Modernism." In George Watson, ed., *Literary English since Shakespeare*. London: Oxford University Press, 1970, pp. 386–407.

Ducrot, Oswald, and Tzvetan Todorov. *Encyclopedic Dictionary of the Sciences of Language*. Trans. Catherine Porter. Baltimore: Johns Hopkins University Press, 1979.

Eagleton, Terry. *Against the Grain: Essays, 1975–1985*. London: Verso, 1986.

———. *The Function of Criticism: From* The Spectator *to Post-Structuralism*. London: Verso, 1984.

———. *Literary Theory: An Introduction*. Minneapolis: University of Minnesota Press, 1983.

Eco, Umberto. *Postscript to The Name of the Rose*. Trans. William Weaver. New York: Harcourt Brace Jovanovich, 1984.

———. *The Role of the Reader*. Bloomington: Indiana University Press, 1979.

———. *A Theory of Semiotics*. Bloomington: Indiana University Press, 1976.

———. *Travels in Hyperreality*. Trans. William Weaver. New York: Harcourt Brace Jovanovich, 1986.

Egri, Peter: *Avantgardism and Modernity: A Comparison of James Joyce's* Ulysses *with Thomas Mann's* Der Zauberberg *and* Lotte in Weimar. (Department of English Monograph Series, vol. 14). Trans. Paul Aston. Tulsa, Okla: University of Tulsa; Budapest: Akademiai Kiado, 1972.

Ehrlich, Hayward, ed. *Light Rays: James Joyce and Modernism*. New York: New Horizon Press, 1984.

Eliot, T. S. *Selected Essays, 1917–1932*. New York: Harcourt, Brace, 1932.

———. *Selected Prose of T. S. Eliot*. Ed. with intro. by Frank Kermode. New York: Harcourt Brace Jovanovich/Farrar, Straus and Giroux, 1975.

Emrich, Wilhelm. *Protest und Verheißung: Studien zur klassischen und modernen Dichtung*, 2d ed. Frankfurt and Bonn: Athenäum, 1963.

Eysteinsson, Astradur. "Baráttan um raunsæið: Um módernisma, raunsæi og hefð." *Tímarit Máls og menningar* 45 (1984): 418–43.

———. "Fyrsta nútímaskáldsagan og módernisminn." *Skírnir* 162 (1988): 273–316.

———. "Hvað er póstmódernismi?: Hvernig er byggt á rústum?" *Tímarit Máls og menningar* 49 (1988): 425–54.

Faulkner, Peter. *Modernism*. London: Methuen, 1977.

Fiedler, Leslie A. "Cross the Border—Close That Gap: Post-Modernism." In Marcus Cunliffe, ed., *American Literature since 1900, History of Literature in the English Language*, vol. 9. London: Barrie and Jenkins, 1975, pp. 344–66.

Fish, Stanley. *Is There a Text in This Class?: The Authority of Interpretive Communities*. Cambridge, Mass.: Harvard University Press, 1980.

Fokkema, Douwe W. *Literary History, Modernism, and Postmodernism* (Harvard University Erasmus Lectures, Spring 1983). Utrecht Publications in General and Comparative Literature, vol. 19. Philadelphia: John Benjamins, 1984.

———. "A Semiotic Definition of Aesthetic Experience and the Period

Code of Modernism: With Reference to an Interpretation of *Les Faux-Monnayeurs.*" *Poetics Today* 3 (Winter 1982): 61–79.

Forster, John Burt, Jr. *Heirs to Dionysus: A Nietzsche an Current in Literary Modernism.* Princeton, N.J.: Princeton University Press, 1981.

Foster, Hal. "The Problem of Pluralism." *Art in America* (January 1982): 9–15.

———, ed. *The Anti-Aesthetic: Essays on Postmodern Culture.* Port Townsend, Wash.: Bay Press, 1983.

Foster, Stephen C., and Rudolf E. Kuenzli, ed. *Dada Spectrum: The Dialectics of Revolt.* Madison: Coda Press; Iowa City: University of Iowa, 1979.

Foucault, Michel. *Language, Counter-Memory, Practice: Selected Essays and Interviews.* Ed. Donald F. Bouchard, trans. Donald F. Bouchard and Sherry Simon. Ithaca, N.Y.: Cornell University Press, 1977.

———. *The Order of Things: An Archaeology of the Human Sciences.* New York: Vintage Books, 1973.

Frank, Joseph. "Spatial Form in Modern Literature." *The Widening Gyre: Crisis and Mastery in Modern Literature.* New Brunswick, N.J.: Rutgers University Press, 1963, pp. 3–62.

Friedman, Susan Stanford. *Psyche Reborn: The Emergence of H. D.* Bloomington: Indiana University Press, 1981.

Friedrich, Hugo. *Die Struktur der modernen Lyrik: Von der Mitte der neunzehnten bis zur Mitte des zwanzigsten Jahrhunderts* (rev. ed.). Hamburg: Rowohlt Taschenbuch, 1967.

Frye, Northrop. *Anatomy of Criticism: Four Essays.* Princeton, N.J.: Princeton University Press, 1957.

Fuchs, Daniel. "Saul Bellow and the Modern Tradition." *Contemporary Literature* 15 (Winter 1974): 67–89.

Gablik, Suzi. *Has Modernism Failed?* New York: Thames and Hudson, 1984.

Gadamer, Hans-Georg. "The Universality of the Hermeneutic Problem." Trans. David Linge. In Josef Bleicher, ed., *Contemporary Hermeneutics: Hermeneutics as Method, Philosophy and Critique.* London: Routledge & Kegan Paul, 1980, pp. 128–40.

———. *Wahrheit und Methode: Grundzüge einer philosophischen Hermeneutik,* 3d ed. Tübingen: J. C. B. Mohr (Paul Siebeck), 1972.

Galloway, David D. "Postmodernism." *Contemporary Literature* 14 (Summer 1973): 398–405.

Gardner, John. *On Moral Fiction.* New York: Basic, 1978.

Garton, Janet, ed. *Facets of European Modernism* (Essays in honour of James McFarlane presented to him on his 65th birthday, 12 December 1985). Norwich, Eng.: University of East Anglia, 1985.

Garvin, Harry R., ed. *Romanticism, Modernism, Postmodernism (Bucknell Review* 25). Lewisburg, Pa.: Bucknell University Press, 1980.

Gass, William H. *Fiction and the Figures of Life*. Boston: Nonpareil Books, 1971.

Gibian, George and H. W. Tjalsma, ed. *Russian Modernism: Culture and the Avant-Garde, 1900–1930*. Ithaca, N.Y.: Cornell University Press, 1976.

Gilbert, Sandra M. "Costumes of the Mind: Transvestism as Metaphor in Modern Literature." In Elizabeth Abel, ed., *Writing and Sexual Difference*. Chicago: University of Chicago Press, 1982.

Gilbert, Sandra M., and Susan Gubar. *The Madwoman in the Attic: The Woman Writer and the Nineteenth-Century Literary Imagination*. New Haven, Conn.: Yale University Press, 1979.

———. *No Man's Land: The Place of the Woman Writer in the Twentieth Century*. Vol. 1—*The War of the Words*. New Haven, Conn.: Yale University Press, 1988.

———. "Tradition and the Female Talent." In Herbert L. Sussman, ed., *Literary History: Theory and Practice. Proceedings of the Northeastern University Center for Literary Studies*, vol. 2, 1984, pp. 1–27.

Goodheart, Eugene. "Modernism and the Critical Spirit." *The Failure of Criticism*. Cambridge, Mass.: Harvard University Press, 1978, pp. 8–27.

Gordon, Mel, ed. *Dada Performance*. New York: PAJ Publications, 1987.

Graff, Gerald. *Literature against Itself: Literary Ideas in Modern Society*. Chicago: University of Chicago Press, 1979.

Greenberg, Clement. "Modernist Painting." In Gregory Battock, ed., *The New Art: A Critical Anthology*. New York: Dutton, 1966, pp. 100–110.

Habermas, Jürgen. *Communication and the Evolution of Society*. Trans. Thomas McCarthy. Boston: Beacon Press, 1979.

———. "The Hermeneutic Claim to Universality." In Josef Bleicher, ed., *Contemporary Hermeneutics: Hermeneutics as Method, Philosophy and Critique*. London: Routledge and Kegan Paul, 1980, pp. 181–211.

———. *Legitimation Crisis*. Trans. Thomas McCarthy. Boston: Beacon Press, 1975.

———. "Modernity versus Postmodernity." *New German Critique*, no. 22 (Winter 1981): 3–14.

———. *Der philosophische Diskurs der Moderne: Zwölf Vorlesungen*. Frankfurt: Suhrkamp, 1985.

Hallberg, Robert von, ed. *Canons*. Chicago: University of Chicago Press, 1984.

Hartman, Geoffrey H. *Beyond Formalism: Literary Essays, 1958–1970*. New Haven, Conn.: Yale University Press, 1970.

Hassan, Ihab. *The Dismemberment of Orpheus: Toward a Postmodern Literature*, 2d ed. Madison: University of Wisconsin Press, 1982.

———. *The Literature of Silence: Henry Miller and Samuel Beckett*. New York: Knopf, 1967.

———. *Paracriticisms: Seven Speculations of the Times*. Urbana: University of Illinois Press, 1975.

——. *The Postmodern Turn: Essays in Postmodern Theory and Culture*. Columbus: Ohio State University Press, 1987.

Hausmann, Raoul. *Am Anfang war Dada*. Ed. Karl Riha and Gunter Kampf. Giessen: Anabas, 1980.

Hebdige, Dick. *Subculture: The Meaning of Style*. London: Methuen, 1979.

Heissenbüttel, Helmut. *Über Literatur*. Olten and Freiburg im Breisgau: Walter, 1966.

——. *Zur Tradition der Moderne: Aufsätze und Anmerkungen, 1964–1971*. Neuwied and Berlin: Luchterhand, 1972.

Hermans, Theo. *The Structure of Modernist Poetry*. London: Croom Helm, 1982.

Hoffman, Michael J. *Gertrude Stein*. Boston: Twayne Publishers, 1976.

——, ed. *Critical Essays on Gertrude Stein*. Boston: G. K. Hall, 1986.

Hoffmann, Gerhard, Alfred Hornung, and Rudiger Kunow. "'Modern,' 'Postmodern,' and 'Contemporary' as Criteria for the Analysis of 20th Century Literature." *Amerikastudien* 22 (1977): 19–46.

Hofmannsthal, Hugo von. *The Lord Chandos Letter*. Trans. Russell Stockman. Marlboro, Vt.: The Marlboro Press, 1986.

Holquist, Michael. "Whodunit and Other Questions: Metaphysical Detective Stories in Post-War Fiction." *New Literary History* 3 (Autumn 1971): 135–56.

Howe, Irving. *Decline of the New*. New York: Horizon Press, 1970.

Hulme, T. E. *Speculations: Essays on Humanism and the Philosophy of Art*. Ed. Herbert Read. London: Routledge and Kegan Paul, 1965.

Hutcheon, Linda. *A Poetics of Postmodernism: History, Theory, Fiction*. London: Routledge, 1988.

Huyssen, Andreas. *After the Great Divide: Modernism, Mass Culture, Postmodernism*. Bloomington: Indiana University Press, 1986.

——. "Mapping the Postmodern." *New German Critique* no. 33 (Fall 1984): 5–52.

——. "The Search for Tradition: Avant-Garde and Postmodernism in the 1970s." *New German Critique* no. 22 (Winter 1981): 23–40.

Inge, W. R. *Modernism in Literature*. London: English Association (Presidential Address 1937), 1937.

Isaacs, J. *The Background of Modern Poetry*. New York: Dutton, 1952.

Iser, Wolfgang. *The Act of Reading: A Theory of Aesthetic Response*. Baltimore: Johns Hopkins University Press, 1978.

——. *The Implied Reader: Patterns of Communication in Prose Fiction from Bunyan to Beckett*. Baltimore: Johns Hopkins University Press, 1974.

Jakobson, Roman. "Closing Statement: Linguistics and Poetics." In Thomas Sebeok, ed., *Style in Language*. Cambridge, Mass.: MIT Press, 1960, pp. 350–77.

Jameson, Fredric. "Beyond the Cave: Demystifying the Ideology of Modernism." *The Bulletin of the Midwest Modern Language Association* 8 (Spring 1975): 1–20.

———. *Fables of Aggression: Wyndham Lewis, the Modernist as Fascist.* Berkeley: University of California Press, 1979.

———. "The Ideology of the Text." *Salmagundi,* no. 31–32 (Fall 1975– Winter 1976): 204–46.

———. *The Political Unconscious: Narrative as a Socially Symbolic Act.* Ithaca, N.Y.: Cornell University Press, 1981.

———. "Postmodernism and Consumer Society." In Hal Foster, ed., *The Anti-Aesthetic: Essays on Postmodern Culture.* Port Townsend, Wash.: Bay Press, 1983, pp. 111–25.

———. "The Realist Floor-Plan." In Marshall Blonsky, ed., *On Signs.* Baltimore: Johns Hopkins University Press, 1985, pp. 373–83.

———. "Reflections in Conclusion." In Ernst Bloch et al., *Aesthetics and Politics.* London: New Left Books, 1977, pp. 196–213.

———. "Ulysses in History." In W. J. McCormack and Alistair Stead, ed. *James Joyce and Modern Literature.* London: Routledge and Kegan Paul, 1982, pp. 126–41.

Jardine, Alice A. *Gynesis: Configurations of Woman and Modernity.* Ithaca, N.Y.: Cornell University Press, 1985.

Jardine, Alice A., and Paul Smith, ed. *Men in Feminism.* London: Methuen, 1987.

Jauss, Hans Robert. *Aesthetic Experience and Literary Hermeneutics.* Trans. Michael Shaw. Minneapolis: University of Minnesota Press, 1982.

———. *Literaturgeschichte als Provokation.* Frankfurt: Suhrkamp Taschenbuch, 1970.

———. *Toward an Aesthetic of Reception.* Trans. Timothy Bahti. Minneapolis: University of Minnesota Press, 1982.

Jens, Walter. *Statt einer Literaturgeschichte.* 5th ed. Pfullingen: Günter Neske, 1962.

Josipovici, Gabriel. *The Lessons of Modernism and Other Essays.* Totowa, N.J.: Rowman and Littlefield, 1977.

Kampf, Louis. *On Modernism: The Prospects for Literature and Freedom.* Cambridge, Mass.: MIT Press, 1967.

Karl, Frederick R. *Modern and Modernism: The Sovereignty of the Artist, 1885–1925.* New York: Atheneum, 1985.

Kayser, Wolfgang. *Entstehung und Krise des modernen Romans* (4th ed.). Stuttgart: J. B. Metzlerische, 1963.

———. *Das sprachliche Kunstwerk: Eine Einführung in die Literaturwissenschaft* (13th ed.). Berne and Munich: Francke, 1968.

Kenner, Hugh. "The Making of the Modernist Canon." *Chicago Review* 34 (Spring 1984): 49–61.

———. "Notes toward an Anatomy of 'Modernism.'" In E. L. Epstein, ed., *A Starchamber Quiry: A James Joyce Centennial Volume, 1882–1982.* London: Methuen, 1982, pp. 3–42.

————. *The Pound Era.* Berkeley and Los Angeles: University of California Press, 1971.

Kermode, Frank. *Continuities.* New York: Random House, 1968.

————. *The Sense of an Ending: Studies in the Theory of Fiction.* New York: Oxford University Press, 1966.

Kiely, Robert, ed. *Modernism Reconsidered (Harvard English Studies 11).* Cambridge, Mass.: Harvard University Press, 1983.

Klinkowitz, Jerome. *Literary Disruptions: The Making of Post-Contemporary American Fiction.* Urbana: University of Illinois Press, 1975.

Knight, Alan R. "Masterpieces, Manifestoes and the Business of Living: Gertrude Stein Lecturing." In Shirley Neuman and Ira B. Nadel, ed., *Gertrude Stein and the Making of Literature.* Boston: Northeastern University Press, 1988, pp. 150–67.

Kofler, Leo. *Zur Theorie der modernen Literatur: Der Avantgardismus in soziologischer Sicht.* Neuwied and Berlin: Luchterhand, 1962.

Kohl, Stephan. *Realismus: Theorie und Geschichte.* Munich: Wilhelm Fink, 1977.

Kohler, Michael. " 'Postmodernismus': Ein begriffsgeschichtlicher Überblick." *Amerikastudien* 22 (1977): 8–18.

Koslowski, Peter, Robert Spaemann, and Reinhard Löw, ed. *Moderne oder Postmoderne?: Die Signatur des gegenwärtigen Zeitalters.* Weinheim: Acta humaniora, 1986.

Kostelanetz, Richard, ed. *The Avant-Garde Tradition in Literature.* Buffalo, N.Y.: Prometheus Books, 1982.

Kristeva, Julia. *Desire in Language: A Semiotic Approach to Literature and Art.* Ed. Leon S. Roudiez; trans. Thomas Gora, Alice Jardine, and Leon S. Roudiez. New York: Columbia University Press, 1980.

————. "Postmodernism?" In Harry R. Garvin, ed., *Romanticism, Modernism, Postmodernism (Bucknell Review 25).* Lewisburg, Pa.: Bucknell University Press, 1980, pp. 136–41.

————. *Powers of Horror: An Essay on Abjection.* Trans. Leon S. Roudiez. New York: Columbia University Press, 1982.

————. *Revolution in Poetic Language.* Trans. Margaret Waller. New York: Columbia University Press, 1984.

Kroker, Arthur, and David Cook. *The Postmodern Scene: Excremental Culture and Hyper-Aesthetics.* New York: St. Martin's Press, 1986.

Krutch, Joseph Wood. *'Modernism' in Modern Drama: A Definition and an Estimate.* Ithaca, N.Y.: Cornell University Press, 1953.

Kubal, David. *The Consoling Intelligence: Responses to Literary Modernism.* Baton Rouge: Lousiana State University Press, 1982.

Kuenzli, Rodolf E. "Dada gegen den Ersten Weltkrieg: Die Dadaisten in Zürich." In Wolfgang Paulsen and Helmut G. Hermann, ed., *Sinn aus Unsinn: Dada International.* Berne and Munich: Francke, 1982, pp. 87–100.

————. "Derridada." *L'Esprit Createur* 20 (Summer 1980): 12–21.

————. "The Semiotics of Dada Poetry." In Stephen C. Foster and Rudolf

E. Kuenzli, ed., *Dada Spectrum: The Dialectics of Revolt*. Madison, Wisc.: Coda Press; Iowa City: University of Iowa, 1979, pp. 51–70.

Lacan, Jacques. *Écrits: A Selection*. Trans. Alan Sheridan. New York: Norton, 1977.

Langbaum, Robert. "The Theory of the Avant-Garde: A Review." *Boundary 2* 1 (Fall 1972): 234–41.

Lemon, Lee T., and Marion J. Reis, ed. *Russian Formalist Criticism: Four Essays*. Lincoln: University of Nebraska Press, 1965.

Levenson, Michael. *A Genealogy of Modernism: A Study of English Literary Doctrine, 1908–1922*. New York: Cambridge University Press, 1984.

Levin, Harry. "What Was Modernism?" *Refractions: Essays in Comparative Literature*. New York: Oxford University Press, 1966.

Libby, Anthony. "Conceptual Space, The Politics of Modernism." *Chicago Review* 34 (Spring 1984): 11–26.

Lippard, Lucy R., ed. *Dadas on Art*. Englewood Cliffs, N.J.: Prentice-Hall, 1971.

Lodge, David. *Language of Fiction: Essays in Criticism and Verbal Analysis of the English Novel*. New York: Columbia University Press, 1966.

———. *The Modes of Modern Writing: Metaphor, Metonymy, and the Typology of Modern Literature*. London: Edward Arnold, 1977.

———. *Working with Structuralism: Essays and Reviews on Nineteenth- and Twentieth-Century Literature*. London: Routledge & Kegan Paul, 1981.

Lotman, Jurij. *The Structure of the Artistic Text*. Trans. Gail Lenhoff and Ronald Vroon. Ann Arbor: University of Michigan Press, 1977.

Ludke, W. Martin, ed. *Theorie der Avantgarde: Antworten auf Peter Bürgers Bestimmung von Kunst und bürgerlicher Gesellschaft*. Frankfurt: Suhrkamp, 1976.

Lukács, Georg. *Essays über Realismus*. Neuwied and Berlin: Luchterhand, 1971.

———. *Die Theorie des Romans: Ein geschichtsphilosophischer Versuch über die Formen der großen Epik*. Darmstadt and Neuwied: Luchterhand, 1971.

———. *Wider den mißverstandenen Realismus*. Hamburg: Claassen, 1958. Trans. John and Necke Mander: *The Meaning of Contemporary Realism*. London: Merlin Press, 1963.

Lunn, Eugene. *Marxism and Modernism: An Historical Study of Lukács, Brecht, Benjamin and Adorno*. Berkeley: University of California Press, 1982.

Lyotard, Jean-François. *The Postmodern Condition: A Report on Knowledge*. Trans. Geoff Bennington and Brian Massumi. Minneapolis: University of Minnesota Press, 1984.

McCormack, W. J., and Alister Stead, ed. *James Joyce and Modern Literature*. London: Routledge & Kegan Paul, 1982.

Macherey, Pierre. *A Theory of Literary Production*. Trans. Geoffrey Wall. Boston: Routledge and Kegan Paul, 1978.

Marcus, Jane. *Art and Anger: Reading Like a Woman*. Columbus: Ohio State University Press, 1988.

Marinetti, F. T. "The Founding and Manifesto of Futurism 1909." Trans. R. W. Flint. In Umbro Apollonio, ed., *Futurist Manifestos*. New York: Viking, 1973, pp. 19–24.

Matejka, Ladislav and Krystyna Pomorska, ed. *Readings in Russian Poetics: Formalist and Structuralist Views*. Ann Arbor: Michigan Slavic Publications, 1978.

Mayer, Hans. *Das Geschehen und das Schweigen: Aspekte der Literatur*. Frankfurt: Suhrkamp, 1969.

———. *Der Repräsentant und der Martyrer: Konstellationen der Literatur*. Frankfurt: Suhrkamp, 1971.

Mellard, James M. *The Exploded Form: The Modernist Novel in America*. Urbana: University of Illinois Press, 1980.

Melville, Stephen W. *Philosophy Beside Itself: On Deconstruction and Modernism*. Minneapolis: University of Minnesota Press, 1986.

Miller, Nancy K. "Arachnologies: The Woman, The Text, and the Critic." In Nancy K. Miller, ed., *The Poetics of Gender*. New York: Columbia University Press, 1986, pp. 270–96.

———. "Emphasis Added: Plots and Plausibilities in Women's Fiction." *PMLA* 96 (January 1981): 36–48.

———, ed. *The Poetics of Gender*. New York: Columbia University Press, 1986.

Millett, Kate. *Sexual Politics*. New York: Avon, 1971.

Moore, Harry T. *Age of the Modern and Other Literary Essays*. Carbondale: Southern Illinois University Press, 1971.

Moretti, Franco. *Signs Taken for Wonders: Essays in the Sociology of Literary Forms*. Trans. Susan Fischer, David Forgacs, and David Miller. London: Verso, 1983.

Mukařovský, Jan. *Structure, Sign and Function*. Trans. and ed. John Burbank and Peter Steiner. New Haven, Conn.: Yale University Press, 1978.

Murdoch, Iris. "The Sublime and the Beautiful Revisited." *Yale Review* 49 (December 1959): 247–71.

Neuman, Shirley, and Ira B. Nadel, ed. *Gertrude Stein and the Making of Literature*. Boston: Northeastern University Press, 1988.

Newman, Charles. *The Post-Modern Aura: The Act of Fiction in an Age of Inflation*. Evanston, Ill.: Northwestern University Press, 1985.

Nietzsche, Friedrich. *On the Advantage and Disadvantage of History for Life*. Trans. Peter Preuss. Indianapolis, Ind.: Hackett, 1980.

———. *Werke in zwei Bänden*. Munich: Carl Hanser, 1967.

O'Connor, William Van. *The New University Wits and the End of Modernism*. Carbonsdale: Southern Illinois University Press, 1963.

Olson, Charles. *Selected Writings*. Ed. Robert Creeley. New York: New Directions, 1966.

Onopa, Robert. "The End of Art as a Spiritual Project." *Tri-Quarterly*, no. 26 (Winter 1973): 363–82.

Ortega y Gasset, José. *The Dehumanization of Art and Other Essays on Art, Culture, and Literature*. Princeton, N.J.: Princeton University Press, 1968.

Owens, Craig. "The Allegorical Impulse: Toward a Theory of Postmodernism." *October*, no. 12 (Spring 1980): 67–86; "Part 2," *October*, no. 13 (Summer 1980): 59–80.

Paulsen, Wolfgang, and Helmut G. Hermann, ed. *Sinn aus Unsinn: Dada International*. Berne and Munich: Francke, 1982.

Paz, Octavio. *Children of the Mire: Modern Poetry from Romanticism to the Avant-Garde*. Trans. Rachel Philips. Cambridge, Mass.: Harvard University Press, 1974.

Perloff, Marjorie. "Pound/Stevens: Whose Era?" *New Literary History* 13 (Spring 1982): 485–510.

Pinsker, Sanford. "Ulysses and the Post-Modern Temper." *Midwest Quarterly* 15 (Summer 1974): 406–16.

Pinthus, Kurt, ed. with an intro. *Menschheitsdämmerung: Ein Dokument des Expressionismus*. Hamburg: Rowohlt Taschenbuch, 1959.

Poggioli, Renato. *The Theory of the Avant-Garde*. Trans. Gerald Fitzgerald. Cambridge, Mass.: Harvard University Press, 1968.

Poirier, Richard. "The Difficulties of Modernism and the Modernism of Difficulty." In Arthur Edelstein, ed., *Images and Ideas in American Culture: The Functions of Criticism*. Hanover, N.H.: Brandeis University Press, 1979, pp. 124–40.

———. *The Performing Self: Compositions and Decompositions in the Languages of Contemporary Life*. New York: Oxford University Press, 1971.

Pound, Ezra. *Literary Essays of Ezra Pound*. Ed. T. S. Eliot. New York: New Directions, 1968.

Pratt, Mary Louise. *Toward a Speech Act Theory of Literary Discourse*. Bloomington: Indiana University Press, 1977.

Quinones, Ricardo. *Mapping Literary Modernism: Time and Development*. Princeton, N.J.: Princeton University Press, 1985.

Reiss, Timothy J. *The Discourse of Modernism*. Ithaca, N.Y.: Cornell University Press, 1982.

Richter, Hans. *Dada: Art and Anti-Art*. Trans. David Britt. New York: Oxford University Press, 1978.

Riding, Laura, and Robert Graves. *A Survey of Modernist Poetry*. 2d ed. London: Heinemann, 1929.

Robinson, Lillian S., and Lise Vogel. "Modernism and History." *New Literary History* 3 (Autumn 1971): 177–99.

Rothenberg, Jerome. "A Dialogue on Oral Poetry with William Spanos." *Boundary 2* 3 (Spring 1975): 509–48.

Russell, Charles. "The Context of the Concept." In Harry R. Garvin, ed., *Romanticism, Modernism, Postmodernism* (*Bucknell Review* 25). Lewisburg, Pa.: Bucknell University Press, 1980, pp. 180–93.

———. *Poets, Prophets, and Revolutionaries: The Literary Avant-Garde from Rimbaud through Postmodernism.* New York: Oxford University Press, 1985.

———, ed. *The Avant-Garde Today: An International Anthology.* Urbana: University of Illinois Press, 1981.

Russell, Francis. *Three Studies in 20th Century Obscurity.* Chester Springs, Pa.: Dufour Editions, 1961.

Schleifer, Ronald. "The Poison of Ink: Modernism and Post-War Literary Criticism." *New Orleans Review* 8 (Fall 1981): 241–49.

Schmidt, Burghart. *Postmoderne—Strategien des Vergessens.* Darmstadt and Neuwied: Luchterhand, 1986.

Schmitt, Hans-Jürgen, ed. *Die Expressionismusdebatte: Materialien zu einer marxistischen Realismuskonzeption.* Frankfurt: Suhrkamp, 1973.

Schmitz, Neil. "Gertrude Stein as Post-Modernist: The Rhetoric of *Tender Buttons*." *Journal of Modern Literature* 3 (1974): 1203–18.

Schwartz, Sanford. *The Matrix of Modernism: Pound, Eliot, and Early Twentieth-Century Thought.* Princeton, N.J.: Princeton University Press, 1985.

Scott-James, R. A. *Modernism and Romance.* New York: John Lane, 1908.

Shattuck, Roger. *The Banquet Years: The Origins of the Avant-Garde in France, 1885 to World War I*, rev. ed. New York: Vintage Books, 1968.

Shils, Edward. *Tradition.* Chicago: University of Chicago Press, 1981.

Sieburth, Richard. "Dada Pound." *South Atlantic Quarterly* 83 (Winter 1984): 44–68.

Silliman, Ron. "'Postmodernism': Sign for a Struggle, Struggle for the Sign." *Poetics Journal*, no. 7 (September 1987): 18–39.

Smith, Barbara Herrnstein. "Contingencies of Value." In Robert von Hallberg, ed., *Canons.* Chicago: University of Chicago Press, 1984, pp. 5–39.

Sontag, Susan. *Against Interpretation and Other Essays.* New York: Delta, 1966.

———. *Under the Sign of Saturn.* New York: Vintage Books, 1981.

Spender, Stephen. *The Struggle of the Modern.* Berkeley: University of California Press, 1963.

Steiner, George. *After Babel: Aspects of Language and Translation.* Oxford: Oxford University Press, 1975.

———. *On Difficulty and Other Essays.* New York: Oxford University Press, 1978.

Stern, J. P. *On Realism.* London: Routledge and Kegan Paul, 1973.

Stimpson, Catharine, R. "Gertrude Stein and the Transposition of Gender." In Nancy K. Miller, ed., *The Poetics of Gender*. New York: Columbia University Press, 1986, pp. 1–18.

———. "The Somagrams of Gertrude Stein." In Michael J. Hoffman, ed., *Critical Essays on Gertrude Stein*. Boston: G. K. Hall, 1986, pp. 183–95.

Sultan, Stanley. *Ulysses, The Waste Land, and Modernism: A Jubilee Study*. Port Washington, N.Y.: Kennikat Press, 1977.

Sypher, Wylie. *Loss of the Self in Modern Literature and Art*. New York: Vintage Books, 1962.

Todorov, Tzvetan. *Introduction to Poetics*. Trans. Richard Howard. Minneapolis: University of Minnesota Press, 1981.

———. *The Poetics of Prose*. Trans. Richard Howard. Ithaca, N.Y.: Cornell University Press, 1977.

Tomkins, Calvin. *The Bride and the Bachelors: Five Masters of the Avant-Garde*. New York: Penguin Books, 1976.

Trilling, Lionel. "On the Modern Element in Modern Literature." In Stanley Burnshaw, ed. *Varieties of Literary Experience*. New York: New York University Press, 1962, pp. 407–33.

Tynjanov, Jurij. "On Literary Evolution." In Ladislav Matejka and Krystyna Pomorska, ed., *Readings in Russian Poetics: Formalist and Structuralist Views*. Ann Arbor: Michigan Slavic Publications, 1978, pp. 66–78.

Tzara, Tristan. "Dada Manifesto 1918." In Lucy R. Lippard, ed., *Dadas on Art*. Englewood Cliffs, N.J.: Prentice Hall, 1971, pp. 13–20.

Valéry, Paul. *An Anthology*. Ed. James R. Lawler. London: Routledge and Kegan Paul, 1977.

Walker, Jayne L. *The Making of a Modernist: Gertrude Stein from* Three Lives *to* Tender Buttons. Amherst: University of Massachusetts Press, 1984.

Wasson, Richard. "Notes on a New Sensibility." *Partisan Review* 36 (1969): 460–77.

Watt, Ian. *The Rise of the Novel: Studies in Defoe, Richardson and Fielding*. Harmondsworth, Eng.: Penguin Books, 1963.

Waugh, Patricia. *Metafiction: The Theory and Practice of Self-Conscious Fiction*. London: Methuen, 1984.

Weimann, Robert. *Structure and Society in Literary History: Studies in the History and Theory of Historical Criticism* (expanded ed.). Baltimore: Johns Hopkins University Press, 1984.

Wellek, René. *Concepts of Criticism*. Ed. Stephen G. Nichols, Jr. New Haven, Conn.: Yale University Press, 1963.

———. *Discriminations: Further Concepts of Criticism*. New Haven, Conn.: Yale University Press, 1970.

———, and Austin Warren. *Theory of Literature*. Harmondsworth, Eng.: Penguin Books, 1976.

Widmer, Kingsley. *Edges of Extremity: Some Problems of Literary Mod-

ernism. (Department of English Monograph Series, vol. 17). Tulsa, Okla.: University of Tulsa, 1980.

Wilde, Alan. *Horizons of Assent: Modernism, Postmodernism, and the Ironic Imagination*. Baltimore: Johns Hopkins University Press, 1981.

Williams, Raymond. *Marxism and Literature*. Oxford: Oxford University Press, 1977.

————. "Realism and the Contemporary Novel." *Partisan Review* 26 (Spring 1959): 200–213.

Wilson, Edmund. *Axel's Castle: A Study in the Imaginative Literature of 1870–1930*. New York: Norton, 1984.

Wimsatt, William K., Jr. *The Verbal Icon: Studies in the Meaning of Poetry*. Lexington: University Press of Kentucky, 1954.

Woolf, Virginia. *Collected Essays*, vols. 1 and 2. London: Hogarth Press, 1966, 1972.

Wunberg, Gotthart, ed. *Die literarische Moderne: Dokumente zum Selbstverständnis der Literatur um die Jahrhundertwende*. Frankfurt: Athenäum, 1971.

Zeraffa, Michel. *Fictions: The Novel and Social Reality*. Trans. Catherine Burns and Tom Burns. Harmondsworth, Eng.: Penguin Books, 1976.

Žmegač, Viktor. "Konvention, Modernismus und Parodie: Bemerkungen zum Erzählstil Thomas Manns." In Peter Pütz, ed., *Thomas Mann und die Tradition*. Frankfurt: Athenäum, 1971.

Index